The Advaitasiddhi
of
Madhusūdana Sarasvatī

Sri Garib Dass Oriental Series No. 102

The Advaitasiddhi of Madhusūdana Sarasvatī

(Chapter I)

Translated into English
by :
Ganganatha Jha

SRI SATGURU PUBLICATIONS
A DIVISION OF
INDIAN BOOKS CENTRE
DELHI-INDIA

Published by :

SRI SATGURU PUBLICATIONS
Indological and Oriental Publishers
A Division of
INDIAN BOOKS CENTRE
40/5, Shakti Nagar,
Delhi-110007
(INDIA)

First Edition : Allhabad. 1917

Second Edition : Delhi. 1990

Reprinted : 2024

ISBN - 81-7030-234-X
ISBN - 978-81-7030-234-6

PRINTED IN INDIA

THE AḌVAIṬASIḌḌHI OF MAḌHUSŪḌANA SARASVAṬĪ.

Preliminary Note.

"*Khaṇḍana—Aḍvaiṭasiḍḍhi—Chiṭsukhī*" constitute the triple "hard nut" of the Neo-Vedantin, to the kernel whereof, in the language of the Pathshalas, the 'beak of intelligence' finds it difficult to reach. The translation of the first having been finished, it is now the turn of the second.

The Aḍvaiṭasiḍḍhi is one of a series of highly polemical works exchanged between the representatives of the 'Shāṅkara' and the 'Māḍhva' Vedanta. The entire series we have not yet been able to trace. But between the *Aḍvaiṭasiḍḍhi* of Maḍhusūḍana (Shāṅkara) and the *Nyāyāmriṭa* of Vyāsa Yaṭi (Māḍhva), the polemical inter-relation is quite manifest. The very names of the *Prakaraṇas* are identical in the two works.

The *Nyāyāmriṭa* with its commentary by Shrīnivāsa has been published by the "Māḍhvavilāsa Book Depot," Kumbakonam. The *Aḍvaiṭasiḍḍhi*, along with its commentary, popularly known as the '*Gauḍabrahmānanḍī*,' appeared in 1892 in a lithographed edition at Benares. Subsequently, the text and commentary were printed in separate volumes in the 'Aḍvaiṭamañjarī' Series at the Shrīviḍyā Press, Kumbakonam, in 1893.

The page-references are to this latter edition.

G. J.

AḌVAIṬASIḌḌHI OF MAḌHUSŪḌANA.

An English Translation.

[The page-references are to the text published in the 'Aḍvaiṭamañjarī Series' Kumbakonam, 1893. Ed. S. Aiyar.]

'Ever supreme is Viṣṇu who, being apprehended of the (absolute unqualified) idea arising from the Shruṭi, has attained, as it were, the beatitude of supreme bliss,—He who is the substratum of all phenomena of false duality, beginning with the notions of the 'cogniser,' that originate from Illusion (Māyā),—Whose very nature consists of Truth, Consciousness and Bliss—Who, having shaken off the false bonds (of illusion) becomes free from all concretions!'

'Salutations to the dust of the feet of the blessed Rāma, Vishvēsvara and Māḍhava, who have realised the real nature of the supreme God, as identical with themselves,—the dust that shakes off the darkness of ignorance!'

'Excellent are the shorter and longer treatises composed by many learned persons for the good of others; this my present effort will verily be for the purpose of doing good to myself.'

'May this *Aḍvaiṭasiḍḍhi*, composed by the sage Maḍhusūḍana, whose sole possession consists in true devotion, after having collected the truths contained in the Scriptures, tend to the acquisition of true knowledge and the subjugation of misguided disputants, by persons who are pressed for time (and hence cannot devote their energies to larger treatises), as also to the delight of the learned!'

CHAPTER I.

ON UNREALITY.

Section 1.

THE METHOD OF INQUIRY.

[The Unity of Brahman can be proved only by proving the unreality of the world; hence the first attempt is towards this latter. This can be proved by the putting forward of proofs in support of the *Siddhānta* and also those against the opposite views.]°

The proof of the truth of *Non-duality* follows from the proof of the unreality of all duality (or plurality). Hence at the very outset, it becomes necessary to prove this *Unreality*. A particular view is established by proving the truth of that view itself, and by refuting all views to the contrary. Both these ends are accomplished by having recourse to one of the three forms of Controversy—(1) discussion (2) disputation, and (3) wrangling. And as what forms the chief factor in a discussion is the doubt arising from a diversity of opinion, it becomes necessary for the impartial 'middleman' to indicate at the very outset, the different opinions.

It certainly is true that the doubt arising from a diversity of opinions does not directly serve any useful purpose with regard to the accomplishment of the character of the true 'Subject' of an inferential argument; as all that is necessary for anything to form such a 'Subject' is that there be a desire on the part of the cogniser to prove something with regard to it, which is not already known through the thing itself. If the presence of doubt were a necessary factor in the character of the true inferential 'Subject,' then, after a man has obtained, with the help of Scriptural passages,

° This synopsis at the head of each section is based on the *Advaitasiddhisiddhāntasāra*, published in the Chaukhambha Sans. Series, Benares, 1903.

a definite knowledge of the Self, he could not, even though he were desirous of doing so, bring forward any inferential arguments with regard to it, as he would have a definite knowledge of the Self, and hence there would be no doubt. Then as for such doubts as are merely assumed (for being set aside by the argument in view),—if this were regarded as a necessary factor in the character of the 'Subject,' then we would be landed on the absurdity of an undue prolongation of the discussion (as there could be no end to such assumed doubts). Nor does this diversity of opinion itself serve any useful purpose with regard to the taking up of the one or the other view by the disputants, as this purpose could be equally well served by the 'middleman' saying to the disputants—"you have got to establish such and such a view,—and you have got to refute it." And thus there would appear to be no use for the statement of the Different Opinions.

Though all this is quite true, and the doubt arising from the said statement is not a necessary factor in the Inference, yet, inasmuch as it is this doubt that has got to be set aside, it does form an integral factor in the discussion. Though in some cases, the Subject may be well-known, and any statement of different of opinions would not create any doubts in the mind of the person knowing the real state of things, yet, by its very nature, a diversity of opinion is capable of giving rise to doubts. Nor is it always that persons entering into discussions are possessed of the definite knowledge of the subject. As for the declaration of old writers that, "two persons having a definite knowledge of the subject carry on the discussion"—this must be regarded as referring to such disputants as are vain of their knowledge; as we often find that a man who is excessively vain, though he himself holds a distinct opinion, takes up, for the moment, some other standpoint, and begins the discussion with the avowed end of establishing this contrary view. For these reasons we conclude that, like the laying down of the rules and regulations of the discussion, it is necessary for the 'middleman,' for the proper fulfilment of his duties, to make a distinct statement regarding the point with regard to which there is diversity of opinion and which forms the subject-matter of the discussion.

As regards 'Unreality' then, the point at issue may be thus stated:—(*a*) Are all things other than Consciousness,—even though they be cognisable as entities, and even though they be such as cannot be sublated (as false) by anything else save the true knowledge of Brahman,—the objects of constant negation at all points of time (past, present and future), with reference to those substrata in connection with which they are ordinarily cognised? (b) Or, it may be stated more simply thus:—Are all such things capable of being denied *real existence* in the aforesaid manner?

Section (2).

WHAT IS THE REAL CHARACTER OF THAT WITH REGARD TO WHICH 'UNREALITY' IS PREDICATED?

[The real character of the 'world' held to be *unreal* is that it is not sublated by any other cognition save the knowledge of Brahman].

In regard to this, it may noted that some people hold that what is sought to be established by the Vedantic inferential argument ('the world is unreal &c. &c.') is the co-extensiveness of the *probandum* (*the character of being the object of negation* &c.) with the 'Subject' (*the thing that is not rejected &c.*) in its particular forms; and in this case, the argument would be open to the fallacy of 'redundancy'; as in a particular case, that of the shell-silver, the *probandum* would be admitted by both parties to be co-extensive with at least a portion of the 'Subject.' In order to guard against this we have added the qualification 'not rejected by anything save the true knowledge of Brahman,'(which takes in everything except Brahman).

There are some people however, who hold that what is proved by the inferential argument in question is the co-extensiveness of the *probandum* with the *Subject in all its forms*; and in this the admission of mere partial co-extensiveness would not make the argument 'redundant.' Hence, in accordance with this view, it would not be necessary to add the aforesaid qualification.

As for the other two qualifications,—the one, 'cognisable as entities,' is added with a view to guard against the fallacy of '*Bāḍha*', 'Annulment', with regard to the absolute void or emptiness,' (which would be *not rejected by anything save the true knowledge of Brahman*, and which would yet *not* be *the object of constant negation &c.*); as no person ever takes the trouble to deny the existence of such a void; but this void is never *cognised as an entity*, the addition of which qualification therefore precludes the fallacy; and the second qualification, 'that apart from consciousness' precludes the same fallacy with regard to Brahman (which is of the very nature of consciousness, and as such becomes excluded).

Or, the 'diversity of opinion' may be stated thus severally, with regard to each individual substance :—'Is the *Ākāsha* unreal or not? Is the Earth unreal or not?' and so forth. In this case, even though each individual substance—such as *Ākāsha* and the like—is made the 'Subject' of the conclusion, yet, even with regard to such things as the jar and the like, the argument could not be regarded as Doubtful and Inconclusive; as these things also would fulfil the conditions of the 'Subject', and as such admit of similar assertions being made with regard to themselves. Then as regards the *doubt* (as to whether these things do actually fulfil the conditions required by the inferential conclusion), the presence of such doubt is a necessary and favourable condition in all inferential processes (as without some such uncertainty there would be no occasion for the inferential argument to be put forward) in fact the presence of doubt or uncertainty can be regarded as objectionable only with regard to the other factors of the inferential Argument (and not the 'Subject'). It is in view of this that we have the following declaration :—" Doubtful Inconclusiveness consists in an uncertainty with regard to the application, or presence, of the Inferential Indicative or Probans (*hētu*) to something that is definitely known to be wholly devoid of the character sought to be proved by the Inference." [That is to say, it is only when we find that the Reason brought forward to prove the presence of a certain character, in a certain thing, may apply also to something which is known to be entirely devoid of that character, then there arises a doubt as to the validity of that Reason]. And as a matter of fact, it is the essential characteristic of the true 'Subject' that with regard to it there should be a doubt as to the presence of the 'Probans,'—or that there should be no definite cognition (before the Inference is duly brought forward) of its possessing the 'probandum,' the character sought to be proved; and thus the character of the 'Subject' would apply to the jar and other things, just as well as to *Ākāsha* and the other substances. And hence with regard to any such things, the argument could not be regarded as Doubtful and Inconclusive.

The *jar and other things* have been spoken of as 'having the character of the *Subject*' (and not as the actual *Subject* of the conclusion in question), because they could not form the subject-matter of that conclusion which would be stated with regard to *Ākāsha*; nor would it be right to define the 'Subject' as that which forms the subject-matter of the *Final Conclusion*; as this could not apply to the case of the *Inference for one's Self*, in which there is no formal *Statement of the Final Conclusion*.

Section (3).

THE UNREALITY OF THE WORLD.

[The World is perceptible—unconscious,—limited; hence it must be unreal; which means—(a) that it cannot be spoken of as existing or as non-existing, (b) or that it is the counter-entity of negation pertaining to all time, (c) or that it is sublated by knowledge, (d) or that it is the counter-entity of the absolute negation subsisting in itself, or (e) that it is something different from the really existing.]

Thus then, the 'diversity of opinion' having been stated in the aforesaid manner, we have the following inferential arguments (in support of Unreality) formulated by ancient writers:—'The object under discussion is unreal,—(1) because it is *perceptible*, (2) because it is *unconscious*, and (3) because it is *limited*,—like the shell-silver.' We are not very particular as to the number of 'factors' necessary in a syllogistic argument (they may be five or three only).

There would be no incongruity in the general and wide form in which the 'Subject' is stated in these arguments,—in view of the specifically particular form in which the 'diversity of opinion' might have been stated (with regard to such things as *Ākāsha*, Jar and the like). Because all these statements could be regulated by conditions favourable to the particular inferential argument. As a rule, after the 'diversity of opinion' has been stated by the middleman, he proceeds to lay down the rules and regulations whereby the discussion should be carried on; and it is after this has been done that the disputants proceed to put forward their arguments and counter-arguments. Thus then, there is always an interval between the statement of the 'diversity of opinion' and the putting forward of the arguments. And though the statement of the 'diversity of opinion' will have ceased to exist at the time that the arguments are put forward, yet the qualifications of the 'Subject' as mentioned in that statement would continue to be regarded as applying by way of 'pointers' to the 'Subject' as put forward in the subsequent arguments. Or, we might even regard these qualifications as actually applying directly to the subsequently-stated 'Subject'; and in this case, we could take the word '*vimatam*' ('the object under discussion') to mean *each and everything that has the character of an object with regard to which the diversity of opinion is present.* And thus there would be nothing incongruous in the form of the above arguments (of the ancient writers).

Definition of 'Unreality.'

"What is this 'Unreality that you seek to prove? On "the strength of the declaration by the "author of the *Pañchapādikā*, that 'the "word *unreal* denotes *undefinability*, anirvachanīyatā,' it "might be held that what is meant by the 'Unreality' of a "thing is that it is *undefinable*; i. e. that it is not the "substratum of either *being* or *non-being* [i. e. that it cannot "be said either to *be* or *not to be*]. But, the opponent of "the Vedantin says, this we cannot admit. For what, we "ask, do you understand by a thing not being the substra-"tum of either *being* or *non-being*?

"Do you mean (1) that the thing is the substratum of "the negation of being *qualified by non-being*? Or, (2) that "the thing possesses the two attributes of *the absolute negation* "*of being* and *the absolute negation of non-being*? Or, (3) "that it possesses the combined property of *the absolute* "*negation of non-being as accompanied by the absolute* "*negation of being*?

"Now the first alternative is not tenable; because, according "to us Logicians, the world is the substratum of *being* only, "and not that of *being as qualified* by 'non-being'; to prove "therefore that the world is characterized by the absence "of *being* qualified by *non-being* is superfluous (because "non-contested).

"Nor is the second alternative tenable—[*i. e.* 'Unreality' "can not be regarded as consisting in the two properties of "the absolute negation of *being* and the absolute negation "of *non-being*]. For as between *being* and *non-being*, the "presence of one necessarily implies the absence of the "other; and hence a combination of the two involves a "self-contradiction. Further, although the world may be "destitute of *being* (*lit.* being-ness—*saṭṭva*—*i. e.* the quality "of being, that which is), in the same way as Brahman, "that possesses no qualities whatever, is destitute of the "*quality* of being, yet it may be (like Brahman) essentially "that which is (*i. e. being* may not be a quality of the world, "but its essential nature, and this is proved by Perception "&c.); and this would establish its *not* being unreal, and thus "you would commit the fallacy of *Arṭhānṭara*; i. e. you would "prove something different from what you mean to prove;— "and lastly, in the case of shell-silver, we find that, though it "is devoid of *being* in the sense of incapability of sublation "(*abāḍhyaṭva*), yet it is not devoid of *non-being* in the sense "of 'capability of sublation'; and hence your definition of "'Unreality' would not apply to this case [for there would "be present the *absolute negation of being*, but not the "*absolute negation* of *non-being*].

"For these same three reasons, we could not accept the "third definition either (according to which 'Unreality' "consists in the presence of the combined property of the "absolute negation of *non-being* as qualified by the absolute "negation of *being*.)"

To this we Vedantins make the following reply:—

First definition of Unreality.

If Unreality be viewed as constituted by the two attributes of absolute negation of non-being and absolute negation of being, no objection whatever can be raised. There is no self-contradiction; for such contradiction could arise only from one of the following three circumstances:— (1) if, between *being* and *non-being* one had the character of the negation of the other; or (2) if the absence of one were invariably accompanied by the presence of the other; or (3) if the presence of one were invariably accompanied by the absence of the other.

In the case in question, however, we find that the *first* of these conditions is not present; since we do not admit of any such mutually negative or exclusive relation between *being* and *non-being*. To explain:—In the case in question, what is meant by *non-being* is not the absence of that true *being* which consists in not being sublated at any time; what we mean by it is not being cognised as existing in any substratum;* it is the absence of such *non-being* which we intend to be included in the *probandum* of our conclusion. Thus then, the *probandum* of our conclusion comes to consist in ***being cognisable as existing in a substratum while at the same time being different from what is not liable to sublation at all time*** (i. e. while yet being liable to sublation at all time). In this manner, this character of the *probandum* (*i. e. unreality* as we understand it) will not be found to be absent in *shell-silver*; for the negation of that *non-being* which consists in liability to sublation does not form an element of the *probandum*. Nor is there any self-contradiction involved in the case of shell-silver; for we have shown just now that *being* and *non-being* are not necessarily mutually exclusive.

Nor is there present the *second* condition of self-contradiction—*i. e.* as between *being* and *non-being*, the absence of the one is not invariably accompanied by the presence of the other; for in Shell-silver, *e.g.*, which is marked by the absence of being, there exists at the same time the absence of non-being in the sense intended; so that there is no invariable concomitance (between *absence of non-being and presence of being*).

And lastly, as to the third condition, we point out that it by no means necessarily implies self-contradiction. For, to

---

* When we say that in the unreal thing there is absence of non-being, we understand by *non being* the incapability of being cognised in a substratum. The *unreal* Shell-Silver *is* cognised in the Shell; the unreal Jar etc. *is* cognised in Brahman.

give an instance, it no doubt is a fact that the class-character of a cow is invariably accompanied by the absence of the class-character of a horse (that which is a cow is not a horse), and *vice versa*; but we observe that the negations of these two class-characters exist together in one and the same substratum, a camel, e. g.—which is neither cow nor horse.

We now turn to the second argument set forth against our definition by the opponent,—viz. that just as Brahman though devoid of attributes and hence of the quality of *being* (*Saṭ-ṭva*), yet essentially is that which is (*Saṭ*), so the phenomenal world also must be said to *be*, and hence not *unreal*; so that, the adversary says, we prove the contrary of what we want to prove.—But this is not so. For as the idea of *being* as attached to all things may be accounted for by one Reality (viz. Brahman) which is present everywhere, there is no reasonable ground for assuming that all the individual things of the phenomenal world should be essentially *being* in the same sense as Brahman is; and moreover with this assumption of *special being* of every individual thing it would be absolutely impossible for us to have any comprehensive conception (of a number of things as included under one concept).

Or (in order to remove all suspicion of *Arṭhānṭara*) we may define *unreality* as being constituted by that difference (*bhēḍa*) which has for its counter-entity *being*, and also by that difference which has for its counter-entity non-being [i.e. the Unreal is that which is different—*bhinna*—from what *is*, and also from what *is not*]. And this will leave no room for the fallacy of '*Arṭhānṭara*' as urged by the Opponent above; because according to none of our opponents would the said *double* 'difference' belong to the world;—as (1) according to the view propounded by Vāchaspaṭi Mishra (in his *Nyāyavārṭika-ṭāṭparya*) the world is both *real* and unreal, (2) according to other writers on Logic, it is only *real*, and (3) according to the Bauḍḍha-Logician, the whole *objective* world is *unreal* [and thus according to none of these would the world be the substratum of *absolute* difference from 'non-being'. Thus then, this form of the *sādhya* not implying any kind of *reality*, even as understood by our opponents, our explanation of the said *unreality* would not involve the fallacy of *Arthāntara*. Nor must it be argued against the above definitions given by us that, since our adversaries also admit a part of our definitions,—viz. that the world is characterized by the absence of non-being, or (according to the last definition) by difference from non-being,—we lay ourselves open to the charge of partial superfluity of reasoning. When the philosopher who holds the so-called '*bhēdabhēda*' view (the view of simultaneous difference and non-difference) argues that 'a quality is at the same time different and non-different from the substance to which it belongs, since the two have a common substratum', the difference is admitted by the Logicians also against whom he argues;—but all the same there is no superfluous reasoning, for the full proposition (i. e. the existence of difference and non-difference) is something *not* proved (before the *bhēdabhēdavādin* proves it). In the same way there is no superfluity of reasoning in the case under discussion, for what has to be proved there is the joint notion of absence of being and absence of non-being. In the former case, since there is no cognition of complete non-difference—such as met with in the case of identical things, such as *ghata* and *kumbha* (both which terms denote the same thing viz. a jar)—what is aimed at is the establishment of combined difference and non-difference. Analogously, in the case of the Vedantic argument under discussion, finding that an absolute non-entity, which is wholly devoid of *being*, is not perceptible, we conclude that it is the combined *presence* and *absence of being* that constitutes the necessary condition of perceptibility; so that what is aimed at is the establishment of that same *combined presence and absence* [and it is this that would form the predicate of our Proposition.] For the same reasons, it would also be right to put forward our proposition in the form that '(all that is perceived) is absolutely devoid of *being* while being absolutely devoid of *non-being*.'

Here the following objection may perhaps be raised :—" Since that combined predicate as well as that qualified " predicate which the Vedāntin sets forth is altogether un-" known from experience, he commits the logical fault of in-" troducing a Probandum which has an altogether unknown " qualification. And if he should plead that he proves a " combined or qualified Probandum on the basis of the sepa-" rate experience of each of the two elements, we reply that he " might as well prove the existence of a hare's horn on the " basis of experience making us acquainted with horns and " hares apart from each other. "

But to this the Vedāntin replies that, as explained above —in the case of shell-silver, we have an actual experience of such a combined predicate (for shell-silver is the counter-entity of the negation of being and of the negation of non-being). Nor finally, must it be objected that, since Brahman is without any attributes and hence devoid of the two attributes of *being* and *non-being*, our definition of Unreality would extend to Brahman also. For as Brahman essentially is *that which is*, it can not be the abode of the absolute negation of *being*; and moreover just because it is without attributes, it cannot be the abode of the attribute of *non-being*.

The Second definition of Unreality.

Or else, we may define the *Unreal* as that which is the counter-entity of an absolute negation with regard to the substratum in which it is cognised—[*i. e.* by calling the jar *Unreal*, what we mean is that it is capable of being absolutely denied in regard to the point of space and time in connection with which it is perceived].

" But ", our Opponent asks, " is this *absolute negation* " itself real or unreal ? If the former, then we have two real "things—Brahman and this *Negation*, and this implies the "abandoning of the Monistic standpoint. If, on the other "hand, the *Negation* be regarded as only *apparently* real "(*prāṭibhāsika*), you superfluously prove what is proved "already [for if the world is the counter-entity of a merely "*apparently real* negation, it is real, and this is just what the "Dualist asserts.] Lastly, if the Negation be regarded as hav-"ing a *practical* (*vyāvahārika*) reality, then you commit the "fallacy of *Arṭhānṭara*, for a negation of this kind (having only "a relative reality) is liable to sublation, and hence not opposed "to the *real* being of the apparent world (which of course "is a conclusion contrary to what is desired by the Vedāntin). "Moreover the Vedic passages declaring Non-duality would, "in this case, say what is true; and the whole phenomenal "world,—which according to the Vedāntin, would be the coun-"ter-entity of a negation only relatively real, and which, *ex-"hypothesi*, has not a mere *apparent* reality—would have to be "regarded as *absolutely* real."

To this we Vedāntins make the following reply:—Even the *reality* of the negation does not imply an abandonment of the Monistic standpoint; for the negation is *non-different* from Brahman, which is the substratum of the negation of the phenomenal world. Nor does the fact of the world being the object of an absolutely real negation imply that the world itself is absolutely real; for we find that no such reality belongs to the shell-silver, which yet is an object of absolute negation. Or else, we may regard the Negation to have no absolute reality. But even in this case, the reality of the Negation is not merely apparent, but rather practical.

"But", our opponent says, "if such be the case, the "negation is something capable of sublation, and hence not "opposed to the reality of its object; and thus your argument "becomes open to the charge of *Arṭhānṭara* [for if the negation "of reality is capable of sublation, what that fact establishes "is *reality*, and not *unreality*]."

This objection, we reply, is unfounded. For ordinary experience shows that a thing seen in a dream is sublated by a negation which itself is a part of the dream [a thing seen in a dream may later on, in that same dream, be judged to be unreal; but the fact of the dream-judgment being itself something unreal, does not make that thing real]. What necessarily implies the reality of a thing negated is not the fact of the negation itself being sublated, but the circumstance of the reality of the negation being lesser in degree than the reality of the thing negated. In the case in question however,—the phenomenal world and its negation have both exactly the same degree of reality (*i.e. practical*, and not absolute, reality); and the denial of this negation, *i. e.* the denial of the absolute reality of this *negation*, does not remove the incongruity of the *absolute reality* of the phenomenal world. [That is to say, the denial of the *practical* reality of the negation of the phenomenal world only implies the *practical* reality of this world, and not its *absolute* reality.]

The opponent may argue that if the negation of the phenomenal world is negated, we have the reality of that world. But this is not so. The negation of the negation of a certain thing establishes the reality of that thing only in those cases where the reality of the thing is actually meant to be established by the negation of its negation, and where, for this reason, we have the negation of the *negation* only; as when e. g. with regard to a piece of real silver we at first have the notion that it is *not silver*, and after some time come to realise that it is really *silver*, then with a view to establishing the reality of the silver, we say 'this is not not-silver' (*i. e.* we deny the previous *negation of the silver* only, not the reality of the *silver* also). In those cases however, where we have the negation of *both* (the *reality of the thing* as well as the *negation of that thing*), the negation of this latter negation does not point to the reality of the thing. As an example we may cite the case of the Absolute Destruction (*Dhvamsa*) of a certain thing, at the time of which we have the negation of the thing destroyed and also of its Prior Non-existence (*Prāgabhāva*) (*i. e.* the thing has been destroyed, and there is no possibility of its coming into existence again) [and this twofold negation does not point to the existence of the thing]. Similarly in the case in question we find that the negation sublates the reality of the phenomenal world, and also the negation of that world ; and hence the negation of this latter negation does not point to the reality of the world. What determines the capability of negation is 'perceptibility' (as apart from consciousness) [*i. e.* all that is perceptible as apart from consciousness is deniable ; and this *perceptibility* we find present in both, the phenomenal world as well as its negation].

The opponent may here further argue that if the Vedic texts declare a negation which is not absolutely real, it follows that these texts are destitute of authority. But this also is unfounded, for what those texts declare to be *not absolutely real* is everything—be it the *phenomenal world* or its *negation—that is not Brahman* ; and texts setting forth this doctrine can not be unauthoritative.

A fresh discussion is started :—" You have defined *Un*-"*reality* as the object of negation ; well, is the world negated in "its own form as known to us (*i. e.* in its own generic "character of 'perceptible,' or in the particular forms of "*Ākāsa* &c.) ? Or, is it only in the form and character of "an absolutely real entity that it is negatived, without pre-"judice to that form and character (perceptibility) of it which is "different from absolute non-entity ? [That is to say, by your "negation of the phenomenal world,—(1) do you mean that "the world has no existence even in the form that we know "it ? (2) or do you mean that though it is *practically* real "so far as it is perceptible, yet it has no *absolute* reality ?] The— "former alternative could not be held, for the simple reason "that as a matter of fact we find—(1) that the origination "&c. of the Ākāsha and other things that constitute the world "are described in detail in the Veda (and what is there des- "cribed cannot be absolutely unreal) ; (2) that they are quite "capable of functioning towards definite useful ends (and this " capability is the only condition of 'reality') ; (3) that they " have (even according to the Vedanta) Nescience for their " material cause (and anything that is unreal cannot have a " material cause); (4) that they are sublatable only by true " knowledge (and an absolute unreality could not stand in need " of any such agency for its sublation) ; (5) that they,—as also " even the shell-silver—have for all intents and purposes, a real " existence, at least at the time that we have the cognition of " them ;—and for these reasons we cannot totally deny the " practically real existence of the world,—an existence which " at any rate, is different from absolute non-existence,—for " all time, past, present and future. Then, as regards the " second alternative, that also is not tenable ; as in that case " you would explain 'absolute reality', the essence of which is " non-capabality of sublation, by means of 'Unreality,' the " essence of which is capability of sublation ; and this would " be moving in a circle. And also if you were to deny the " absolute reality of the world *in its own form as we know it*, " you would be open to the objections that have been put " forward against the former alternative ; and if this *absolute* " *reality* were to be denied not in the *practical* sense, but in " the *absolute sense*,—then too we would have a *regressus ad* " *infinitum* [as it would be necessary to put forward an *abso-* " *lute reality* with regard to every negation, and there would be " no end to it]."

To the above the following reply is made :—

As a matter of fact, it is admitted that it is in its own form that the phenomenal world, as also the shell-silver, is an object of negation, extending to all time, past, present and future. For instance, when one mistakes the piece of shell to be silver, as soon as he discovers the real character of the thing perceived, the idea that he has is that—'*it is* not silver, it *has* never *been* silver, and it *will* never *be* silver'—wherein we have the negation of the silver in its own form; and in the case of the phenomenal world also the text 'there is nothing that is diverse' expresses the negation of the world in its own form. It might be argued that in the case of the erroneous cognition of silver what is the object of negation (by the subsequent sublative cognition) is only that silver which, ordinarily, is regarded as *absolutely* real [so that it is not right to say that the *absolute* reality is *not* the object of negation]. But this would imply that the erroneous cognition and the sublative cognition refer to two different things [the former cognising the *apparent*, and the latter the *absolute*, reality of silver]; and it would further imply the negation (by the sublative cognition) of something for the negation whereof there is no occasion [what is *denied* by the negation being *not* the same thing that has been *asserted* in the preceding cognition]. It being thus proved that the phenomenal world, like the shell-silver, is in its own form an object of negation extending to all times,—the objection might be raised that, "if the world in its own form, were capable of negation extending to all times, there would be no possibility of its *origination* (*continuance* and *dissolution*, as described in Vedic texts, and as admitted by the Vedantin in his very definition of 'Brahman')." But as a matter of fact, for the origination, (continuance and dissolution) of a thing it is not necessary that the thing should, in its own form, be incapable of negation,; as our opponents, the Naiyāyikas, themselves deny the origination &c. of *Ākāsha* and such other eternal substances, though every one of these is admitted by them to be things that cannot, in their own form, be negated. In fact, it has to be admitted that what determines the origination &c. of a thing is something entirely different,—some such thing for instance as the 'nature of the thing itself'. And this 'nature of things' we Vedantins also admit,—although it be (like everything other than Brahman) a mere fiction.

"Your view," the opponent says, "implies the abandoning of the view (expressed in an authoritative Vedanta work (viz. the *Vivaraṇa*) that—'Of absolute negation, the counter-entity, *in its own form*, may be (empirically real) Silver as it is found in the silversmith's shop, or the counter-entity, *in its absolutely real form*, may be merely apparent silver.'"

But this is not so. For what the teacher (the author of the *Vivaraṇa*) here means to say is that the counter-entity of the negation is nothing else than apparent silver, which is conceived (by the misconceiving person) as identical with empirically real silver. What the 'or' is meant to indicate is that the author is not particularly concerned whether this apparent silver be negated in its own form (as conceived at the time) or as absolutely real silver. The form in which he expresses his meaning is intended—(1) to dispel the notion that the silver is cognized only as indentical with *the object before the man*,—and (2) to intimate that it is cognised also as identical with ordinary empirical silver. This is the view set forth in the *Tattvadīpikā* also. Old Teachers have expressed themselves in the following way:—'In the negation 'this is not silver' it is ordinary empirical silver that is the counter-entity of the negation'. This statement is to be understood in the following way—Since it is observed that a man desirous of silver takes action with regard to the thing before him (*i. e.* stoops and picks it up), it is evident that what he actually cognizes at the time is practically real silver, and it is this cognized ordinarily real silver which is the object of the negation 'at no time this thing is empirically real silver'.

The sense of all this may be explained as follows:—There is the general law that in all cases of negation, where the thing negated and that with reference to which it is negated are denoted by words having the same case-termination, the negation expresses the mutual negation (*anyonyābhāva*) of the two things; as *e. g.* in the negation 'the jar is not the cloth' (where *ghaṭaḥ* and *paṭaḥ* are both in the nominative case). In the same way the sentence 'this is not silver' expresses the mutual negation of *this* and *silver*; and as the cognition of the object expressed is equal in character to the cognition produced by the sentence, the cognition that arises in us through the sentence 'this is not silver' has for its object the mutual negation of these two. Thus, in the case of the negation 'this is not silver' we have the mutual negation between the object before the eyes—which is denoted by '*this*'—viz. the apparent silver,—and the ordinary empirical silver which is denoted by the word '*silver*'; and this *implies* the unreality (*mithyātva*) of the apparent silver. ('This silver seen by me is not empirically real silver; it therefore is unreal'). Where, on the other hand, the denial is made in the form 'there is no silver in this place' (*na atra rajatam*), the cognition expressed by the sentence has for its object the absolute negation of silver in that place, in agreement with the general rule that where the two terms of a negation are expressed by words having different case-endings (*atra*, *e. g.* being a locative case, and *rajatam* a nominative), the word *not* signifies the absolute negation of the one with regard to the other. The cognition therefore, in the case under discussion, has for its object the empirical reality of silver; and the unreality (of the apparent silver) follows as a matter of course [as *empirical* reality is of a grade higher than *apparent* reality; so that the negation of the former implies that of the latter]. The general conclusion therefore is that, if we regard the negation of reality also as unreal, we do not thereby abandon our main position,—nor do we come into conflict with authoritative Vedanta writers: Hence our view is not open to any objection.

The Opponent proceeds to raise a fresh objection against "the proposition that *the phenomenal world is unreal*:—"Thus "then, in the way that you define 'unreality,' it would come to "this that the phenomenal world has *no existence* at all. Be-"cause *the character of being the object of an absolute negation* "*in connection with the substratum occupied by it* must necess-"arily imply the capability of being absolutely negated "*at all times and in all places*; and this character, accord-"ing to you, belongs to all such things of the ordinary world "as the *jar* and the like, which are admitted by all to have no "existence in certain cases (in the case of the misconception of "the jar, for instance); and this would mean that these things "have *no existence* at all. As otherwise, it would become possi-"ble to assert that they have an existence even in those cases "where they are universally admitted to have no existence; and "you have distinctly asserted that no such existence is "possible. And under the circumstances, what would be "the difference between these things of the world and those "things that have no sort of existence at all. As the "*non-existence* of such impossible things as the 'hare's horns' "and the like would not in any way differ from the *non-*"*existence* of these things of the world, as you explain it. "(a) You can not every well say that the 'non-existence' of these "things of the world is *undefinable* (*nirupākhya*); since in "saying this you would actually be *defining* it as 'undefin-"able'; and so it could not very well be spoken of as 'un-"definable'. (b) Then, you might say that the 'non-exis-"tence' of the things of the world consists in their 'non-"cognisability'; but this too could not hold; as if that which "is 'non-existent' were *not cognised*, then we could "not have any such cognition as that 'such and such a thing "is different in character from that which is *non-existent*', "nor could we have any sublation of the cognition of the "*non-existent* thing; nor lastly, could we ever use the word " 'non-existent' at all. (c) Nor could you define 'non-exis-"tence' as *the character of being not cognised as something* "*directly perceptible*; for such non-existence would come to "apply to all eternal supersensuous things (as none of "these are ever cognised as 'directly perceptible')."

To the above we make the following reply:—It is quite true that the character of *being the object of absolute negation at all times* belongs to that which has no existence at all, as well as to that which has an undefinable existence; but that which has no existence at all has also the character of being such as can never be cognised in any substratum, real or assumed; and as a matter of fact, we know that this latter character does not belong, either to the shell-silver or to the phenomenal world, until these objects are sublated by subsequent True Knowledge. For this reason, neither the shell-silver nor the phenomenal world would be absolute non-entities, even according to our view. Because in the case of the shell-silver, as also in the case of the phenomenal world, we find that until we have the sublating cognition—in the form of 'this is not silver', or 'this world is not real'—the silver, as well as the world, is distinctly cognised as *existing*; it is this fact that is indicated by the word '*upādhi*', 'substratum', in the condition set forward as necessary in proving a thing to be an absolute non-entity. [And thus not having this *non-cognisability*, they would not be absolute non-entities].

As for the *Shūnyavādin*, the Bauddha Nihilist, he does not admit of any mistaken cognition with a real substratum; and so with reference to the shell-silver and to the phenomenal world, he would never admit the presence of *the character of being cognisable as existing in a certain substratum*,—a character which serves to differentiate ordinary things from absolute non-entities, which are not cognisable as having an existence in any substratum. [So it is the Nihilist who will be open to the charge of regarding the phenomenal world as an absolute non-entity; and not the Vedantin, who fully admits of mistaken cognitions with real substratum, the ultimate real substratum for all things being Brahman].

Objection:—" Now then *Unreality* comes to consist in " being the object of an absolute negation that has for " its substratum *things having real existence*. And in " that case, your argument would become 'superfluous', "even as against the *Naiyāyika*; specially with reference " to such all-pervasive substances as the *Ākāsha* and the "like; as these substances, according to the Naiyāyika, are " such as have their *absolute* negation nowhere (in any " substratum); and as such your 'unreality' would not apply " to such all-pervasive substances (and as for other substances, " the Naiyāyika also does not hold them to be *permanent* reali- " ties). It might be argued that—what is meant by the "'unreality' of a thing is that it is capable of being negated " with regard to that entity (which appears in the mistaken " cognition that we have of the thing) as its substratum. But " in that case too the Inferential Argument would be 'super- " fluous'; as such 'unreality' would be one that is admitted "(even by the Logician) to belong to all entities. As for " instance, that which would be the substratum of the " cognition of the jar by the relation of *contact* (*i. e.* that " which would be in contact with it) would certainly be the " object of the absolute negation of that which would *inhere* " in (*i. e.* form a constituent part of) that jar; and conversely, " that which would *inhere* in the jar would be the object of " absolute negation with regard to that which would be in " *contact* with it [and in both cases, the substratum would be " a *real entity*, in the form of the *jar*; and yet the 'unreality' "as above explained would be admitted by all to apply to all "things.] In order to guard against this, it might be said "that—what is meant by 'Unreality' is that the thing is capable of being negated with reference to that relationship which "that thing bears to the real entity that may form its substratum. But then too the argument would be 'superfluous'; "as this 'Unreality' also would be admitted by the Logician, "as belonging to all things that are not all-pervasive (*i. e.* "things that have only limited extension) [That is to say, "for instance, the jar, being in contact with one part of "space could certainly be negated with regard to another "point in space, even with reference to the same relationship "of *contact*; as the jar could not, at one and the same time, "be in contact with all points in space.]."

Reply:—None of your objections is well taken; as what is distinctly indicated by the word '*praṭipanna*' in our definition of *unreality* is that 'unreality' consists in being the object of negation with regard to a certain substratum,—this negation being with reference to that form in which the substratum has been 'occupied', or taken possession of, by that which is negated; and this 'form' always consists in a certain *relationship* and a certain differentiating *characteristic.* Certainly the spot on earth is never cognised as the *substratum* of the jar, except through a certain definite relationship between them; nor is the tree the subtratum of the contact of the monkey, unless this contact forms a distinguishing characteristic of that particular tree. Thus then, the 'unreality' of a thing, according to us, comes to mean this:—when a certain thing can be cognised as having another thing for its substratum, either through some relationship or through some distinguishing characteristic,—if that something can be absolutely negated with regard to that same substratum, and that too in reference to the same relationship and the same distinguishing characteristic,—then that thing is '*unreal*'. And now, tell me, in what way can there be any 'superfluity' in our argument?

At this stage the Opponent may come forward with the following argument :—"In the case of *Ākāsha* we find that it "can never form the object of either *prior negation* (as we "do not know of any time at which it did not exist) or "*destruction* (as it is never found to be destroyed); and in "the same manner, it is quite reasonable to hold that it cannot "be an object of *absolute negation* (at any rate prior to your "conclusion being established). (1) Because evidences for the "denying of *Ākāsha* being an object of *absolute* negation are "exactly similar to those for denying its being the object of "the other two kinds of negation; (2) because we can never "have any such notion as that 'there is no *Ākāsha* in this "place'; (3) because any inferential argument that might be "brought forward would be absolutely wanting in any corro- "borative instance; and if we were to attach any importance "to mere inference from particulars (without any corrobora- "tive reasoning pointing to a universal premiss), then we "might as reasonably prove that *Ākāsha* is the object of *prior* "*negation* as well as of *destruction* (as we know of many "particular substances that are such objects); specially as the "denial of the conclusion of such an inference would not "lead us to any incongruity with regard to any well-known "effect. In the same manner, there would be no evidence "for declaring the absence of the jar *in the relation of inherence*, "in a place where the jar exists *in the relation of contact*; "and so it would be much simpler to regard the *absolute* "*negation of jar* to consist in the incompatibility of the co- "substrateness of that jar (with any point in space or time),— "than to introduce the factor of any peculiar relationship (as "that of *contact* or *inherence* and the like); specially as the "cognition of the absolute negation of the jar that we have "may always be explained as referring to the absence of the "*inherence* of the jar (*i. e.*, the non-existence of the jar *by* "*relation of inherence*); because as regards the relation of the "container and the contained (as between the jar and the "place occupied by it), this is actually perceived as existing; "and so there never can arise any doubt as to the real exis-"tence of the jar by this latter relationship. Nor could you "have any inferential argument for establishing the absolute "negation of the jar; as we have already shown that in the "absence of any corroborative reasoning, no such mere in-"ference from particulars could be effective. Nor could "the jar &c. be said to be the common substratum of contact "and *non-contact* (and as such incongruous); as it is "quite possible for one and the same thing—the tree, for "instance,—to be the substratum of the contact of the monkey, "*at its top*, and at the same time to be the substratum of the "non-contact of that same monkey, *at its base*; and certainly, "there would be no incongruity in this."

In view of these objections then, we may now accept 'unreality' to be that character which consists in being the *object of the absolute negation of all being.*

Objection:—"If your argument be meant to establish "this 'unreality',—then, there being no incompatibility "between *presence* and *absence* (as we have shown in regard "to the *tree* and the *monkey*), the cognition of the one would "not set aside the other (*i. e.*, the cognition of the absence of "the phenomenal world would not necessarily set aside all "cognitions of its existence)."

Reply:—Not so; because though it is true that there is no incompatibility between presence and absence as located in different substrata, there would be a distinct incompatibility between them as located in one and the same substratum; as for instance, if *in regard to any particular place* we recognise the practically absolute negation of the jar, then we must have the cognition that *the jar has no practical existence at that place.*

Objection:—"If it were so, then, in the case of the "declaration 'this is shell and not silver',—the negation "spoken of and cognised would be *practical*; and as such "what would be denied by this negation would be only the "*practical reality* of the silver believed to exist before the "eyes; and as such the cognised or *apparent* reality of that "silver would not be denied; and hence even after the said "negation, it would be possible to have the *idea* that 'this "is silver' (as this would have for its object the *apparent* 'reality which would not have been denied by the negation "in question)."

Reply:—The assertion 'this is shell' brings to our mind the direct or immediate cognition of the shell; and this direct cognition sets aside the ignorance (of the shell) that had given rise to the *apparent silver*; and the removal of this *ignorance* deprives the silver of its *apparent* reality also; because the *apparent silver* owes its existence to the observer's *ignorance* of the shell; and so when this *ignorance* (the cause) has been removed (by the cognition of the shell), the removal of its effect, the *apparent silver*, follows as a necessary consequence. It is for this reason that, it is only in a case where the cognition of the substratum (of delusion) not being direct, there is no cessation of ignorance that has given rise to the misconception or delusion,—that, though we have the denial of *practical* reality, there is no denial of *apparent* reality. For instance, in the case of the misconception 'sugar is bitter', we find that unless there is a direct sensuous cognition of the fact of the sugar being *not bitter*, the misconception remains undisturbed (*i. e.* the *apparent reality* of the *bitterness* of sugar remains undenied). Exactly in the same manner, in the case of the phenomenal world, so long as we do not obtain the *direct* perception of the Impartite Brahman, and our sole cognition of it is only indirect (obtained only by means of such words as 'Brahman only exists' and so forth),—

even though we have the denial of the *practical* reality of the phenomenal world, the idea that *the world is real* continues undisturbed (*i. e.* the *apparent* reality of the world remains); but as soon as the ignorance of the real substratum (Brahman) has been removed by direct perception, the idea ceases (and so also the *apparent* reality of the world).

The above arguments also serve to set aside the following objections:— "(1) If by the word '*upādhi*', 'substratum' "(in your definition of 'unreality') you mean any and every "sort of substratum, then your argument proves an undesir-"able conclusion; for instance, even though Colour is the "object of that negation which has for its substratum *Air* "(*i. e.* it does not exist in the Air), yet it is not unreal. (2) If "you mean by the word '*upādhi*' the *adhiṣṭhāna*, the *receptacle* "or *container*,—then, as this receptacle of the negation would "be that same object which would be the subject of the "Ignorance that gives rise to the misconception, there would "be a mutual interdependence:—as the *unreality* of the object "would depend upon the cognition being a mistaken one, and "the mistaken character of the cognition would depend upon 'the unreality of the object".

These arguments are refuted by explaining the *substratum* in the manner described above: which leaves no room for any valid objections.

Another objection is raised against the above definition of 'Unreality':— "We meet with such sentences in the "Upaniṣads as— 'He alone below, He above, &c. &c.'— "which speak of Brahman as occupying definite points in time "and space; but Brahman in reality does not exist at any "such special points of time and place (according to the 'Vedāntin at any rate); and hence being the object of nega-'tion with regard to the substratum occupied by It, Brahman "should be 'unreal' (according to your definition); and "thus your definition would come to have an application that "is too wide for you."

Reply:—This is not quite correct; as by Its very nature, Brahman is devoid of properties; and as such It could never have the property of being the object of any negation.

Objection:—"If Brahman is devoid of all properties, then "It could not have *reality* either (as this also is a property); "and this denial of the reality of Brahman would contradict "many such Vedic passages as—'Brahman is real, conscious-"ness; endless &c. &c.'."

Reply:—We do not admit of any *negation* apart from the substratum (*i. e.* the *negation* of the jar in any place is nothing more than that *place by itself*); and hence the *negation of the said Unreality* would be nothing more or less than the *Reality* itself (which is the substratum of the Unreality, the negation constituting the Unreality being with regard to, and having for its substratum, the Reality); and this *Reality* would be quite compatible with the nature of Brahman.

In the same manner the 'self-luminous', and other characters of Brahman, would be quite compatible with Its nature. As 'self-luminousness' consists only in *the absence of the character of being manifested by something else*; similarly 'eternality' is *the absence of the character of being limited by time*; 'omnipresence' consists in *the absence of the character of being limited in space*; 'absoluteness' is the absence *of limitation by anything*: and so forth. And thus even though Brahman be totally devoid of any positive property (all its characters being mere absence of some positive property), there would be nothing incompatible in the nature of Brahman consisting in the absence of all properties.

And thus no exception can be taken to the second definition of 'Unreality' given above.

We may also define 'Unreality as *the character of being set aside or discarded by cognition (true knowledge)*.

Third Definition of Unreality.

An objection is raised against this definition:—"If we "accept this definition of 'Unreality', then as every cogni- "tion would be set aside by the cognition following it, all "cognition would be 'unreal', and on the other hand, the jar, "which is set aside or destroyed by a stroke of the stick "(and not by any *cognition*), would not be 'unreal'.

"Then, it might be urged that what we mean is that the "unreality of an object consists in its *being such a cognition* "*or idea as is set aside by a cognition.* But then too, the "definition does not cease to be objectionable; as in that case, "there would be no 'unreality' in the shell-silver; because "this is set aside by the direct perception of the substratum "(shell), and yet it is not a *cognition* (being a mere *miscon-* "*ception*); and thus the very 'probandum' of your argument "becomes vitiated

"Then again, it may be explained that what is meant by "a thing being 'unreal' is that it is rejected or set aside "by a cognition that appears in a character belonging to "*Cognitions as such, in general.* But such an 'Unreality' "would belong also to the Impressions left on the mind by Cog- "nitions; as these Impressions are actually set aside by subse- "quent Remembrances which are possessed of the generic "character of 'Cognitions, [and if Impressions were unreal, "then the Impression left behind by the True Knowledge "of Brahman would also be 'unreal'; and thus there could "be no permanent reality for this knowledge]."

Reply:—It is not so; what is meant by a thing being *rejected by cognition* is that it has its existence denied by a general negation proceeding from the true knowledge of the substratum. This 'existence' may be in two forms:—the thing might exist either in its own form, or in the form of its cause,—the latter in accordance with the doctrine that the effect or product has an existence even prior to the operation of the cause. And hence when the jar is smashed by the stroke of the stick, even though it ceases to exist *in its own form* (of the jar), yet its existence in the form of its material cause (the particles of earth) continues (and the jar lies latent in these particles). And this twofold Existence of anything could be negatived only by the true knowledge of Brahman. Thus our definition of 'Unreality' would not be inapplicable to the jar and such other things that existed in the past. For this same reason, our argument will not be open to the charge of invalidity as regards the case of that cognition which would be sublated by the cognition following it,—a sublation that is admitted by all parties, and as such would make the Vedantic argument open to the charge of being 'superfluous'. Nor, on the other hand, could we be taunted with the remark that, inasmuch as such things as the *Ākāsha* and the like have their cognitions set aside only by the *Knowledge of Brahman* (and not by any ordinary cognition), they could not be regarded to have the same 'unreality' as the cognition set aside by any ordinary cognition coming after it. Neither of these charges could be reasonably brought against us; because, as regards the former case what happens is that the previous cognition becomes merged into the succeeding cognition; and as such it contrives to exist *in the form of its cause*; and hence there can be no denial of its *existence* altogether. In the case of such things as the 'hare's horns' and such other non-entities, though there is an absolute denial of their existence altogether, yet as this denial is not by means of any cognition (such as that 'the hare's horn does not exist), our definition of 'unreality' cannot apply to such non-entities (that are never known as *entities*). In the case of the *shell-silver* we have to admit the *apparent* reality of the *silver* for the time being, as otherwise we could not account for the fact of the man actually perceiving it; and this *apparent* reality does not cease until we have the subsequent cognition denying the reality (*i. e.* the cognition—'this is not silver'): and thus the character of the subject of our argument becomes applicable to it (as this also has its existence denied by a cognition).

It is with a view to all this that the author of the *Vivaraṇa* has made the following declaration:—'The *bāḍha* of a misconception consists in its being sublated by cognition, along with its effects either latent (in the form of impressions) or apparent (in the form of gross materials).'

The author of the *Vārṭika* says:—'As soon as there appears the true knowledge arising from such declarations as *That Thou Art* and the like, Nescience, along with its products, neither is, nor was, nor will be.' What is meant by 'nor was' is that nescience ceases along with those of its products that have become merged into it; 'nor will be' means that it ceases and with it cease all its future products or emanations; but this latter fact does not concern us at present.

The fact remains that as soon as we have perceived the real substratum (the shell) in its real form, the ignorance or misconception of the *silver* that we have had ceases forthwith, along with all its products, present as well as past—the latter being such as have become merged into it. And thus we find that each misconception caused by the ignorance of the real character of a thing is set aside by the knowledge of that thing; and thus there being as many 'ignorances' as there are misconceptions, each of these would be set aside by the realisation of the true knowledge of its own substratum (and it is not that ignorance being set aside by the knowledge of Brahman only, there would be no cessation of any misconceptions before this knowledge is gained). And thus the object of our inferential argument (*i. e. the character of being set aside by knowledge*) does not fail in applying to the corroborative instance (of the case of shell-silver). As all parties are agreed on this point—that, as after the falling of the stick on the jar (the jar is broken. and) we have the notion 'the jar is no longer,' so in the same manner, after the true knowledge of the substratum (shell) has been obtained, there appears the notion 'the ignorance of the shell, as also the silver in it, is no longer.'

Nor is there anything objectionable in regarding 'Unreality' as consisting in the character of being precluded by a cognition from appearing in a character concomitant with the generic character of 'Cognitions'. Because when one cognition (an ordinary cognition, not a misconception) sets aside another cognition preceding it, it does so, not in any character that is concomitant with the generic character of 'cognitions', but in the character of a specific quality of the Self, like Desire &c.,—or in the character of being an all-pervasive quality; that is to say, when we have one cognition following the other, the one sets aside the other, not because this latter is a *cognition*, but because it is a specific quality of the Self (and as such cannot admit of another quality at the same time; just as at the time that one desire appears it does not admit of the presence of any other desire at the time). And thus our argument would not be open to the charge of being superfluous'. [That is to say, if such 'Unreality', as would belong to all cognitions merely by reason of their being cognitions, were meant to be proved by the Vedantin with regard to the whole phenomenal world, then alone, as there would be no one to object to such an 'Unreality', the putting forward of such an argument would have been absolutely useless and superfluous.]

Nor would this definition of 'Unreality' apply to the Mental Impressions which (it has been argued), though not set aside by Desire &c., are set aside by Cognitions in the form of Remembrances. Because we have no evidence to show that an Impression is ever actually *destroyed* by the subsequent Remembrance; on the contrary, when the Remembrance appears, the idea that we have is that the Impression (giving rise to that Remembrance) has become *strengthened*; and this 'strength' can consist only in the multiplication of the number of Impressions (with regard to to the object remembered); and thus we find that the case of Impressions does not affect our explanation of 'Unreality'.

As a matter of fact, one cognition sets aside another, only when the former is of the character of *direct* or immediate cognition, and as such none of the aforesaid objections is applicable to this view of the case.

Nor again would our definition of 'Unreality' apply to 'Doubtful Cognitions' (such as 'is this a jar or not?') merely by reason of its *being set aside* by 'certainty' (in the form 'this is a jar') which is a property common to *all kinds of cognition* (immediate or mediate, perceptional as well as inferential) [That is to say, we have said that 'Unreality' consists in being set aside by direct or immediate cognition; and Doubtful Cognitions are set aside, not merely by 'immediate' cognition, but by definitely certain cognitions of all kinds; hence the 'doubtful cognition' could not be rightly said to be 'set aside by immediate Cognitions'; consequently the said definition of 'Unreality' would not apply to these].

Fourth Definition of Unreality.

The '*Unreality*' *of an object may be defined as the character of being negated by the absolute negation located in its own substratum*; this would mean that it is cognised as the substratum of its own absolute negation; and herein would lie the difference of this definition from the second definition. The objections too against this definition would be set aside in the manner shown above. [The absolute negation must be in reference to the same kind of relation in which the unreal object is at first cognised]. In the case of the relation of *Contact* we find that before the jar is produced and comes into contact with a certain point in space, there is an 'absolute negation' of it even in regard to the point in space with which it is to come into contact; and so also after the jar has been destroyed; similarly in the case of the relation of *Inherence* also we find that the colour of the unbaked jar, which resides in it by the relation of Inference, is destroyed by the baking that the jar undergoes; and as such there is an absolute negation of the *inhering* colour also. So we find that it is quite possible for us to have an absolute negation also of things related either by Contact or by Inherence. Nor would the possibility of such negation make impossible our conception of the *material* cause [the conception whereof is based upon the undissolubility of the relationship between the cause and its effect,—an undissolubility which would appear to be impossible in the face of the aforesaid possibility of the absolute negation]. Because just as in regard to Time, we find that both the *presence* and the *absence* (absolute negation) of the jar in the earthenware pieces that form its material cause are possible at different periods of time,—so both its presence and absence in its material cause would be possible at different points in space also; and secondly, because as a matter of fact we find that the character of the *material cause* is quite compatible with the 'prior non-existence' of the product [*i. e.* the jar has no existence before it is produced, and this previous non-existence does not interfere with the fact of the earthenware pieces being its *material* cause]. [And similarly there could be no incompatibility of the nature of this cause with the absolute negation of the product also].

It might be argued that, "even the *prior negation* of "an object would not be possible in a substratum where we "have its *absolute negation* (as 'prior negation' means that the "object is brought into existence after this negation; and this "would not be possible for that of which we have an *absolute* "negation)."

But as a matter of fact we find that in regard to Time, there is no impossibility of the 'prior negation' of that which is also an object of 'absolute negation'.
[That is to say at the time that the jar is at the point of being produced we have the 'prior' as well as the 'absolute' negation of the jar].

Objection :—" As regards *Time* we admit of this co-exist-"ence of the *prior* and *absolute* negations, on the strength "of such ideas as—'at the present time we have the *absolute* "negation or non-existence of the jar'—and 'at this time we "have the *prior* negation of the jar'; but as regards *Space*, we "have no valid grounds for admitting of such co-existence "of the two kinds of negation."

Reply :—For admitting this we do have sufficient grounds, in the form of—(1) the Inferential cognition that we have of the *Unreality* of all things, and (2) the Vedic texts pointing to such co-existence (and consequent *unreality*).

We have already shown above how there is no incongruity or incompatibility in the co-existence of the affirmation and negation of two different kinds of existence [*i. e.* the affirmation of the *apparent* existence of a thing would not be incompatible with the negation or denial of its *practical* existence.]

It might be argued, that, " this fourth definition of 'Unreality' would not apply to an absolute non-entity." But such would not be the case, as what is meant by the definition is the character of *being cognised* as existing in that which is the substratum of its absolute negation. [And a non-entity could very well be *cognised* as such, though having no existence].

Objection :—" We meet with such Vedic texts as—' Some "say there was *nonentity* in the beginning'; and as this "sentence distinctly points to the *real existence* of the *non-en-*

"*tity*, your definition of 'Unreality' would unduly include this "*Nonentity* also (and thus you would be going against a direct "Vedic declaration)."

Reply:—What the passage speaks of is only the *absence* of the idea—'this was entity or real in the beginning'; [*i. e.* it means that in the beginning people had no such idea as 'this was real' &c.] and it does not mean to assert the *existence of non-entity*; as if it meant the latter, then there would be self-contradiction in the passage (as the sentence '*Asaḍēva &c.*' is followed immediately bythe sentence '*saḍēva &c.*). And thus there is no impropriety in the application of the definition to *nonentities*.

Over and above this, all that we have said above in connection with the other definitions would apply to this last definition also. Hence we desist from further argumentation.

Fifth Definition of 'Unreality'.

We may define the 'Unreality' of an object to consist in *its being something distinct from existence.* That an object exists means that it is recognised by the valid means of knowledge; and the 'validity' of the means of knowledge consists in its being unaccompanied by (free from) discrepancies or deficiencies. So that 'Unreality' comes to be the character of being distinct from that which is recognised or established by the valid means of knowledge; that is, all that is not thus recognised is 'unreal'; like dreams (dreams being known by means of knowledge under the influence of the deficiencies imposed by sleep). Though the character of *being recognised by valid means of knowledge* is invariably concomitant with *non-deniaiblity* (*i. e.* that which is known by valid means of knowledge is never capable of being reasonably denied),—yet this explanation of the former character would not be as effective in the present connection as the one we have given above [*viz*: the character of being recognised by such means of knowledge as are free from discrepancies].

This definition however as it stands would apply to absolute non-entities as well as to Brahman who is devoid of all qualifications; as a non-entity would be 'distinct from existence' and Brahman also is not believed by the Vedantin to have 'existence'. Hence with a view to guard against This it becomes necessary to supplement the definition further thus:—'The *unreality* of an object consists in its being distinct from existence, and yet *being cognised as existing*'. This now could not apply to either non-entity or Brahman; as neither of these is ever *known as existing* (*lit.* is never the object of a cognition qualified by existence).

This same reasoning also serves to set aside the following objection:—" In your definition, 'distinct from existence', " what do you mean by 'existence'? Do you mean—(1) that " which is the substratum of the general essence of 'existence or " being'? or (2) 'which is incapable of being denied'? or, (3) " 'which is of the nature of Brahman'? In the case of (1), inas- " much as you admit the ordinary objects like the jar &c. to be- " long to, and be possessed of, the general essence of 'Nescience' " (which is believed by the Vedantin to be beginningless, and as " such to have an existence),—the definition of 'Unreality' " would consist simply in 'undeniability' [and thus this fifth " definition of yours would not in any way differ from the one " given before]. Lastly, in the case of (3), your proposition " and arguments would be superfluous; (as none of your op- " ponents holds the phenomenal world to be *of the nature of* " *Brahman*; and so this 'Unreality' they would never object to]."

All this is rejected by the very fact of our not accepting any of the three alternatives here put forward. And here we might recall all the reasonings that we have shown in connection with our first definition, where 'unreality' has been shown to be distinct both from 'existence' and 'non-existence.' We shall have something more to say in this connection, in the chapter on '*Ḍrishṭārṭhasiḍḍhi*'?

Thus ends the section on the Definition of 'Unreality.'

Section (4).

THE UNREALITY OF 'UNREALITY'.

['Unreality' is also unreal; nor does this make the world 'real'; it only proves that the world is *practically* real, endowed with a relative, not absolute, reality].

Says the Opponent:—"Is this *Unreality* of yours 'real' "or 'unreal'? If it is 'unreal', then the

P. 10. "World (of which it is the *Unreality*) would "be 'real'. As it is a universally recognised rule that when "two contradictory properties are suspected to belong to "one and the same object, the 'unreality' of any one of "these properties would necessarily imply the 'reality' of "the other. [Hence between 'Unreality' and 'Reality' as "suspected to belong to the Phenomenal World, the 'unrea-"lity' of the 'Unreality' would necessarily imply the 'reality' "of the 'Reality']. On the other hand, if the *Unreality* "be *real*,—then just as this would be real, so would the "World also be *real*. And thus in either case, there would "be no chance for 'Monism' [*i. e.* in any case there would "be no truth in the theory that the only one reality is "Brahman]."

To the above we make the following reply:—It is not so; as the 'unreality' of the *Unreality* of the world would not make this *World real*. Because the law—that of two contradictory properties the unreality of one implies the reality of the other—is true only of cases where the conditions of unreality are not the same in both the properties; as for instance, in the case of the *shell* we find that of two mutually contradictory characters of 'silver' and 'non-silver', [the two mutually exclusive characters of 'silver' and 'something other than silver'], the unreality of the one implies the reality of the other; and in this and similar cases we find that the conditions of the unreality of one property are totally different from the conditions of the unreality of the other. In the case of the

Phenomenal World and its Unreality however we find that the conditions of unreality are exactly the same,—both being regarded as 'unrèal' simply by reason of their '*perceptibility*' and such other characters.

As a similar case we may cite that when the two characters of the 'horse' and the 'cow' are denied with reference to the Elephant, the condition of the unreality of both the characters consists in the fact of both being concomitant with the absolute negation or absence of the character of the 'Elephant'; and hence in this case, the unreality of the one (the character of the 'horse') does not imply the reality of the other (the character of the 'cow').

Then again, we shall show later on that 'Reality' and 'Unreality' are not contradictory terms,—nor are they invariably concomitant with the negation of each other. But, even if the two were contradictories, there could be no actual contradiction between the two in a case where each would pertain to a different kind of existence; f. i. though the 'unreality' of *practical* existence would be contrary to, and would preclude, the 'reality' of the *practical* existence, yet it would not affect the reality of the *apparent* existence.

And further, we find the Logician admitting of the co-existence, in one and the same substrate, of two contradictories,—such as '*Contact*' and '*Absence of Contact*' (*i. e.* the 'monkey on the tree' would be in contact with the tree as regards the branch on which it is sitting, and would not be in contact with it as regards the base); and in the same manner, there would be nothing incongruous in the co-existence of 'Reality' and 'Unreality'.

Then again, between any two things we find that when that which establishes the existence of the one precludes the existence of the other,—all that this shows is that the existence of the two things is of different kinds; as for example, between the *Shell-silver* and the *Not-shell-silver,* we find that the cognition 'this is not silver' denies the former and asserts the latter; and in this what is proved is the fact of the former having only an *apparent* and the latter a *practical* existence. But in a case where we have both things precluded by one and the same negation, the existence of the two things is of the same kind; for instance, the cognition 'this is shell' denies the 'silver-in-the-shell,' and also the fact of the thing being '*something other than shell*'; and here we find that both of these latter have only *apparent* existence. And in the case in question we find that the 'Reality' of the Phenomenal World as well as its 'Unreality' are both precluded by one and the same agency, viz., the true knowledge of Brahman; and thus the existence of both must be of the same kind; and hence that which would preclude 'Unreality' would also preclude the reality of all phenomenal diversity; and so the unreality of 'Unreality' would not affect the ultimate 'Unity' of things.

Thus ends the Section dealing with the Unreality of Unreality.

Section (5).

[What is meant by the World being 'perceptible' is that it is the object of the 'Vṛiṭṭi' of cognitions not produced by Authoritative Word, or (b) that it is the object of qualified or limited cognition, or (c) that it forms the object of consciousness, or (d) that it is dependent upon a cognition which is different from itself, or (e) that it is not self-illumined.]

Objection:—"You have put forward the 'perceptibility' of "the phenomenal world as a reason for its 'unreality', and "it behoves you to explain what you mean by a certain "thing being 'perceptible'. Do you mean—(1) that it is "pervaded over by the '*vṛiṭṭi*' (*i. e.* the shape taken by "the organic modification of the mind moving outwards)? "or, (2) that it is pervaded over by (*i. e.* identical with) "the resultant shape of the manifested '*vṛiṭṭi*'? or (3) "that it is both of these? or, (4) that it forms at some "time and in some way the object of consciousness? or, "(5) that for its own activity, it depends upon something "apart from itself, in the form of Cognition? or, (6) that "it is not self-illumined?

"It could not be the *first*; as such 'perceptibility' would "belong to the Self also, which is pervaded over by the '*vṛitti*' "produced by the Veḍānṭa texts (*i. e.* the Self forms the "object of cognition produced by these texts). [And so "the Self also would become 'unreal']. For this same "reason it could not be the *third*. Nor could it be the "*second*; because as a matter of fact we find that eternal "substances and substances not perceptible by the senses, "and also such misconceived things as the *shell-silver*, are "never actually identical with the resultant *vṛitti* [*i. e.* "the eternal substance has an existence of its own, independ-"ently of any '*vṛitti*' of the internal organ; imperceptible "substances too can never be identical with any sensuous "'*vṛitti*; and lastly, the *shell-silver* has no existence at all, "and as such cannot be regarded as having any shape identi-"cal with the *vṛitti*]; and hence an 'unreality' based upon "such 'perceptibility' would not apply to all things, and as "such your argument would be open to the fallacy of *Incom-"pleteness*, and would also be deficient as regards its subject "(as even the 'unreality' would not apply to such univers-"ally admitted unrealities as the shell-silver and the like). "Nor could it be the *fourth*; as Brahman also would be such "an object; as we have such ideas as 'Brahman which "was not known before, is *known* now by means of the "Veḍānṭa texts'; and thus your 'unreality' would apply "to Brahman also. Nor again could It be the *fifth*; as an "'unreality' based upon this also would apply to Brahman; "as in regard to Brahman also we find that as It is spoken "of as 'without a second' and so forth, It stands in need of "other cognitions than its own. Nor, lastly, could it be "the *sixth*; because 'non-self-illuminedness' is nothing "more than 'non-cognisability' coupled with 'incapability "of direct or immediate recognition'; and as this incapabil- "ity is not found to belong to the shell-silver, which is cog- "nised directly, the 'unreality' would not belong to this shell- "silver, and this would vitiate the Vedantic argument."

Reply : Not so; because with the sole exception of the *second* all the other five explanations are capable of standing water (the closest scrutiny). For instance, it has been argued that if 'perceptibility' consist in being pervaded by '*vṛitti*', then that would apply to Brahman also; or otherwise Brahman, would not be the object expressed by the Vedanta texts, which therefore would become absolutely meaningless and useless. But it is not so; because as a matter of fact the *Pure* or Absolute Brahman is not 'perceptible'; as is distinctly stated in such texts as 'That which is imperceptible'; what *is* 'perceptible', however, is the *conditioned* Brahman, and this conditioned Brahman is also 'unreal'; because at the time that Brahman becomes an object of the '*vṛitti*', it is no longer *pure*.

1. Perceptibility' consists in being the object of Vritti.

It might be argued that, this view of the case would be contradictory to such declarations of ours as—'becoming fixed in the form of Brahman, which is *cognisable* by all cognitions' &c. &c. But there would be no such contradiction; as this declaration also refers to the *conditioned* Brahman only.

Objection :—"If such be the case, then you could never "establish the existence of the pure Brahman."

Reply :—The *pure* Brahman is self-manifest, and as such has Its existence established by Its very nature.

Objection :—"Unless the thing is known, we cannot either "assert or deny any property with regard to that thing: "hence in denying the 'perceptibility' of the pure Brahman, "you admit its 'cognisability' (and this would be enough, "to establish Its unreality). It might be argued that, being "self-manifest, Brahman has its existence established by Its "very nature, and that which is denied is only the fact of "the pure Brahman being 'perceptible' *by the Vṛiṭṭi*. But "if the pure Brahman were not perceptible or cognisable "*by the Vṛiṭṭi*' produced by the words 'the pure Brahman "is self-manifest', then its self-manifest character could "never be recognised."

Reply :—At the time that the '*vṛiṭṭi*' actually appears, anything that is characterised by that '*vṛiṭṭi*' could not be 'pure'; and hence the pure Brahman could never form the objective of any '*vṛiṭṭi*'. Consequently the sentence 'the pure Brahman is self-manifest' is taken as expressing by *indirect indication*, the fact of the *impure* (*conditioned*) *Brahman being not-self-manifest.* And thus the *pure* Brahman is saved from being the object of verbal cognition; and this preclusion of the *self-manifest character* from the *impure Brahman* would naturally imply that it belongs to the *pure* Brahman; just as the preclusion of 'diversity' implies 'Unity.'

Objection :—"If the *pure* Brahman be not designated, either directly or indirectly, then there would be no use for the use of the texts at all."

Reply :—But it is actually found serving the useful purpose of supplying the implied meaning just pointed out.

Thus then, what the assertion that *the pure Brahman is not perceptible nor unreal* means is that *perceptibility* and *unreality* are concomitant with *impurity*; and this implies the absence of '*perceptibility*' and *Unreality* in the *pure Brahman.*

This also serves to set aside the following assertion of of the Shūnyavāḍin, the Nihilist :—"It would be much simpler "to regard *Appearance* alone as the necessary condition of "*Unreality*; and Brahman also would be *unreal*, as that also "*appears*, even though by itself [*i. e.* even if It is self-"manifest, yet It has *appearance* all the same]." For the character of *self-appearance* we do not find in any such admittedly *unreal* things as the *shell-silver* and the like, as what actually *appears* is not the *silver*, but the *shell*; and as for mere *appearance* (the character we find in such unreal things), this we do not know of as belonging to Brahman.

Objection:—" As a matter of fact, we find that whenever " we have the idea of a thing as *qualified* by a certain " character, this idea includes or implies the idea of the *thing* " itself; and hence when we find Vedic texts affording us " the idea that *qualified* (conditioned) Brahman is 'percepti- " ble', this idea would imply also the idea that *Brahman* " *itself* is also 'perceptible'; and thus too your reason (' per- " ceptibility ' as proving ' Unreality') would become fallaci- " ous. It might be argued that, in such sentences as *viṣ-* " *ṇavē shipiviṣṭāya &c.* we find the Veda speaking of Viṣṇu " *as qualified* by a certain character to be the deity of a " certain sacrifice; and in the same manner the passages " in question may be regarded as pointing out the *perceptibil-* " *ity* of the *qualified* or *conditioned* Brahman; or again, as we " find *Agni* and *Soma* mentioned as the two *together* form- " ing the deity of a certain sacrifice, so too we may re- " gard *perceptibility* as mentioned with reference to the " *qualified* Brahman and the *qualification* (that of being con- " ditioned) as taken together; and thus *perceptibility* could " not belong to the *pure* or *unconditioned* Brahman. But " this could not be; for if 'perceptibility', and the conse- " quent 'unreality' were to belong to the two (the *qualified* " and the *qualification*) only when taken together (and not " to either by itself), then the qualifications also (that limit " and condition Brahman) would not be 'perceptible' and " 'Unreal'; and so your reasoning would *fail partially* (not " proving the unreality of the qualifications)."

Reply:—There could be no such undesirable contingency; as we do not deny the 'perceptibility' of Brahman *when It has become qualified*; as we regard the *conditioned* Brahman to be as perceptible and Unreal as anything else.

This same reason also sets aside another similar objection—that, "if *perceptibility* belongs to the *conditioned* Brahman it must belong to *that which is conditioned* (*pure* Brahman) also." Because in its *conditioned* form Brahman is held by us to be *unreal.*

Nor would there be any 'partial failure' of our reasoning (by reason of the *qualification* by itself, of Brahman, not being 'perceptible' and 'Unreal'); as the qualifications that are perceived as belonging to Brahman are such as are perceived also elsewhere apart from Brahman; and in such cases it will have been found to be 'perceptible' and 'Unreal.' [The knowledge of the qualified Brahman however can never be had apart from Brahman Itself].

Objection:—"According to you the Vēḍānta texts are "productive of a single impartite *Vṛiṭṭi*; now if this "*Vṛiṭṭi* had for its object the *conditioned* Brahman, "then,—inasmuch as at the time that the *Vṛiṭṭi* would "be present (which could be only at the time of the "realisation of the 'true knowledge' described in the texts), "there could be no other limiting *condition* for Brahman,—the "only limitation possible would be the *Vṛiṭṭi* itself; and as "the object of the *Vṛiṭṭi*, would be Brahman as conditioned by "the limitation of the *Vṛiṭṭi*, you would have the absurdity of "the *Vṛiṭṭi* having itself for its object. Nor could this be "desirable for you; as in all cases of verbal cognition "nothing is cognised that is not present in the word (as its "denotation); and so when we have the verbal cognition "produced by the Vēḍānta texts, we could not have any "cognition of the *Vṛiṭṭi* which is not in any way present in "the words (of the texts). [And hence the texts cannot be "regarded as producing any knowledge of the *conditioned* "Brahman]. In fact, even if this were possible, this know-"ledge could not set aside Nescience and its products. "Because the Cognition that is capable of setting aside "Nescience and its products is only that which has nothing to "do with this Nescience &c. (*i. e.* of which Nescience &c. do "not form the object). [And in the case in question, according to you the knowledge produced by the Vēḍānṭa texts has "for its object Brahman *along with some limitation*—, and this "limitation is a product of Nescience; so the knowledge "having for its object a product of Nescience, could not set "aside the Nescience itself]. Otherwise (*i. e.* if a knowledge "having for its object Nescience and its products could set "aside Nescience itself), such cognitions also as 'I am ignorant', "'this is a jar' and the like, would set aside Nescience,— "these also having for their object something *conditioned by* "*limitations.*"

Reply:—Not so; because what we hold is that the *Vṛiṭṭi* that serves as the limitation of Brahman is such as is manifested by the verbal operation (of the words); as has been well said by the author of the *Vēḍānṭakalpaṭaru*:—'The *Vṛiṭṭi* that has for its object the *pure* Brahman, whenever it does appear, it sets aside *all* the limitations of Brahman, including itself (*i. e.* the *Vṛiṭṭi* sets aside itself along with the other limitations); for the simple reason that it is itself as good a limitation as any other; and thus the *unconditioned* Brahman can never be the *object*; then [as regards the *object* being Brahman *as conditioned* by the limitation of the *Vṛiṭṭi*, we would not have the absurdity of this *Vṛiṭṭi* being its own object; because] the limitation of the *Vṛiṭṭi* on Brahman exists only as a differentiating factor (distinguishing the *conditioned* from the *pure* Brahman), and not as a factor to be itself cognised as part of the '*object of cognition*'.

The sense of this may be thus explained:—Though the character of the 'Perceiver' (Witness) belongs to Brahman *as conditioned by Nescience*, yet 'Nescience' does not enter into the constitution of the 'Perceiver' (Witness) for the simple reason that Nescience is something totally devoid of consciousness (while the character of the 'Perceiver' is consciousness itself); in fact 'Nescience' forms a factor in *that which is perceived or witnessed* (the object cognised); in the same manner, though the character of the 'object' belongs to Brahman *as conditioned by the Vṛiṭṭi*, yet the *Vṛiṭṭi* does not enter into the constitution of the 'object'; for the simple reason that it could not form its own objective; in fact though not an 'object' itself, the *Vṛiṭṭi* imparts the objective' character to the Consciousness (of Brahman); and there can be nothing incongruous in this.

The above explanation also applies to the point of one and the same thing (Brahman) being the object of 'Nescience' as well as of 'knowledge'. That is to say, 'Nescience' applies to Brahman only when this is conditioned by Nescience; for the simple reason that at the time that Nescience does not cast its limitation on Brahman, it has no existence at all. Thus then, both 'Nescience' and 'knowledge' have for their objective, not any limitation, but Brahman as conditioned by the limitation; and hence both have actually one and the same thing for their objective.

From this it also follows that 'Nescience' can not be removed by the 'knowledge' of mere limitations; as 'Nescience' has no limitation for its objective, and it is only when the Knowledge and the Nescience have the same objective that they remove or set aside each other.

II. 'Perceptibility' consists in being the object of Vṛiṭṭis other than those produced by Words.

As a matter of fact however, 'Perceptibility' consists in *the character of being the object of Vṛiṭṭi other than that produced by words.* If we do not admit this explanation, then Perceptibility' would belong even to such absolute non-entities as the 'hare's horns' and the like; as even such non-entities form the objects of verbal cognition by means of words, such as—'the hare's horn is an absolute non-entity'; and on the other hand, this 'Perceptibility' would not belong to the *pure* Brahman which is the object of only such *Vṛittis* (cognitions) as are produced by the Vedanta texts. As neither the *absolute non-entity* nor the *pure Brahman* is regarded as the object of any *Vṛittis* or cognitions other than those produced by Words.

III. 'Perceptibility' consists in being the object of a definitely qualified Vṛitti.

Or, we may define 'Perceptibility' as the *character of being the objective of a qualified Vṛitti*; and this 'qualification' would be a definite and definable property. And thus it would not apply either to the *pure* Brahman, which is the 'object' of an *undefinable* cognition, or to the *absolute non-entity*, which is the object of a cognition qualified by an *undefinable* property. Then as regards Negation, the said 'Perceptibility' would apply to that also; as all Negation is *definable*, and as such, is the object of *definable or definite cognitions*. As for the fact of the 'qualification' being something known as 'existing', that is a point that does not affect the case in question.

The fourth definition of 'Perceptibility'.

In the same manner as a reason for 'Unreality' we may have that 'Perceptibility' which consists in *the character of being the object tending to the ordinary worldly activity*—a character that is common to that which is pervaded over, or affected by, the *Vṛitti* as well as that which is affected by the result of the *Vṛitti* (*i.e.* the cognition resulting from the *Vṛitti*). How this will not apply to Brahman or to an absolute Non-entity, we have already explained above.

The fifth definition of 'Perceptibility'.

Or again, we may define 'Perceptibility' as *the character of being the object of consciousness.* This character forms the reason for 'unreality', inasmuch as it consists in the fact of being in some way related to consciousness.

This character could never belong to the *pure* Consciousness (*i. e.* Brahman), for the simple reason that relationship of any kind always presupposes a certain difference between the members related; and hence there could be no relationship between Consciousness and consciousness. And as regards the absolute non-entity, how the character in question does not apply to it may be easily explained [*i. e.* by a further qualification, in the form of *being the object of the idea of 'existing'*, which latter cannot belong to the absolute non-entity.]

Sixth definition of 'Perceptibility'.

Or, as a reason for 'unreality' we may have that 'Perceptibility' which consists in *the character of always depending, for its usage or activity, upon the cognition or idea of something other than itself.* The word 'idea' (*samvit*) here used may be taken as denoting either—(1) the consciousness as manifested in the object, or (2) the consciousness manifested by the *Vritti* (organic extension of the transformed inner perceptive organ), or (3) the pure Consciousness itself. As a matter of fact, we find that all activity with regard to the ordinary things, such as the jar and the like,—and even with regard to eternal and supersensuous things (like *Ākāsha*) —which are manifested (rendered cognisable) by the *Witness* or Perceiver, depends upon the idea of something other than the things themselves; and hence the 'unreality' based upon such 'perceptibility' would apply to all these things. The 'activity' here spoken of might be in the form of '*sphuraṇa*', 'appearance', or '*abdhivadana*', 'being spoken of', and so forth (*i. e.* 'being desired' &c.) [When a thing *appears*, there is a '*vyavahāra*' in connection with it; and so also when it is *spoken of*, *desired* &c. &c.] And as regards Brahman,

Page 13.

inasmuch as the only *vyavahāra* or 'activity' with regard to It is in the form of 'appearance', and this is ever present in its accomplished form, there is no need for the idea of anything apart from Itself. [And hence the definition of 'Perceptibility' does not apply to Brahman]. The word '*niyaṭa*', 'always', in the definition serves to preclude all possibility of deficiency in it; as the word makes the definition applicable to *all activity* in connection with the things, which depends upon the idea of something else.

Seventh definition of 'Perceptibility.'

In the same manner we may explain 'Perceptibility', as the basis of 'Unreality', to consist in *the character of being not self-luminous. The 'Self-luminousness'* of a thing consists in its not depending, for its direct cognition, upon anything else; (and this character belongs to Brahman alone) as declared in the passage— 'That which is by itself directly cognised is Brahman'. And this character finally comes to lie in the character of being directly cognisable independently of everything else. And thus the fact of a certain thing being the substratum or object of distinction or differentiation due to this character (*i. e* the absence of this character) would form the basis of 'Unreality'.

This character we find present in all that is never directly cognised, as well as that which is cognised by the help of something else;—such for instance, as the *jar* and the like. It might be argued that, "this character "would apply to Brahman also, as there is some sort "of an *assumed* distinction between the Brahman "that is cognised and the Brahman (Consciousness) "that cognises it (and so the cognition of Brahman also de-"pends upon something different from itself); and as a "matter of fact, even in the case of the ordinary things, "like the *jar* &c., all distinction is merely *assumed*, there "being no distinction or difference (according to the Vedantin) "that is not assumed."

But this is not true; because the distinctions that we have with regard to Brahman are not based upon the aforesaid character of *independent direct cognisability*; as a matter of fact, those distinctions are based upon such totally different characters as those of the '*Jīva*' (the Individual Self), the '*Ishvara*' (God) and the like.

Eighth Definition of 'Perceptibility'.

In the same manner we may have as the reason for 'Unreality', that 'Perceptibility' which consists in *the character of being not uncognisable, and yet incapable of being regarded or treated as directly cognisable.*

Objection:—" As a matter of fact we find that, just as " in Brahman, so in Nescience, in the Inner Organ, and " even in the shell-silver and such other things,—we find the " said *capability of being regarded as directly cognisable which* " *is qualified by the character of being the object of the activity* " *resulting from the cognition* [*i. e.*, just as Brahman, so " Nescience &c. also are incapable of forming the object of " actions proceeding from their cognition]; and as such if " you were to make this character your 'reason' for 'Un- " reality', then your argument would be open to the fallacies " (1) of being 'unknown' (not recognised by all parties), and " (2) of the *Probandum* being defective."

Reply:—Not so; as what we mean by the 'character of being regarded as directly cognisable' is the *capability of forming the object of such Vṛitti or cognition as sets aside ignorance*; and certainly this latter *capability* does not belong either to Nescience &c., or to the shell-silver and such things; and as such our argument would not be open to any of the above mentioned fallacies. Then, as for the capability of the jar, &c., to form the object of the resultant activity (following from cognition), this we shall explain later on.

In accordance with the view that the 'cessation of Nescience' is a fifth kind of things (as apart from the *absolutely real*, the *practically real*, the *apparently real* and *absolute nonentity*), it would be necessary to postulate as the reason for 'Unreality', the 'Perceptibility' as *qualified* by existence at the time of the ignorance; and this would make this reason inapplicable to the said 'cessation of Nescience' (as this cessation does not exist while ignorance exists). And the same qualification would preclude the reason from all *absolute non-entities*.

In the same manner we may go on showing how there would be no objection to regarding 'Perceptibility' as the reason for 'Unreality.'

When however, we regard 'Unreality' as nothing more but 'difference from real being,' then there could not be the least chance of our argument applying either to the 'absolute non-entity' or to the 'cessation of Nescience' regarded as the fifth condition things.

Section (6).

[What is meant by the '*Jadatva*' or 'Unconsciousness' of the World is (*a*) that it is not of the nature of Cognition, or (b) that it is not-Self.]

Question :—"What do you mean by this '*jadatva*', '*Un-*
P. 13. "*consciousness*? Is it—(1) the character of the "*non-cogniser*? or (2) the character of *non-cognition* "(*or ignorance*)? or (3) the character of the *not-self*?

"It could not be the *first*; because according to the Vedantin "the object of the notion of 'I' is also included in the 'phenomenal world', the 'Unreality' whereof he seeks to prove; and "it is this 'I' whom he holds to be the 'cogniser'; and as such "the *character of the non-cogniser* would not be present in the "whole of the 'phenomenal world'; and so the Reason would "fail with regard to that particular factor of it. And "further, the *character of the non-cogniser*, would be present "in the *pure* Self, whom the Vedântin regards to be the

" *non-cogniser*; and so the Reason for 'Unreality' would " become applicable to the *pure* Self also.

" Nor could 'Unconsciousness' be regarded as the *charac-* " *ter of ignorance*' (or non-cognition); as according to the " Vēdāntin, 'cognition' being only 'consciousness as " affected by the *Vṛitti*', either the '*vṛitti*' by itself or " the *pure* consciousness by itself would not be 'cognition'; " and hence even though the said *character of non-cognition* " may, on this ground, be shown to be applicable to the '*Vṛitti*', " yet the undesirable fact would remain that the said charac- " ter would be present in the *pure Consciousness* (which also " having the *character of non-cognition*, would have to be re- " garded as 'Unreal').

" Nor lastly, could 'Unconsciousness' be regarded as the " *character of the Not-self*; because it cannot be easily " ascertained what the *character of the Self* is [and hence it is " all the more difficult to understand the character of the " Not-Self]. The 'Self' cannot be regarded as a parti- " cular *class*, for the simple reason that the Vedantin " admits of but one Self (and no *class* can be formed of a " single thing); and even though there is a multiplicity " of *qualified* or *conditioned* Selves, these would all, according " the Vedantin, be included in the 'phenomenal world', whose " Unreality he seeks to prove. Nor again could the *charac-* " *ter of the Self* consist of '*bliss*'; as, if this 'bliss' were " 'material bliss', then, as there would be no '*jadatva*' " apart from this, this *Jadatva* as apart from the " 'Bliss-Self' would be something altogether *unknown*, " and hence fallacious as a reason; and if this 'material " bliss' be regarded as the character of the *Self*, then, " this view would become open to the objections that " have been urged against the view that 'Unconsciousness' is " *the character of non-cognition* [*i. e*, if the *pure* Conscious- " ness were of the character of 'bliss', then this also would " become 'Unreal', and so forth]."

To the above we make the following *reply*:—There is nothing objectionable in the *second* and *third* explanations suggested. For instance, if we regard 'Unconsciousness' as *the character of non-cognition*, it would never apply to Brahman ; as even during the state of Liberation, Brahman does not lose Its character of consciousness, which by itself consists in illumination (or manifestation) with an objective taint [of the '*Vṛiṭṭi*' during the liberation-state pertaining to all knowable things]. [And as such, what is meant by the 'character of non-cognition' would *the character of that which is not pure Consciousness*].

Objection:—" Just as all negation implies the counter-" entity (the object that is negatived), so all Desires and all " Cognitions, by their very nature, imply their objectives; " and hence as in Desires, so in Cognitions also, the reality of " the existence of the object, would be similar and equal to " that of the Cognitions. [So that Consciousness would be " coeval with the object, and no *pure* Consciousness apart from " the object would ever be possible]."

Reply:—It is not so; because the fact of the Cognition having an object consists only in the Cognition *being related to* the object; and this *relationship* is not *real*, but *erroneously surmised, aḍhyasṭa*; we shall show later on how it is impossible to find out any *real* relationship between the Cognition and its object. For this simple reason the 'objectivity' of Cognitions cannot be regarded as *natural*; for certainly the *silver* is not *natural* in the *shell*. Thus then, as regards Desires, the 'objectivity' of these also cannot be *natural*, as the objectivity of Desires is based upon the objectivity of Cognitions in general [and as it has been found to be *erroneously surmised* in the case of the latter, it could not be *natural* and *real* in the case of the former].

Page 14.

It might be argued that,—" if such be the case, then—as " we have (according to the Vēdāntin) cognitions or conscious-

"ness independently of the relationship of objects—so too we "could have Desires independently of objects."

But this could not be ; as for anything to have an independent existence, the necessary condition should consist in the fact of that thing having an existence more extensive than the existence of that on which its existence would be dependent; while in the case of Desires we find that their existence is not more extensive than that of the objects to which they pertain. [And hence no Desires could ever exist independently of their objectives].

Objection:—"The Vedāntin holds that in the Liberation-"state, the Self is free from all taint of objects; and hence "according to this view, in that state there would be no "manifestation (or experience, by the Self) of *bliss*; and thus "this 'bliss' could not be the 'highest end' of man."

Reply:—In the Liberation-state, what we have is a manifestation *in the form of* (identical with) Bliss,—and not a manifestation *of* Bliss; and we have already shown that in that state also we have a manifestation or illumination with the objective taint; and as such this 'manifestation' does not lose the character of 'Cognition' (in which the objective taint is a necessary condition). [During Liberation the Consciousness of the Self pertains to *all things*, the Self being omniscient.]

Objection:—"Even then, as there would be no 'Cogniser' "at the time of Liberation (the notion of 'cogniser' being a "product of Nescience) according to the Vedāntin, there "could be no 'cognition' at the time. Just as when there is "no 'eater' there is no 'eating'. It might be said that,— "'inasmuch as the *Cognition* (that we have at the time "of Liberation) is beginningless, it has not the character "of an *action*; and hence is not necessarily dependent upon "a *Cogniser*.' But this could not be; because we find many "beginningless things that are not so independent; for

"instance,—(1) Antecedent Negation (*Prāgabhāva*), which "has no beginning, depends upon that of which it is the "negation; (2) the Universal essence (*Jāti*), which is beginningless, is dependent upon the Individuals which it "comprehends; (3) the Differentiation between the Personal "Self (*Jīva*) and Brahman is without a beginning, and yet it is "dependent upon these two co-relatives; (4) Nesicence, "though without beginning, depends upon the *substratum* "wherein it subsists, and the *object* (the unknown thing to "which it pertains); and (5) the existence of B ahman being "beginningless, is yet dependent upon the Agent (Brahman "that exists); if it were not so, then we could not have any "such expression as '*Brahma asti*' (Brahman exists), where "we have the *active* conjugational affix (in '*asti*') denoting "the Agent or Nominative character (of 'Brahman'). In "the same manner, in the case of the cognitions of the past "and the future, and also in that of the cognition of God, "we find that, even though there is no need of the actual "presence of the objects of cognition (at the time that the "cognition appears), yet the cognitions appear in the form "of these objects (and thus far they are dependent upon "these); and hence it cannot be denied that Cognitions have "their forms always defined by their objects and by the "Agent (who cognises); otherwise we could have no such "idea as—'*I know this*' (a form of Cognition in which the "forms of the *cognised* and the *cogniser* enter as necessary "factors). And further, a denial of this would be a direct "contradiction of the *Vivaraṇa*, which declares that 'the "Cognition consists in the manifestation *of the object to* "*the Cogniser*.'

Reply :—Not so; because, as regards the Universal Essence and the Individuals constituting it,—though it is true that the former is distinguishable only by means of the latter, yet it is quite possible for it to subsist without any definite relationship with a particular individual; and the reason for this lies in the fact that the extension of the limit of its existence is much wider than that of any conditions or circumstances regulating its relationship with individuals.

For this same reason, it is not a necessary factor in the nature of *Cognition* that it should have an *object* ('Cognised') and an *Agent* ('Cogniser'). For, what do you mean by the *Cognition* 'having an *object*'? Does it mean—(1) that the *Cognition* is *produced* by the object? (2) Or, that it is invariably concomitant with it? It could not be the former; because such *production* is not possible in the case of *non-immediate* Cognition (*i. e.* Cognition other than that *produced* by sense-contact), and in the case of God's cognition (which is eternal and as such not 'producible'). Nor could it be the latter; because such a 'concomitance' would mean, with reference to *time*, that whenever the *Cognition* is present, its *object* is also present; while as a matter of fact, we do not find such to be the case, as shown just now (with regard to non-immediate Cognition); and as regards the 'concomitance' with regard to *place*, it is absolutely untenable that the *Cognition* occupies the same place as its *Object*.

Objection:—"No objection can be taken to the 'concomi-" tance' in regard to *time*, as it cannot be denied that 'when-" ever immediate (perceptional) Cognition is present, its" object is present'; and as for the Self, that too (according" to the Vēdāntin at any rate) is in the form of an *Immediate*" *Cognition*, as described in the Vedic passage—'That which is" direct and immediate (Cognition) is Brahman'; and thus the" Self also would be invariably concomitant with the cognised" object."

Reply:—Such 'concomitance' between the Cognition and its Object is not possible in the case of God's Cognitions, or in that of the cognitions of persons endowed with occult perceptive faculties. As regards the 'concomitance' that 'whenever there is *sensuous* Cognition the *object* is present',—this is admitted by all parties. And certainly this *sensuous* character does not belong to the Cognition that constitutes the nature of the Self; and hence the absence of the latter 'concomitance' in the case of the Self would not be objectionable.

Objection:—" If you do not admit of the 'concomitance' in
" the form that, 'whenever there is *immediate* Cognition, the
" *Object* is present', then you cannot establish your point
" that—'in the case of the misconception of silver in a piece
" of *shell*, what we have is the *Silver in an undefinable or inex-*
" *plicable form*'; because the only reason that you have for this
" is that, unless some such thing is assumed, it cannot be
" explained how we have an *immediate* Cognition (of *silver* in
" the case); as we have the *immediate* Cognition (of 'silver'),
" even in the *absence* of the *object cognised* (*i. e. Silver*).
" [The *silver* is not in contact with the sense-organ; so that
" the *immediateness* of its cognition could not be due to its
" *sensuous character*]".

Reply:—It is not so; because, as we shall show later on,
Page 15. the 'silver' is regarded to be in the *inexplicable* form, (not on account of the reason you speak of, but) because we cannot find any other objective substratum (save the 'inexplicable' Silver) for the Cognition that we have (in the case of the misconception under consideration) in the form—'I know or perceive *this silver*' (there being no *silver* in reality, and yet the Cognition being *of silver*, we cannot but assume the *silver in its inexplicable form* as the substratum of that Cognition). It is for this same reason that in all cases of direct or immediate misconception, the objective substratum is regarded as existing in an *inexplicable* form. Then again, the 'concomitance' of the Cognition with an *Object* is necessary, only as regards the cognitions that are *produced* (and not that Cognition which, in the form of the Self, is *eternal*). [And as regards the evanescent Cognitions, such concomitance being necessary according to the Vedantin also, the objection brought forward with regard to the misconception of silver loses its force entirely; the mis-

conception being evanescent; the Cognition of God however is eternal, and as such need not be invariably concomitant with its Object]. And as regards the cognitions of persons endowed with occult perceptive faculties,—such cognitions cannot be regarded as 'immediate.' Hence the assumption of the presence of *silver in the inexplicable form* cannot in any way vitiate our position.

Similarly we ask—what do you mean by the Cognition 'having a cogniser'? (1) Do you mean that the *Cognition* is produced by the *Cogniser*? (2) or, that it is invariably *concomitant* with the *Cogniser*? The former could not be accepted; as the Cognition of God is never *produced*; as we shall prove later on that all Cognitions are eternal (and as such the Cognition of God also must, *as Cognition*, be regarded to be eternal, and as such not *produced* by Him).

As regards the latter alternative, that too could not be maintained for just as Cognitions are not *produced* by *Cognisers*, so would they also not inhere or subsist in (and thus be concomitant with) them. Then again, as Cognitions are not regarded by us to be either Qualities or Actions, there could be no inference of the fact of their inhering or subsisting in a Substance (the Self). [This anticipates the Naiyāyika argument that, being a *quality* or an *action*, the Cognition must subsist in a *Substance*]. It does sometime happen that there is some sort of a relationship between the Cognition and the Cogniser; and this is what accounts for the ordinary idea entertained by the common people (that 'Cognitions subsist in the Cogniser,'); and it also explains the assertion that we find in the *Vivaraṇa* to the effect that 'Cognition is the manifestation of the object to the *Cogniser*'.

Then as regards the expression '*Brahma asti*', 'Brahman exists', the conjugational affix in '*asti*' does not denote the fact of Brahman being the *agent* of Its *existence*; as Its existence or *being* is eternal, and as such could not have any agent (to bring it about). The affix therefore must be regarded as appearing only for the sake of imparting to the verb the correct grammatical form.

Objection :—" As a matter of fact, there is no cognition " apart from True Cognition (*pramā*) and False Cognition " (*apramā*); and as for the Cognition that forms the nature " of the Self, this cannot be regarded as *true*; as if it were " true, then the objects of such cognition—Nescience and the " rest—would have to be regarded as *real*. Nor could that " Cognition be regarded as *false* ; as if it were false, it would " have to be regarded as proceeding (like all misconceptions) " from certain discrepancies or deficiencies in the cognitive " agency."

Reply :—The Logician regards the Cognition of God to be neither 'true' nor 'false'; so in the same manner, we also can regard the Cognition in question to be, by its very nature, neither 'true' nor 'false'. Because in the case of the cognition of the Logician's God also, if it were 'true,' then it would have to be accepted as produced by certain favourable accessories in the cognitive agency [and being thus *produced* it would not be *eternal*] ; and if on the other hand, it were 'false,' it would have to be attributed to certain deficiencies in the cognitive agency. Then again, the Logician holds that Abstract Cognition is totally devoid of any determining characteristics or qualifications ; and for this reason such a cognition could not be regarded either as 'true' or as 'false'; because a 'True Cognition' is defined as the Cognition that appears as determined by certain characteristics, with reference to an object actually possessing these characteristics; and 'False Cognition' is regarded to be that which appears in connection with a certain object that does not possess the characteristics that determine or qualify that Cognition [so in both cases, the Cognition is regarded in its *determined* or *qualified* form]. For us, as a matter of fact, it does not matter if there be a hard and fast rule that a cognition to be either 'true' or 'false' must be *produced* and *determinate* or concrete; because, even though in its pristine nature, Self-cognition is absolutely pure (free from all functions and operations), and as such, cannot be regarded as either 'true' or 'false', yet by being tainted by the peculiar forms of 'true' and 'false' cognitions, it can be regarded as 'true' and 'false'.

Question :—"[What do you mean by the 'Unconsciousness' of the World?] (1) If you mean by it *the character of* "*being something not directly denoted by the word* '*Cognition*', "then this 'Unconsciousness' (and the consequent 'Unreality') "would not apply to the adventitious determinants (*upādhis*) "of Cognitions; for the simple reason that these are directly "denoted by the word 'Cognition.' (2) If however you mean "*the character of being something not indirectly indicated by the* "*word* '*Cognition*',—then such a character would fail to apply "to such ordinary objects as the jar and the like,—as all these "are actually *indicated* by the word 'Cognition.'"

Reply :—What we mean by 'Unconsciousness' is *the character of being something distinct from that which is qualified or pointed out only by the idea produced by the word 'Cognition'*; and this is not open to either of the two objections urged (as neither the determinants nor the jar &c., are *pointed out only* by such an idea).

In this same manner we can also show that the Not-Self is something that is distinct from Bliss. Because all *bliss*, even those pertaining to material things, is of the nature of Brahman or Self,—the productions and destructions pertaining only to the adventitious determinants of the *bliss* (and not to the *bliss* itself).

Objection:—"Even Brahman is *assumed* to be something "*distinct from Cognition and Bliss* [such assumption being "absolutely necessary for the explanation of such declarations

" as 'Brahman is Cognition', 'Brahman is bliss', which would " be impossible unless we assumed some sort of a distinc- " tion between the subject and the predicate of the " sentences] ; and so the aforesaid definitions of the *Not-Self* " would apply to Brahman (Self) also. "

Reply :—Not so ; because the 'distinction' mentioned in the two definitions in question is such as is co-existent and coeval with the object distinguished by it [and certainly there can be no distinction co-existent and coeval with Brahman]. Or the 'distinction' herein meant may be said to be such as is *not adventitious* (but natural in the thing) [and all distinctions with regard to Brahman are only *adventitious*].'

It has already been explained how this 'distinction' cannot apply to the *absolute non-entity*, or to the *cessation of Nescience*, regarded as the fifth condition of things (as apart from the four admitted by the ordinary *Vedantin* :—*absolutely real*, *practically* real, *apparently* real and absolute Nonentity).

Lastly 'unconsciousness' may also be defined as 'non-self-luminousness'; and how this is real, we have already explained above.

Section (7).

[By Limitedness, 'Parichchhinnatva' as *the Third Reason for 'Unreality'*, is meant that it is limited in time, limited in space and circumscribed by objects.]

Limitedness also is a reason for Unreality. And there are three kinds of 'limitation': *viz.*—(*b*) limitation in space, (2) limitation in time, and (3) limitation by objects. Of these 'Limitedness in Space' consists in the character of being the object of absolute negation [*i.e.*, when a certain thing is such as can have no existence at all in certain places, it is said to be limited *spatially*]; 'Limitedness in Time' is that character whereby a thing is capable of destruction ; and 'Limitedness by objects' consists

Page 15.

in being the object of mutual negation [*i.e.* when one thing can be said to be not-another-thing, then it is said to be limited *objectively*].

Objection:—" As regards the 'absolute negation' that you " speak of under 'limitedness in space,' if you mean by that " that a thing is 'limited in space' when it can be absolutely ne- " gatived in regard to the relationship of *inherence* (*i.e.* when a " thing does not exist in a certain place by the relation of in- " herence, then you regard that thing to be 'spatially limited') " then such 'limitedness' would belong to Brahman or Self " also; as like *Ākāsha*, the Self also does not exist anywhere " *by the relation of inherence*. If however, you mean that the " thing is 'spatially limited' when it is not *in contact* with " something,—then such 'limitedness' would not apply to " such things as *Ākāsha*, as *Ākāsha* is universally known to be "*in contact* with all material things. [Hence such absolute " negation and consequent *limitedness* would not belong to " *Ākāsha*, which therefore would not be 'unreal']. If (for the " purpose of including *Ākāsha*) you were to say that a thing " is 'spatially limited' when it is such as is not in " contact with non-material things,—then such 'limitedness' " would apply to the Self (which also does not exist in contact " with any material or non-material things). If then, you " were to hold that thing to be 'spatially limited' which does " not exist (in certain places) by any sort of relationship, then " too it would apply to the Self, which does not exist any- " where by any sort of relationship; and it would not apply " to Nescience, which (according to the Vēdāntin) exists every- " where by all kinds of relationship. Secondly, as regards " the 'capability of destruction' (which you make the condition " of 'limitedness in time'), it would not apply to *Ākāsha* and " such other substances as are regarded by other philosophers " to be indestructible. Lastly, as regards the 'capability of " mutual negation' (which you make the condition of 'objec- " tive limitedness'), this belongs to the Self, with regard to "which you must say 'Self is not unconscious' (and which "therefore becomes 'capable of mutual negation'); and if "you were not to deny 'Unconsciousness' of the Self, then "It would have to be regarded as 'Unconscious.'"

Reply:—The absolute 'negation' and the 'mutual negation' that are meant are such as are co-existent and coeval with the object negatived; and such a negation could not apply to the Self (as none of the negations put forward by the objector are co-existent with the Self); and as regards *Ākāsha* and *Nescience*, they are universally recognised as being the objects of such absolute and mutual negations as are co-existent with them. In case Nescience, *Ākāsha* and the rest be regarded as having only *practical* and not *absolute* reality, the aforesaid 'negations' must be qualified as *having an existence not in any degree less than that of Ākāsha, etc.*; and thus the reason (for Unreality) would not be inapplicable to such things, like the *shell-silver*, as have only an *apparent* reality, and are objects of the negation of *practical* reality (as this negation is not in any degree less than that of the *shell-silver*). Nor again would this 'reason' for 'unreality' be the same as 'unreality' itself; as none of the various forms of 'unreality' described above has such a character (as we ascribe to 'limitedness'). Then as regards *the character of being the object of destruction*, this is not inapplicable to such things as *Ākāsha* and the rest; because in many such Vedic passages,—as 'from that Self was born *Ākāsha* &c. &c."—*Ākāsha* is spoken of as something *produced*; and from this destructibility would be naturally inferred. Then as regards the declaration—"The Self is all-pervading like *Ākāsha*, and eternal,"—here we have *Ākāsha* put forward by way of an example of something that *pervades all things while it exists*, and continues to exist till Universal Dissolution. That such is the sense of the passage is shown by the Vedic sentence, 'all else is destructible,'—which distinctly says that *everything* except the Self, is destructible.

Thus then we find that there can be nothing objectionable in the following assertion made by Ānandabodha :—" All ordi'nary objects, like the jar, etc., are regarded by us to be mere'ly assumed in, or imaginarily projected upon, the Real 'Substance (Self) that pervades, in manifestation, over such 'objects; this view is specially supported by the fact of the 'objects in question being differentiated (regarded as differ'ent) from the All-pervading Substance. What we mean is 'that just as in the case of the *rope-serpent* (the rope 'mistaken for the serpent) we find that the miscon'ception that we have is in the form—'*this* is a serpent'; and 'in this we find the differentiation of the notion of the ''serpent' from the notion of 'this' which forms a part of 'the 'rope' and pervades it in appearance (*i.e.* the notion of ''this' is quite correct as regards the *rope*, so far as it goes; 'and the mistake comes in only when the 'this' is identified 'with the 'serpent'); and in the same manner, from the all'pervading Brahman we have the differentiation of all such 'objects as the *jar* and the like, in such assertions as—'the 'jar is *an entity*,' 'the Cloth is *an entity*' and so forth."

In this passage what is meant by 'differentiation' is that *limitedness* of the object which consists in its being the object of a negation co-existent and coeval with itself; and as such this 'differentiation' could never apply either to Brahman or to an absolute non-entity (the latter because it has no existence at all).

Objection :—" In the case of such assertions as—'the ox is "defective,' 'the ox is hornless' &c.—[what we find is that "something is asserted of an *individual* ox, and] we have no "assumption or projection of the *individual ox* upon the *Uni-* "*versal Essence* of 'ox,' which essence pervades, in manifesta"tion, over all individuals. And so it cannot be admitted "that in the case of all ordinary objects we have such an as"sumption or projection."

Reply :—This objection has no force against us ; as we do not admit of any such *Universal Essence* as that of the 'ox' or any such thing, apart from the *Universal Essence* of 'Being.' Even if we could admit of the Universal Essence of the 'Ox,' we could never admit of any such characteristic as would serve to make that Universal Essence manifested. Because according to the Logician the manifestive characteristic of the *Universal Essence of the 'Ox'* consists either in the individual oxen taken one by one, or in all of them as included in the general notion of 'the animal possessing the dewlap etc.'; but as a matter of fact, all ordinary usage with regard to the 'ox' could be more simply explained as being based upon the fact of the one All-pervading *Universal Essence* of 'Being' itself, being specified or individualised by each *individual ox* [and there would be no necessity for postulating an intervening Universal Essence of the 'ox'].

This also explains the following passage from the *Brahmasiḍḍhi* :—'The jar and such other objects are all projected 'upon the form of *Being* ; as each of them is cognised as per'vaded by It ; just in the same manner as each reflection of 'the moon in the numerous waves is pervaded by the single 'moon.'

Objection :—"How could Brahman ever form the real subs"tratum of the idea 'the jar exists',—when It is (according to "the Vedāntin) without any such distinguishing characteristic "as that of *Colour* and the like, and is obscured by Nescience "as long as the phenomenal world exists,—specially as "Brahman is held to be cognisable only by means of words "(*Vedic texts*) ? Then again, as a matter of fact, we find that "the idea expressed by the phrase 'the jar is transient' is that the "*transient character* belongs *to the jar* (even according to the "Vēdāntin) ; and from this it would be only natural to conclude "that the idea expressed in the phrase 'the jar exists,' is that "*existence* belongs *to the jar*. It might be urged that, 'as in the "case of Rāhu (the shadow cast on the Moon during Eclipse) "we find that, though by itself Rāhu is invisible, yet it becomes "visible by its contact with the Moon, so, in the case in ques- "tion also, though by Itself Brahman is imperceptible, It is "made perceptible by its contact with (or qualification "by) such objects as the jar and like.' But this could "not be; if we were to admit of such vicarious perceptibility, "then we would have to regard the *Ākāsha* as 'audible,' by "reason of its being qualified by 'Sound' (which is audible). "As regards the case of Rāhu, the fact is that it is of a dark "colour and as such not visible at a distance; but when the "brilliantly white light from the moon falls upon it, it "becomes visible."

Reply:—All this is not true; because it is not in its pure form of 'Being' that Brahman is regarded as 'obscured' by the Root-Nescience (the first Nescience with which differentation begins); in fact It is 'obscured' by such Nescience as has its forces characterised or qualified by the jar and such other objects of the world. And thus there would be nothing objectiona ble in the view that in the case of the perception of the jar as *existing*, what occurs is that the particular 'Nescience', (with reference to the jar) obscuring Brahman for the time being, is removed by the functioning of the perceptive organs—of vision (in this particular case),—and on being thus unobscured, Brahman manifests Itself.

Objection :—"Such a view would be set aside by the "impossibility of Brahman being visible because of Its being "without colour."

Reply :—The presence of Colour and such other qualities is necessary for (visual) perception only in the case of such objects as are perceptible by means only of certain particular organs; Brahman, however, in the form of 'Being,' is perceptible by *all* the organs of perception; and hence even though It is devoid of colour, there can be no obstacle to Its being visible. As a matter of fact, our Opponent (the Logician) also holds that 'Being' is perceptible by all the organs of perception Thus does the author of the Vārṭika (Surēsvarāchārya) declare :—'Of all the sense-organs, the Eye and the rest have for their object only *Cognition*, the character of which is unknown,— this Cognition is self-existent and with regard to this are the organs the means of valid knowledge.' Then again, the Mīmāmsaka and others admit the fact of Time, which is devoid of colour &c., being perceptible by all the sense-organs

Objection:—"But in that case *Ākāsha* as qualified by Sound would have to be regarded as *audible*!"

Reply:—Not so; as a matter of fact we find that when a certain object is, by its nature, perceptible,—if its perceptibility happen to be obstructed by certain causes, then alone can a qualification come in and make it perceived; as for instance, we find in the case of the shadow cast on the Moon,—the shadow is made imperceptible by reason of the extreme distance, but regains its perceptibility by reason of the Moon's light. In the same manner, the perceptible Brahman, having, Its perceptibility obstructed by the *covering of Nèscience*, regains it by help of the *jar* and such other objects. As for *Ākāsha* on the other hand, it is by its very nature imperceptible; and it has not its perceptibility merely obstructed by some fleeting cause; and as such it could not be rendered perceptible by any such agency as that of Sound.

Or, we may offer another explanation :—It is only for the perceiving of *Substances* that the Eye stands in need of *Colour*, and Brahman is not a *substance*,—the character of 'Substance' being precluded by the denial, with regard to It, of all the four kinds of Dimension (of one or the other of which a *Substance* must be possessed), in the Vedic passage :—'It is neither gross nor subtle, neither short nor long'; and as such there can be no incongruity in our view. Or even granting that Brahman is a *Substance*,—we find that Qualities, Actions

&c.,—on which the character of 'Substance' is merely projected (assumed for the purpose of explaining their perceptibility)—are perceptible; and yet they have no *colour* &c. (as the Logician denies the subsistence of qualities in qualities); and this fact leads us to conclude that the Eye stands in need of colour, in the case of only such objects as have their 'substantiality' coeval and co-existent with their existence [i. e. such things as are always '*substance*', and not those whose character of ' substance' is merely assumed, as in the case of Qualities]; and in the case of Brahman we find that Its 'substantiability' falls far short of Its 'existence' (as the character of 'Substance' can, at best, be only *assumed* for the purpose of explaining Its *perceptibility*): and hence for the perceiving of Brahman, the Eye cannot stand in need of *Colour*. What we mean by a certain character being 'assumed' is that it *appears* to be present in the object which has its own natural character otherwise,—or that it is such as is denied as soon as the real character of the object is understood. But this is a different matter, and need not detain us here.

Thus then we find that 'Limitedness' also is a reason for "Unreality."

Section (8).

[The *composite character* of the world also proves its unreality, as pointed out by Chitsukha.]

Chitsukhāchārya (*Pratyaktattvapradīpa*, Kā. 8) has declared in one place, thus:—' The cloth is the object of negation in the yarns (*i.e.* it does not exist in these)—because it is the *composite whole*—just like other composite things.' And here, it may be noted, that the yarn is mentioned only as a representative of the whole class of *material* or *constituent causes*; hence in accordance with this view, a thing would be 'unreal' when it would be capable of being absolutely denied with regard to its material causes.

Objection:—"The Sāṅkhyas hold that the Effect is non-"different from its material cause; and for these people the "effect cannot be said to be *contained* in the cause; conse-"quently they will not deny the fact of such 'unreality' "belonging to things; and your argument would thus become "open to the fallacy of '*Siddhasādhana*' (proving that which "is already admitted by the Opponent). And again, "all that your argument would prove would be that the effect "(Cloth) is *not contained* in the cause, or that it is contained, "not in its cause, but in something else,—both of these "conclusions being compatible with the said 'denial'; and as "such your argument would become open to the fallacy of "'*Arṭhānṭara*' (proving a conclusion entirely different from "what it was meant to prove)."

Page 18.

Reply:—It is not so; because if we were to admit of an absolute identity between the cause and its effect, then there would be an end to all causal relationship (as a relationship is possible only when there is some sort of distinction between the members related); so that it is absolutely necessary to accept some sort of difference between the cause and its effect.. Nor would this militate against the 'non-difference' of cause and effect, laid down under Brahma-Sūṭra II—i—14; because all that is meant by that *Sūṭra* is that the effect or the product has no existence apart from its material or constituent cause. [Thus then, our argument is free from the fallacy of '*Siddhasādhana*']. Then, as regards the fallacy of '*Arṭhānṭara*,' this too does not apply to our argument; because of the two conclusions that the Opponent makes our argument lead to, that which would refer to *the product not being contained in anything*, is found to be rejected (by other and more valid cognitions); and the other conclusion (that the product may be *contained in something else*), we could very well guard against by adding a qualifying adjunct to the 'subject' of our argument, in the form that it should be a product that is *contained in that particular cause only* (and is yet the object of denial &c., &c.)

It might be argued that the conclusion of the Vedāntin also is such as is rejected by other and more valid cognitions. But we are going to show later on how no such rejection of the Vedāntic conception is possible.

Objection:—" We have still got a loophole, in the question " as regards the validity or invalidity of the 'absolute denial' " that you make the basis of 'unreality'."

Reply:—But this question has already been settled.

Objection:—" The piece of cloth in question may be in " contact with certain yarns (*i.e.* yarns other than those it is " itself composed of); and any denial with regard to this cloth " (being related to yarns) would be wrong; and as such the " said 'unreality' would not apply to this case."

Reply:—What we deny is the fact of the Cloth being contained *in those yarns wherein it inheres* (*i.e.* which enter into its composition); while what you bring forward against us is the case of the Cloth in relation to the yarns with which it is only in *contact*; thus your argument becomes open to the charge being of '*Pakṣasama*' ('Change of Subject').

Objection:—" Your argument might prove only that the " *Cloth does not pervade over the whole of the yarns* (and this " would be something different from its not being *contained* " in it at all); and thus your argument would be open to the "fallacy of '*Arthāntara*.'"

Reply:—If the conclusion were in the form that you put it, then it would come to this that the *Cloth*, as well as its *negation*, would co-exist in the yarns! And this would certainly put an end to all ideas of 'contradiction' in the world. Then again, as a matter of fact, we do not admit of the co-existence, in the same substratum, of contact and its absence (as the *Naiyāyika* does in the case of the monkey sitting on the top of the tree, and not at its root). [Hence when the non-pervasive existence would, according to us, not be possible even in the case of *contact*, how could it ever be possible in the case of *Inherence ?*]. But even if we were to admit of the said *co-existence*, we might guard against the consequent incongruity by making the 'absolute denial' *pertain to any and every sort of existence* (by Contact or Inherence) in the *yarns*. In the same manner we can further specify the 'denial' as pertaining to the particular *time*; and this will save us from the fallacy of '*Arthāntara*' that might be brought forward against us by making the 'denial' refer to some other time [and hence not applying to the case at the time that the cloth and its unreality are meant to be cognised, by the Vedāntin].

Objection :—" Such denial of the Cloth in regard to the " component yarns would be in direct contradiction to, " and hence sublated by, the direct sensuous cognition that " the cloth subsists in these yarns' (the cognition that every " body has whenever he sees a piece of cloth)."

Reply :—This conception might well be relegated to the category of 'misconceptions'; as its validity is always open to doubt, just like the validity of the conception that the moon is a few inches long (which is also a sensuous conception, the moon being actually *seen* as such); and hence the said conception could not serve to sublate the denial (that is otherwise valid). This we shall explain in further detail when we come to deal with the question of refuting all possibility of 'sublation' (with regard to the Unreality of the world).

Objection :—" The piece of cloth, which does not inhere " in anything else could not rightly be spoken of as 'compo- " site' unless it inhered in the yarns that compose it. And as " such your 'probans' (in the reasoning 'the cloth is...because " it is composite') is 'contradictory' (proving the contrary of " your conclusion)."

Reply:—The 'Compositeness' of the cloth would not in a way be incompatible with our conclusion; because, even though the Cloth might be the object of absolute denial with regard to the particular yarns composing it, yet there could be nothing incongruous in its inhering in those yarns; for the simple reason that the fact of one thing being incapable of being absolutely denied with regard to another thing does not constitute the necessary condition for the former inhering in the latter. If it were so, then, in accordance with the view of our opponent, the Logician, all such properties as pervade over the whole of a certain object would have to be regarded as *inhering* in it (as an all-pervading property could never be denied even partially with reference to the object it pervades over). As a matter of fact, what does form the necessary condition for one thing inhering in another, is the fact of the former being the object of a 'previous negation' with reference to the latter (*i.e.*, when the relationship between the two is such that the one did not exist in the other before, but has subsequently appeared); and certainly this would be quite compatible with the fact of its being an object of absolute denial with regard to that thing [*i.e.*, when one thing is capable of being absolutely denied, it is certainly capable of being denied with reference to any previous time as well; and so in both cases the conditions necessary for 'inherence' would be present]. This we shall show in detail later on.

Then again, what is meant by one thing 'inhering' in another is that the one forms the material or constituent cause of the other, and not that any sort of constant relationship subsists between the two (as held by the Logician); in fact, we do not admit of any such 'constant relationship.'

The Pūrvapakṣin says:—"Against your argument, the "following counter-argument may be put forward— "'This cloth is not capable of being absolutely denied "with reference to these yarns (composing it),—because it "has been made out of these yarns,——and another cloth "which is so denied is not found to be made out of these "yarns,'—the instance being one that corroborates the "proposition *per dissimilarity.*

"It might be urged against this argument that,—'inas- "much as the person putting forward the argument does not "admit of the 'capability of the cloth of being absolutely denied "etc.,' the argument, in the form put forward becomes "open to the fallacy of *Aprasiddhavishēṣaṇa* (a certain "qualifying factor being such as is not admitted by one of the "two parties).'

"But, as a matter of fact some such *deniability in general* "is certainly admitted by us; specially in view of the "following argument:—The absolute deniability of the cloth "must pertain to something,—because it comes under the "category of the *capability of relative negation,*—just as we "have in the case of the capability of 'previous negation'. "[What is meant by this is that the Logician does admit of "the cloth being absolutely deniable *with reference to some-* "*thing,* and as such his above-mentioned argument is not open "to the technical fallacy of '*aprasiddhavishēṣaṇa*'; but he "denies the fact of the cloth being capable of being denied "*with reference to the yarns composing it*].

"Another objection may be raised:—'In the case of *Ākāsha* "and the jar, we find that the absolute negation of the former "with reference to the latter would be included in the category "of *Relative Negation*; and yet as the absolute negation of "*Ākāsha* would be all-pervading, it could never form the object "of negation with reference to any thing, and as such your "premises would fail with regard to this case.'

"This is not right; because as a matter of fact we find "that the absolute negation of *Ākāsha* exists in a property "which is all-pervading, and which on this account is not the "object of any relative negation; and as such the said "absolute negation would not come under the category of "'deniability by relative negation'; and as this particular case "could not come under our *premiss,* there could be no objec-"tion to our premiss as such."

Our answer to the above is as follows:—As regards the truth of the universal negative proposition —'The piece of cloth that can be absolutely denied with reference to a certain yarn can never be composed of that yarn,'—we find that it is invalidated by a 'vitiating condition' (Upāḍhi) in the shape of 'the previous non-deniability of the cloth with reference to the yarns.' For we find that this latter 'non-deniability' means that with regard to the cloth it cannot be said that it had no existence in the yarns in question, (and as in all cases of the production of cloth from yarns, such denial is absolutely necessary, the cloth having no existence *previous* to its being produced) *the character of being not composed of the yarns in question* is found to be invariably concomitant with the said 'non-deniability;' and yet this 'non-deniability' cannot be asserted of the 'subject' of your argument (viz., the 'Cloth'); because the *absolute deniability* of this cloth with regard to the yarns in question is still a matter of doubt (sought to be removed by the argument here propounded); and as such this *absolute deniability* could not yet (until your conclusion is established) be regarded as invariably concomitant with the aforesaid *previous non-deniability* with reference to the yarns in question. And we shall show later on how we refute all reasonings put forward against 'Perceptibility' and the other reasons (for deniability) put forward by us.

Page 19.

For this same reason *the character of not being produced out of these yarns* cannot serve as a 'vitiating condition' in the above reasoning propounded by Chitsukhāchārya. Because it has already been explained that a 'vitiating condition' invalidates the reasoning, only when it is found that it is possible to prove the negation of the *probandum* of that reasoning by the negation of the 'vitiating condition' in question; and this is not possible in the reasoning under discussion [as there is no validity attaching to any such proof, which could only be done by means of the following argument:—"This cloth contains the negation of the counter-entity of the absolute negation of these yarns,—because it contains the negation of being not produced out of these yarns"—]; (1) because this argument is subject to the 'vitiating condition' pointed out above (Text, top of page 19); (2) because such a reasoning would become 'too wide,' in accordance with the view (held by the Logician) that *Conjunction does not subsist over the whole of an object.* [Because the conjunction between the cloth and the yarn would subsist in certain parts of the yarn and not in certain other parts]; and (3) because in accordance with the same view in regard to conjunctions, the 'vitiating condition' under discussion fails to be recognised as being the invariable concomitant of the *probandum* of the reasoning,—a fact which could be recognised only in this form:—'wherever there is the character of the counter-entity of the absolute negation subsisting in these yarns, there is present the character of not being produced out of these yarns.' And this is not possible; as any such general statement would be found to fail in the case of Conjunctions [consequently the 'vitiating condition' is not a true *vitiating condition* at all].

Thus then there is nothing objectionable in the following argument propounded by Viḍyāsāgara:—'The thing under discussion (the phenomenal world) has no existence apart from consciousness,—because it is never cognised apart from consciousness,—just like a dream.' What is meant here by 'non-existence apart from consciousness' may be any one of the various forms of 'unreality' described above;

and what is meant by the thing being 'non-cognisable apart from consciousness' is that it is cognisable only when there is an illumination of consciousness. And so no objection can be taken to the said argument.

In the same manner may be explained all the other arguments put forward by the various standard writers on Vedanta.

Section (9).

OBJECTIONS ANSWERED.

[The Arguments put forward in proof of the world's unreality are not open to the charge of being invalidated by vitiating conditions].

Objection (brought forward by Maḍhvāchārya):—"The "Reasons—'Perceptibility' and the rest—that you have put "forward are all invalidated by 'vitiating conditions' (Upāḍhis); "because an argument is said to be so vitiated whenever a "certain 'term' (or character) can be found which, while conco- "mitant with Probandum, is not concomitant with the Probans, "(and thus puts an end to the universal character of the major "premiss); and in the case in question we find that we have "such terms or characters—(I) The first is in the shape of *cog-* "*nisability due to a certain derangement in the perceptive facul-* "*ties which has not been set aside by that which is admitted to be* "*the sublator of it* [*e.g.* in the case of the cognition of *shell-* "*silver*, we find that when this cognition is due to a derange- "ment in the man's perceptive faculties which has not been "set aside by the admitted sublator in the form of the idea "'this is shell,' then the *shell-silver* is 'unreal'; and thus as "regards this, the said 'cognisability' may be said to be conco- "mitant with 'Unreality,' which is the 'Probandum' propounded "by the Vedāntin; and yet we find that it is not concomitant with "'perceptibility', which is the 'Probans' put forward by him; "for instance, in the case of such things as the Ākāsha and "the like, we find that these are not known to be cognised by "any derangements set aside by the 'sublator'; and as these are

"'perceptible', the said 'cognisability' will not be concomi-
"tant with this 'perceptibility'];—and (II) the second is in
"the shape of *the character of being an object of denial with*
"*reference to a certain sublator which is not set aside by the*
"*sublator of the thing cognised* [*e. g.* in the case of the cogni-
"tion of *shell-silver* we find that it can be denied with
"reference to the idea 'this is not silver,' which idea is not
"set aside by the idea 'this is shell,' which is the admitted
"'sublator' of the cognition of *shell-silver*; and thus this cha-
"racter may be regarded as concomitant with 'Unreality,'
"the 'Probandum' of the Vedantin's reasoning; but at the
"same time we also find that it is not concomitant with
"'perceptibility'; because *Ākāsha* is 'perceptible'; and yet the
"said character does not belong to it; as the idea of the 'absence
"of *Ākāsha*' is, according to the Vedāntin at any rate, subla-
"ted by the 'knowledge of Brahman' which is also the subla-
"tor of the idea of *Ākāsha* itself]. These characters are all the
"more vitiative of the Probans, because they are entirely absent
"in your '*vipaksha*,' *i e.* Brahman,—which according to you is
"free from 'Unreality'. And as such the concomitance of
"these characters is similar in extent to that of your Probans
"('Perceptibility'). Thus the 'vitiating conditions' are
"of the kind known as '*Vyatirēkavyāptimat*' [*i. e.* that
"which is capable of entering into a Universal Negative pro-
"position—*viz.* 'Whenever these *conditions* are not present,
"*Unreality* is not present.']"

Reply:—(I) These characters, that you bring forward do not vitiate our Reason. *Firstly*, because as a matter of fact, they are not concomitant with all cases of 'Unreality'; inasmuch as we find that they are not present in the false *identification of the Soul with the body*, which is rejected only by the *Knowledge of Brahman. Secondly*, because the 'characters' are similar in character to what are called '*pakshētara*' (something wholly distinct from the 'Subject' of the Argument, which is held by all parties to be no proper 'vitiating condition'); as they are accompanied by qualifications that serve to preclude all such phases of the 'Subject' as have the 'Probans' subsisting in them (while they do not preclude the 'Contradictories of the Subject' from containing the Probans); just as in the case of the argument 'there is fire in the mountain, because there is smoke', *the character of being something distinct from things existing in the parts of the mountain* is not regarded as a proper 'vitiating condition' [because with regard to such a condition it still remains to be seen if it is concomitant with the Probandum, the *presence of fire*].

Objection:—"The vitiating condition in question would "be quite effective, because of its being such as is indicated "by the *Bāḍha* (*nugatory character*, of the Vedāntic argument)."

Reply:—But we are going to show later on that no such '*nugatory character or nullification*,' is possible (and hence no validity can attach to any condition that would be indicated by such *nullification*).

Then again, as a matter of fact, the Probandum could be regarded as concomitant with only that thing, the negation of which would prove the negation of that 'probandum'; simply because in support of any further phase (even of that thing), there would be no corroborative instance. For instance, in the case of the argument, 'The earth is not produced by a Creator, because it is not produced by a material body.'—we find that all cases of *being produced by a creator* are not concomitant with the character of *being produced by a material body*; because the qualification '*by a material body*' is absolutely useless (as regards the validity of the argument as a whole). And in the same manner, in the case in question we find that, in any such argument as—"the *Ākāsha* and other things are not unreal, because they have not their cognisability due to a certain derangement in the perceptive faculties which has not been set aside by that which is admitted to be the 'sublator' of these things" [this is the argument which the Opponent has in mind when he puts forward the first of the two 'vitiating conditions'],—we find that there is absolutely no use for the qualifying clause '*which is not set aside etc.*,'—at least so far as the negativing of 'Unreality' is concerned; and hence 'Unreality' cannot be said to be concomitant with *cognisability due to a certain derangement in the perceptive faculties which has not been set aside by that which is admitted to be the sublator of the thing.* What is actually concomitant with 'Unreality' is merely *cognisability due to certain derangements* (in the cognitive faculties). And as regards this latter 'cognisability,' it is concomitant with our 'Probans (*i.e.*, 'Perceptibility) also; and as such no such *cognisability* could serve as a 'vitiating condition' invalidating our argument; specially as the fact of *Ākāsha* and other things having such a cognisability is also proved, like 'Unreality,' by the very same 'Probans' of 'Perceptibility' and the rest.

(II) In the same manner, as regards the second 'vitiating condition' put forward by the Opponent, the qualification '*with reference to a certain sublator which is not set aside by the sublator of the thing cognised,*' is absolutely useless, as regards the proving of the negation of 'unreality;' and as regards the rest of the character (*i.e.*, that of *being an object of denial*), this is found to be such as is concomitant with 'unreality' as well as 'perceptibility'; and as such this also could not be a 'vitiating condition' invalidating our argument.

(III) This same line of argument also serves to set aside another 'vitiating condition' put forward in the following manner:—"In regard to the argument of the Vedantin, we have a vitiating condition, in the shape of *the character of being the object of such cognition as is produced by causes tainted with such discrepancies as are coeval and co-existent with that which is regarded as the substratum of that cognition.* In this case the qualification, 'as are coeval and co-existent &c., &c., ' is not useless; as Brahman also, according to the Bauddha, is the object of momentary "cognitions produced by discrepancies" [and as the discrepancies, being momentary, would not be coeval with Brahman, the said character would be concomitant with 'Unreality,' but would fail to be concomitant with 'perceptibility']. Nor again, would this character be a mere '*pakṣētara.*"

This 'vitiating condition' also is not effective; because just as the said character does not belong to Brahman, so also does it not belong to such unreal properties as 'momentariness' and the like imposed upon Brahman; [because the cognition of the momentary character is not coeval with its substratum, Brahman or Its properties]; and as such the said character, not being concomitant with 'Unreality,' cannot be regarded as an effective 'vitiating condition.' And we have already said that such qualifications are absolutely useless as regards the proving of the negation of 'Unreality.'

P. 20.

(IV). Nor could *the character of forming the subject-matter of Shruti* be brought forward as a 'vitiating condition' invalidating our argument. Because it is Brahman alone that forms the real subject-matter of *Shruti*; and hence the absence of this character would certainly cover all cases of 'perceptibility' [and thus one of the main features of the 'vitiating condition' would be absent].

(V). Nor again could there be a 'vitiating condition' in the form of *the character of having an apparent existence.* Because this character is the same as that of being set aside by something other than 'Brahma-knowledge' [It is the *practical* reality of things that is set aside by Brahma-knowledge alone, for putting an end to merely *apparent* reality we do not stand in need of that knowledge] and this character we find absent even in that wrong conception of the Body as *self* (as this is set aside by Brahma-knowledge alone); and so it is not found to cover all cases of our *probandum* ('unreality'). [Hence the main feature of a 'vitiating condition' is absent]; and as regards the negative proposition (Ākāsha &c., are not unreal &c.,) the qualification becomes useless [as the Vedantin also admits of the *Apparent* reality of *Akāsha* &c.].

(VI) Lastly, we could not have as a 'vitiating condition' *the character of having no existence apart from appearance.* (1) Because such a character would cover all cases of 'perceptibility' and the rest (that form the *probans* of our agreement), in accordance with the doctrine of the *Dṛiṣṭisṛiṣṭivāḍa**; and (2) because any such character is not admitted by the Opponent himself.

Section (10)

[Refutation of Fallacies urged against the Vedantic arguments *for Unreality.*]

"We have such reasonings as— (1) 'the world has "*apparent* reality, because it is perceptible' 'and (2) "'Brahman is unreal, because It forms an object of ordinary "phenomenal activity, or because it differs from an absolute "non-entity, like the shell-silver'; and we find that the "fallacies that might be urged against these would apply "with equal force to the Vedantic Arguments [(1) 'the world "has practical reality, because it is perceptible', and (2) "'Brahman is real, because it is *not* an object of ordinary "activity, &c.'] And thus the Vedantin's arguments would be "open to the charge of *Abhāsasāmya*' (the same invalidating "conditions being present in both sets of arguments)."

Reply:—As regards your *first* argument, if you deny the *practical* reality of the world, then you make impossible all worldly activity. And as for the *second* argument, the

* According to the doctrine of the *Dṛiṣṭisṛiṣṭivāḍā*, the *saṭṭā*, *esse*, of a thing is not different from *ḍṛiṣṭi*, *percipi*; there is nothing to prove this difference. The opposite doctrine is called *Sṛiṣṭiḍriṣṭivāḍa*, according to which the *sṛiṣṭi*, or emanation, of things from Brahman—which constitutes their *saṭṭā*—precedes our knowledge of them, *ḍṛiṣṭi*. (Venis; Intro. to *Vēḍānṭasiḍḍhānṭamukṭāvali*).

unreality of Brahman would make *all things* non-entities, and that would land us in absolute Nihilism (*Shūnyvāḍi*), Then again, your reasonings are such as are easily set aside by stronger reasonings to the contrary; while as for our arguments, we shall show later on how there can be no valid reasonings against them.

Further, (as regards your *first* argument, we ask)—what do you mean by the '*apparent* reality' of a thing? Do you mean, (1) that it is set aside by something other than Brahma-knowledge? or (2) that it has no existence apart from its appearance? (1) If you mean the former, then such an 'apparent reality' being the 'probandum,' the argument would not apply to the identification of the Self and the Body; and further, in this case, the Probans would fail to prove the conclusion [as 'Perceptibility' would not necessarily point to 'being set aside by something other than Brahman'.] (2) If however you mean the latter, then the argument becomes 'redundant,' in view of the *Dṛiṣṭisṛiṣṭi* doctrine (according to which such an *apparent reality* would be readily accepted by the Vedantin). Similarly, as regards the argument put forward to prove the 'unreality' of Brahman, there is 'redundancy,' if Brahman *in the limited phenomenal condition* is what is meant (whose 'unreality' is admitted by the Vedantin); while if it is Brahman *in Its pure state* that is meant, then the *Probans* ('because it forms an object of ordinary phenomenal activity') would not apply to It (as the *pure* Brahman can never be such an object). If, with a view to avoid this difficulty, it be argued that the Vedantin admits the fact of Brahman being the *object* of the *cognitive operation* proceeding from the scriptural texts (which are held to be the means of *knowing* Brahman),—then (we reply that) in that case the *Probans* would fail to prove the desired conclusion [as even though Brahman itself might be *real*, it could form the *object* of an *unreal operation*; and hence the latter fact could never be accepted as proving *unreality*.]

In the same manner, as regards the second '*Probans*' that has been put forward by the Opponent to prove the 'Unreality' of Brahman [*viz. Its being different from an absolute nonentity*],—we may point out that this cannot apply to Brahman. Because what is meant by a thing *being an absolute nonentity,* is that it is incapable of being cognised in connection with any condition or state; and hence a thing could be spoken of as 'different from an absolute entity' when it would be contrary to this,—*i.e.* when it would be cognisable in connection with a certain condition or state; and as a matter of fact this latter character cannot belong to the *pure* Brahma [and as regards the *conditioned* Brahman, we also admit it to be *unreal*].

Objection :—" A thing is regarded as an *absolute nonentity* " when it is capable of being rejected; and the opposite of " this, 'unrejectibility,' is certainly present in Brahman. [And " hence the reasoning would be quite applicable to Brahman]."

Reply :—In that case your argument comes to this :— 'Brahman is *unreal*—i.e. *capable of being rejected,*—because it is *unrejectible,*—and this would be a purely self-nugatory argument!

Lastly, the corroborative instance of the 'shell-silver'* that you bring forward, is such as can have no connection with the *Probans* [as the 'shell-silver', being an absolute nonentity, can never be said to be 'different from an absolute nonentity'). And as regards the doctrine of Nihilism, we are going to refute it later on [and we have said above that if we regard Brahman as *unreal,* we would be landed in Nihilism].

Thus then, we find that the reasonings that we have put forward above (to prove the 'unreality' of the world) are not open to the charge of '*Abhāsamsāya*'.

Section (11).

[There is no real contradiction between the above Inferential Arguments in support of the unreality of the world and the ordinary facts of Sense-perception].

"The arguments set forth by the Vedāntin, on the basis of *visibility* and the like, in order to prove the *unreality* of the world, are such as are nullified by ordinary perception expressing itself in forms such as the jar exists (is real)."

Not so, we reply; you are unable to give a satisfactory explanation of such *real existence* (*sattva*) opposed to 'Unreality,' as would be capable of immediate perception by the eye or other sense-organs. You cannot say that what has real existence is—(*a*) either that which is the object of true cognition (*pramā*); or (*b*) what is capable of true cognition; or (*c*) what is not the object of erroneous cognition. For 'real existence' is often found to be the subject of several such true and erroneous cognitions as are not to be apprehended by the senses, and hence it cannot be said to be always cognisable by the senses; and moreover each of the above definitions is open to special objections which we will now detail:—

(*a*) The first definition,— *viz.* 'that is *real* which is the object of true cognition'—is unacceptable for the following reason. Since the means of knowledge do not operate with regard to the non-existent, *real existence* must be allowed to the thing previous to its becoming the object of the senses, and hence real existence must be something different from being the object of the senses. Moreover true cognition (*pramā*) is to be defined as cognition which has for its object a really existing thing; *i.e.* it cannot be defined unless through the definition of what really exists; and this implicates us in a vicious interdependence of definitions. And further, you admit that even such avowed unrealities as the connexion of the Shell and Silver are the object of true cognition, in so far, that is to say, as they enter into the judgment, 'I cognize silver'. (which expresses a true fact); and directly in so far as they are the object of the (true) sublative judgment 'this is not silver.' [From all which it would follow that shell-silver and the like also have 'true existence']. (*b*) Nor is your second definition of 'real existence' as *capability of true cognition* tenable; for 'capability of', or 'suitability for', true cognition is itself still undefined. (*c*) Nor finally is the third definition tenable. For that things should not be the objects of erroneous cognition, is something quite non-established; since it is admitted that all things are the objects of such erroneous cognition, as when *e. g.* they are held to be merely momentary (as by the Bauḍḍhas).

(*d*) For this same last reason we also cannot accept a further definition of *real existence*; *viz.* that a real thing means a thing which is not the object of such an erroneous cognition as does not apprehend non-existence; moreover this definition would imply a vicious interdependence (since it avails itself of 'non-existence' to define 'true existence').

(*e*) Nor *fifthly*, can you define a *real thing* as that which is the object of a true cognition which apprehends existence; for this would be defining a thing (*existence*) by itself.

(*f*) Nor can you define a *really existing* thing as that which is not the object of an erroneous cognition that apprehends non-existence; for this definition also moves in a circle.

(*g*) Nor can a *really existing* thing be defined as that the real existence of which in its recognised substrata does not admit of being negated at any time; for this definition also presupposes what has to be defined.

(*h, i, j*) Nor will it avail you to define the *real* as that which possesses the class-character of 'Being-ness' (*saṭṭā*); or as that which possesses causal efficiency, or as that which is different from the non-existing; for as all these characters are not contradictory to what we understand by Reality, sensuous perception of them does not refute the inferential arguments set forth above to prove the Unreality of the world.

(*k*) Nor can the *really existing* be defined as that which does not possess Unreality in the sense of the Vedānta; for this definition would apply to absolute non-entities also.

(*l*) Nor is the *really existing* that which, while different from absolute non-entities, is not superimposed (falsely surmised). For a thing's not being superimposed means its not being the object of superimposition; and this character does not belong to the things concerned; for all things are (as the view of the Bauḍḍha shows) objects of the superimposition of momentariness, &c.

" Let then the following definitions be proposed—(*m*) A real thing is that which, at sometime or other, is the direct object of a true cognition,—or (*n*) that which has a relation to time. ' Existence' in the former definition means not real being (*Saṭṭva*), but only the attribute of existing (*varṭamānaṭva*); and hence the definition is not open to the charge of pre-supposing what has to be defined; and as past things also *existed* at some time, the definition takes in these also. And as for the latter definition, anything that is falsely superimposed is indicated by a sublative cognition to be that which has no relation to any point of time; and hence the definition does not unduly extend to ' superimposed' (or falsely surmised) things."

But these definitions also we reject. For since true cognition apprehends and pre-supposes *existence*, and is not amenable to the operation of the eye and other sense-organs, the former definition is open to the objections stated above; and further a thing's being the object of a true cognition apprehending the *character of existing* (*varṭamānaṭva*) does not preclude its being *unreal*. [For the *unreal* thing also may be truly cognised as *present*, when, for instance, we speak of the *shell-silver* as being *present* in the man's consciousness;—and further, at the time that the man has an idea of the shell-silver, this silver is *existing* for him, and the cognition also is, for him, quite true, for the time being.] Nor also does the latter definition preclude the Unreality of the thing so defined. For shell-silver also has a relation to the time when it presents itself to consciousness; and although the subsequent sublative cognition ('this is not silver') negates the *real* relation of that silver to any point of time, it does not negate its *unreal* relation.—Nor may you prop up your last definition by declaring that the really existing is that which has a *real* relation to time. For we are yet to ascertain the character of that Reality by which you qualify the relation; and if that character be considered as ascertained already, the remainder of the definition becomes superfluous.

"Well", the opponent here resumes, "if you reject the above definitions of the *real*, listen to what follows. By the *reality* of the world I understand exactly what you understand by the *reality* of Brahman; in accordance with what the following verse declares—'To the world belongs the same kind of reality as belongs to Brahman; if the reality of Brahman is something undefinable, that of the world also is undefinable.' Nor must it be objected that the reality of Brahman consists in *unlimitedness*, which certainly does not belong to the world. For a non-entity also is something *unlimited*, but is not on that account allowed to have real being; hence *real being* does not consist in *unlimitedness*, but must be something else; and this something must be held to belong to shells and the like, no less than to Brahman; since those things are the substrata of erroneous cognitions."

You have heard, the Vedantin replies, of the bridegroom who, when at the time of marriage, being questioned by the bride's father as to his *Goṭra* (*i. e.*, his clan or family) replied 'my *Goṭra* is exactly the same as yours;'—of that bridegroom you are the true brother. For if father-in-law and son-in-law belong to the same gotra, the marriage cannot take place; and in the same way, if the world and Brahman had the same kind of *being*, the world would be absolutely unreal. For the being of Brahman consists therein that it is self-illumined, non-dual intelligence;—now if this constituted the true nature of the world also, which is admittedly non-intelligent (*jaḍa*), then—in the same way as the shell-silver is false because its true being is constituted by the shell which is incompatible with silver—so the world also would be proved to be essentially unreal because its true being would be constituted by self-illumined reality which is incompatible with its inherent non-intelligence (*jaḍatva*). And as it is intelligence only which—as being the object of all nescience, whether limited or unlimited—is admitted to be the universal substrate of all erroneous cognition, you cannot prove the reality of shells and the like on the ground of their being the substrates of error.

P. 22. "Well then," our Opponent resumes, "let non-being "(*asattva*) be defined as that which is the "correlate of a negation existing in all places "and all points of time. Non-existence thus understood "belongs equally to the absolutely non-existing (the merely "futile) and the inexplicable (the *unreal* in the Vedantic sense); "and we then define the truly existing as that in which there "is absence of such non-existence. And existence in this "sense belongs to Brahman and the world alike. Nor must "you object to this definition that it does not take in Conjunc-"tion (which is a really existing thing like others). For we "do not hold the view that conjunction does not reside in the "whole of the things conjoined [if the quality of Conjunction "resided only in certain parts of the things conjoined, it would "be the correlate of a negation residing in the other parts, and "hence would not be *sat* in the sense defined]. If, however, "conjunction should be held to be non-pervasive, then—in

" order to make the definition applicable to Conjunction, we " would define it by specifying that the *absence* of non-exis- " tence is to be understood as extending over the whole of " the things conjoined. Nor would this make the definition " inapplicable to *Ākāsha*, which is all-pervading. Because we " do not admit that the absolute negation of *Ākāsha* is present " at all times and places; and as such the definition would " be quite applicable to it; for certainly there is no point " of time or place where there is a negation of *Ākāsha*; if " there were any such, then *Ākāsha* would cease to be all- " pervading and eternal. But even if one were to admit " that the absolute negation of *Ākāsha* is present at all " times, [*i. e.*, that *Ākāsha* is mere void] then the afore- " said, 'absence' of non-existence would be further " qualified as that which has for its correlate something that " has *existence* ".

All this reasoning we Vedāntins oppose on the ground that such real existence as you define rests on a number of factors which are no suitable objects for the sense-organs, and hence cannot be apprehended by sensuous perception. No person has ever perceived by means of his senses a thing's 'being the correlate of a negation that is connected with all place and time,' and hence a thing's *not* being the correlate of such a negation (which according to you constitutes the real existence of the thing) can also not be perceived. And even if you omit the two subsequent qualifications—that the absence should be pervasive and that it should have for its correlate something that has existence,—the fact remains that the two circumstances of something being connected with all time and place are not suitable objects for sense-perception. "But," our opponent resumes, "it is a matter of perception that a certain thing is not the correlate of a negation residing in its own time and place (*i. e.*, that the thing is present here and now); and as the present time is included in all time, and the particular place occupied by the thing in all place, we *do* perceive the thing's not being a correlate of a negation residing in all time and place, and on the basis of such perception we can certainly not accept the inference as to the thing being the correlate to a negation abiding in all time and place, *i.e.*, being unreal (*mithyā*) in the Vedântic sense !"

This is not right, we reply, as a matter of fact, none of the sense-organs is found capable of perceiving the character of being an object of all negations with reference to the particular time and place; and hence it is all the less probable for the absence of this character to be *perceived* by them. Then as regards the character of not *being the object a few such negations*, such a character would not necessarily be contrary to *unreality* (and as such this could not be a correct definition of *Reality*).

Then again, inasmuch as no absolute negation or denial of any thing is known to us, we could never have any idea of any thing being the object of an absolute denial,—specially as regards such things as form objects of universal affirmation, and also such ordinary things as the jar and the like, which cannot be absolutely denied at least with reference to *all kinds of relationship;* and then, we shall ask—does this character of being the object of absolute denial &c, consist, (1) in non-subsistence in *all* substrata of the absolute denial, or (2) in non-subsistence in only a few such substrata? In either case, the objections urged above would be applicable.

Thus then, there being no other method of defining *Reality*, and no other definition being actually contrary to *unreality*, you must regard *reality* as consisting in the character of *not being an object of any absolute negation whatsoever*; and certainly this character can never be perceived by the sense-organs, as we have already said before.

Opponent:—"In connection with all such objects as the "jar and the like, we find that we can actually *perceive* their "character of not being the object of *any* absolute negation "whatsoever with reference to the particular time and place at "which they exist; as all such negations are brought to view "(rendered perceptible) by reason of their proximity (close "relationship) to the *particular negation* with reference to "*any particular* time and place that we may happen to be "cognisant of (by the law that the *universal* is always present "and perceived in the *particular*). And for this reason we "could never perceive in the jar the character of being the "object of any absolute negation *with reference to all times and* "*places* [and so it could never be regarded as *unreal*, as this "character which is a necessary factor in *unreality* would be "absent in it].

Reply:—Even though all the denials may be brought to view by the law of the 'Perception of Universals', yet it would be absolutely impossible to perceive, by the sense-organs, any such thing as the *absence of the character of being the object of such denial.* Because only such negation or absence could be perceived by the senses as pertains to objects that are perceptible; and certainly the object of *all denials* would always be beyond the reach of the senses. In reality there can be no sense-contact with *Universals*; and we have nothing to show that there is such contact.

Our opponent here formulates an objection:—"If," he says, "there were no perception of Universals, then, since the in- "variable concomitance of smoke and fire is apprehended "(through the connection with the sense-organs of the) fire- "place in the kitchen only (not in the mountain), we could "not infer fire from the smoke on the mountain. If, on the "other hand, we admit that there is contact with Universals "also, such as the *general character of smoke* (*dhūmatva*), the "perception of smoke in the fire-place will involve the percep- "tion of smoke in its universal character, and then this universal "character will be apprehended in the case of the smoke on the "mountain also, hence the concomitance of the two will be "apprehended there also, and the inference (that there is fire "on the mountain) will take place."

Not so, the Vedântin replies; what takes place in this inference, is as follows:—At the time when the sense-organ and the smoke of the mountain come in contact, there is also *remembrance* of the *generic* form of 'smoke' whose concomitance (with fire) has been previously perceived; and it is this remembered concomitance which, being found to qualify the particular smoke seen, leads to the inference (of fire in the mountain); and hence for the sake of this inference, it is by no means necessary that we should admit of the sense-contact of the *generic* form of 'smoke'. Specially as all that is necessary in the cognition of the *particular* smoke as qualified by the generic or universal character of 'smoke', is that we should not have any cognition or idea of there being no connection between the object seen, the sense-contact and the desired qualification [*i. e.* so long as we do not actually have the notion that the smoke we see has *no* connection with the generic character of 'smoke', we have all the conditions necessary for the recognition of the relationship between the two]. Just as we find in the case of the proposition—'Sandalwood is fragrant' [where even though what is *perceived* actually is only the Sandalwood, and there is not yet any contact of it with the organ of smell, still we have the notion of its being *fragrant*, because we are not cognisant of any want of connection between the *wood* and *fragrance*; and for putting forward the proposition it is not necessary that the *fragrance* should be actually *perceived at the time* that the assertion is made; in the same manner, for the purpose of asserting the invariable concomitance of the *universal character of smoke* with *fire*, it is not necessary that that character of 'smoke' should be actually *perceived* at the time].

Or (to mention another possible view), the cognition of the minor premiss (which asserts the connection between the

Subject of the conclusion, the mountain—and the Probans, (the smoke) may be held to lead to the conclusion through the remembrance of the invariable concomitance of smoke and fire.—Even then, though the invariable concomitance may have been *perceived* and subsequently *remembered*, with reference to the smoke *in the culinary hearth*,—yet, the perception of smoke in the hearth may be taken as the cognition of the smoke in the mountain also; and this would be accomplished without admitting of any actual sense-contact with the *universal character* of 'smoke'; and this would be enough for our inferential conclusion.

Objection:—"If you do not admit of a sense-contact with "generalities or Universals (and the smoke in the mountain be "regarded as the same as that in the hearth) then, you could not "have any doubts with regard to the non-concomitance or "otherwise of the *smoke* with *fire* (and it is this *doubt* that forms "the only incentive to the inferential reasoning); because "the particular *smoke* that is already known (as perceived in "the culinary hearth) would *ex hypothesi* also be known as "concomitant with fire, and as for the unknown, *smoke*, there "could be no idea of it at all."

Reply:—The invariable concomitance that is definitely recognised is that with regard to the particular or individual smokes that have been previously perceived in such places as the culinary hearth and the like; and hence it is quite reasonable that we should have a doubt as to the concomitance of the universal character of 'smoke'. In fact even the author of the *Tattvachintāmaṇi* (an authoritative work on Nyāya) has declared thus:—"Though we know the jar to be, *as jar*, different from all other things, yet we have a doubt with regard to the *universal* character of 'Earth' as subsisting in it; and hence it is this earthy character of the jar that we seek to prove by means of an inferential reasoning." We may have doubt as to the concomitance of smoke with fire, arising from the uncertainty as to whether or not the universal character of 'smoke' is concomitant with something else, which can never be concomitant with *fire*; just as even in regard to a thing that we cognise definitely, we have a doubt as to the truth of this cognition, due to an uncertainty as to the validity or otherwise of the means whereby we may have cognised it. This same explanation applies also to the doubt that we have as to Air being coloured or not.

Objection:—"As a matter of fact, there is no desire to "prove what is already established; it is only something not "yet established that is sought to be proved; this desire is "produced by the cognition of the object with regard to "which it appears; and this cognition would not be possible "without some sort of 'perception or sense-contact of "Universals' (*i. e.* of the generic form of that object). It "might be argued that,—'in the case of *pleasure* we find that "the desire for the unexperienced pleasure proceeds from "the cognition of a pleasure that has been already ex-"perienced; especially as the only condition necessary for "such appearance of desire is that it should pertain to a "thing that is *similar* to something already known (and not "that both should belong to one and the same category).' "But if it were so, then, silver having been cognised as *silver* "(and as such something desirable), we would have a desire "for *silver* even in regard to such diverse objects as the "*jar* and the like. It may be added that it is the charac-"ter of being the substratum of the character (*of silver* f.i.) "to which the desire pertains. But in that case we could not "account for the appearance of desire *for silver* with refer-"ence to the *shell* (as the shell would not be the substratum "of the character of the desired silver). And it must be "admitted that when the character of the things to which "the desire and the cognition pertain is the same, it follows "as a necessary corollary that the object of the two must be "the same. This same argument serves to set aside the "view that in accordance with the theory of '*Akhyāṭi*' (*i.e.* "the theory that in the case of the misconception of Silver in "a piece of shell, there is *no perception* of the silver at all), "what urges the person to pick up the shell is only the "*remembrance* of silver seen somewhere else."

Reply :—This is not true; because in the case of the misconception that you cite, it is a fact that the desire that arises from the misconception of silver is not with regard to the *shell*, but with regard to an *undefinable* silver, as we shall show later on, under the section on '*Anirvachanīya-khyāṭi*.'

Then again, by means of the arguments that you have brought forward you may succeed in frightening the up-holder of the '*Akhyāṭi*' theory, who holds also that for the appearance of desire with regard to a certain known thing, it is necessary that it must be known as the substratum of the character with reference to which the desire appears. But if this were a necessary condition, then the theory of '*Anyaṭhākhyāṭi*' also would be rendered untenable [as by this theory, in cases of misconception the *shell* is actually *perceived* as *silver*; and then the thing as desired would have the character of silver, whereas the thing with regard to which it would appear would be known *from before* only as *shell*.]

Objection :—"If such be the case, then there would be no "*misconception* at all; because in the case in question, the "Cognition that is regarded as a 'misconception' is in the "form 'this is silver' and herein it would not be admitted "that this misconceived silver has a character other than "the actual silver."

Reply:—But a cognition is regarded as a 'misconception', simply because it is found to be sublated after sometime,—and not because it pertains to a character different from the actual state of things; as we shall show later on that this latter condition also is only indicated by the sublatability of the cognition.

Objection:—"(If we do not admit the 'perception of "Universals) then, no perceptibility could belong to Darkness; "because it is nothing more than the *absence of all light* "*capable of illuminating things*; and as a matter of fact, no "*absence* or *negation* can be perceived without a knowledge "of its counter-entity; so unless we admit of the 'sense-"contact of the Universal *Light*, (the counter-entity of "Darkness), we cannot in any way explain the perception "of Darkness; as without the sense-contact and perception "of the *universal Light* we could not have any conception "of Light at the time (and without some conception of *Light* "we could not have any perception of *Darkness*)."

Reply:—But we hold *Darkness* to be a distinct substance by itself (and not mere *absence of Light*).

Objection:—"In any case the perception of Darkness "would require the *Absence of Light*; and it is only such "absence that could manifest it."

Reply—True; but what is necessary for the manifestation of Darkness is that there be an *absence of light*; and not that this absence should be actually cognised; as we have no grounds for this latter view.

Even for those who donot ragard Darkness as a distinct substance, though it would be necessary for them—in the perception of Darkness—to require the actual cognition of the *absence of light*, yet as this cognition could be obtained by the mere cognition of the characteristics of Light (such as that of illuminating things), it would not be at all necessary to have any 'sense-contact of the *universal Light'*: Nor would it be right to argue that, 'the cognition of the *absence of the cow* is brought about by the cognition of the universal character of the *cow*; and as this *universal* character is only that which subsists in *all cows*, while subsisting in nothing that is not a cow, this could never be cognised without the sense-contact of the universal *cow'*. This view, we say, would not be right; as the universal character of the 'cow' belongs to (and may be cognised in) only a few individual cows (and not necessarily to *all cows*).

This same reasoning applies also to the perception of the 'Previous Negation'' of things. Further, inasmuch as the cognition of Previous Negation would presuppose the cognition of something which is yet in the future, it could be obtained only by means of Inference (and not by Sense-perception, pure and simple). This fact is thus stated in the *Nyāya-kusumāñjali*—'Whenever there is a doubt (as to a certain concomitance with regard to any point of time other than the one at which the inquiry is held), there is an Inference; and when there is no such doubt, then of course there is all the greater chance for the Inference; and a properly constituted reasoning marks the limit to all doubting; and as regards the objection that this reasoning would also need an invariable concomitance, (and thus there would be an unending circle),—this objection is to be set aside by the reasoning (that if such inferential processes were rejected on the ground of this vicious circle, then people would never be cognisant of the concomitance of fire and smoke, and as such they would not take to the kindling of fire when they would want smoke).'—In this passage it is distinctly implied that it is from Inference alone that we obtain the idea of something still to come—an idea which serves to set aside doubt.

And the inference with regard to that which is yet to come would be somewhat in the following manner:—'The *present cooking* precedes another cooking,—because it is a cooking,—like the *cooking in the past* (which preceded the present cooking). It might be argued that this conclusion would be wrong with regard to the *final cooking* (which would have no *cooking* coming after it). But the very idea (that we may have now) of the possibility of any such thing as the *Final cooking* would be based upon the conclusion in question; as it is only when we accept the fact of the present cooking as preceding another cooking, that we can carry on the reasoning further, and thereby believe in the existence of the *final cooking*; and thus the discrepancy that you urge with regard to this cooking would itself presuppose the truth of the conclusion, and as such could not vitiate it. If in this case, such a discrepancy were really to vitiate the argument, then the propounder of this discrepancy would be met with the argument—if from the present cooking we can rightly infer the future cooking, then the 'discrepancy' becomes futile; and if we cannot rightly infer any future cooking, then we can have no idea of the *final* cooking upon which you base the 'discrepancy.'

And then again (even if we were to reject this inferential cognition), we have a *verbal* cognition of *all smokes* and *cookings* &c. (and thus too it is not necessary to assume the 'sense-contact of universals'). It might be argued that—"it is not absolutely necessary that the necessary word should be recalled in every case that we have a doubt (that gives rise to the inference, of 'fire' from 'smoke,' for instance)." True; but all the factors in an inference must be those whose verbal expressions are known to the person concerned; and hence if the man knows the word, even though it may not be actually recalled previous to the 'doubt', yet the idea of *all* the *individuals* denoted by the word is present in his mind; and this idea helps him to have the notion of the invariable concomitance (of *all* smokes with fire), which leads to the inference.

Says the Opponent:—"As a matter of fact an inferential "cognition is produced by the cognition of the qualification "(*i. e.* it is necessary to recognise the fact of *smoke in general* "having the qualification *fire*); and this proves the necessity "of the 'sense-contact of Universals'; nor could the cognition "of this qualification be said to be obtained by means of "another inference; as this would give rise to the assumption "of inferences *ad infinitum*."

It is not so; as the inference with regard to the 'Subject' (Mountain) as qualified by the 'Probandum' (Fire) is brought about by the cognition of the *peculiar character* (as ascertained through the 'invariable concomitance' expressed in the premises) of the 'qualification' (smoke) [and it is by no means necessary that we should have the cognition of 'smoke' *in general*].

This same argument serves to set aside the 'cognitive or ideal sense-contact' that has been assumed by the Logician for the purpose of explaining the composite sensuous perception in the form 'this peice of sandalwood is fragrant' [where the direct sense-contact is that of the Sandal with the eye, and yet we have the idea of *fragrance*, which, it is held, has a sort of ideal sense-contact with the organ of smell]. Because as a matter of fact, the *fragrance* is only *inferred* from the fact of the peice being *sandalwood*. If we do not admit this, then in all cases of Inference, we could regard the cognition of the '*Subject*' *as qualified by the* '*Probandum*' to be sensuous (the 'Subject' being in *direct* sense-contact, and the 'Probandum' in *ideal* sense-contact); and thus we would have no such thing as *inferential cognition.*

Objection:—" In the case of an inference where the ' Pro- " bandum ' is a negative term, and the conclusion an universal " negative proposition;—a knowledge of the ' Probandum ' is " not a necessary factor; and hence in such cases the inferen- " tial conditions that are well ascertained, would be infinitely " stronger than those of sense-perception (which would have " to be assumed) [and hence the postulating of the *ideal* "*sense-contact* cannot be said to put an end to all Inference]."

Reply:—No such Inference (of Universal negatives) is admitted by us, who hold ' Presumption ' to be a distinct *means of Cognition. [The example cited of such an Inference is—' The earth is not any other substance, because it has smell '; and the conclusion of this is regarded as got at through Presumption on the basis of the presence of smell].

There can be no incongruity in the admitting of an inferential cognition wherein the ' Probandum ' would appear as *qualified* by the ' Subject ', (in the form ' the Fire is qualified by the mountain '),—this conclusion following from the Premises in the form—' the *smoke* that exists in the mountain is invariably concomitant with *fire* '. Because there are no reasons for insisting upon the fact of the ' subject ' always appearing in the conclusion as the *qualified* (and not as the *qualifying factor*).

Then again, as a matter of fact it cannot be admitted that whenever we have the cognition of smoke, there is an actual sense-contact with the universal ' smoke ' *in reality*. Because, if it were so, then, in a case where we infer the existence of *fire* upon seeing a cloud of dust and mistaking this for smoke, it would not be possible for us to form any idea of the invariable concomitance of *all smokes* with fire; as in this case we would perceive what is *not smoke*; and as such there would be no sense-contact with the *universal smoke in its real form* (and without this latter we could not have any notion of the required concomitance). Nor can this non-cognition of the invariable concomitance be regarded as desirable; as without the cognition of the said concomitance, you could not account for the subsequent conclusion, which is found to follow even on the mistaken notion of *smoke*.

The Opponent might urge that in view of such cases he would assume the *cognitive* or *ideal sense-contact* with regard to *universal smoke* (and certainly there is an *idea* of smoke even in the case of the mistaken notion of smoke). But as a matter of fact, in the case of actual sense-contact of *smoke*, there is no such *ideal sense-contact*, before the smoke before us is actually perceived; specially as there is no evidence to show that there is an abstract or non-determinate perception (preceding every concrete perception); and also because we do not admit the view that the *cognition of the qualified* is the effect of, or is brought about by, the *cognition of the qualifying factor*; and as a matter of fact, all our activities are carried on only by notions of well-ascertained causal relationships [and in the case of perception, the only well-ascertained cause that we know of is *sense-contact*, and nothing else].

P. 25. There is nothing to show that after the perception of the *particular smoke* before our eyes, there follows a similar cognition of another *smoke*, which is not before our eyes; because whenever we perceive smoke, the only idea that we have is in the form—'I perceive *as smoke* that which is before my eyes, and not any other that is outside the range of my vision'; if what the Opponent says were true, then the idea in our minds would be in the form—'I am perceiving all the smokes that exist on the surface of the earth.' And certainly, people, who (like the Logicians) base all their notions upon direct experience, cannot admit of any such idea as this latter.

Then again, if we were to admit of any such thing as the 'sense-contact of universals,' then in the case of persons cognising and putting forward such propositions as—'that which is knowable is also predicable' or 'that which contains the knowable also contains the predicable,'—we would have to admit that they are omniscient (the said propositions persupposing the sense-contact of all things in the world.] And such omnisicence would certainly not be acceptable. Because if we were to admit this, we could not account for the presence of doubts as to whether the object cognised by another person is really the object that he cognises [Because when this other person would be omniscient, at any rate as regards *all jars*, no such doubts would be possible].

Objection:—" As a matter of fact, what is incompatible " with a doubt with regard to the *jar*, is the definite and " well-ascertained cognition of the jar, *as such* (i.e. as qualified " or conditioned by the universal character of the 'jar'); and " it would not be incompatible with any notions of *knowables*; " because though the notion of *knowables* would include the "*jar* also, yet it could never be regarded as qualified or con-" ditioned by the universal character of the jar. [And as " such even in the face of the aforesaid omniscience, the doubt "could exist all the same."

Reply:—It is not so; because what is meant by a cognition being *qualified* or *conditioned* by a certain thing, is that this thing appears among those that impart to the cognition its peculiar character; and certainly it cannot but be admitted that the character of the 'jar' appears among things imparting their peculiar character to the cognition of 'knowables.'

The opponent may say that any definite cognition conditioned by the character of 'jar' can follow only from the notion *of the 'jar'* (and as this notion is not present at the time that we have the notion of 'knowables,' his position remains unshaken).

But it is not so; because you can regard the *notion of the 'jar'* to be thus productive (of the cognition conditioned by the character of *jar*) only on the ground of its being a necessary qualification in this latter; and we have already shown that no such qualification is possible. Then, if you should seek to establish this causal relationship on the basis of mere '*Svarūpasambandha*' (a relation due to the very nature of things), then it would come to the same thing as to say that it is 'inexplicable'.

Many such other objections might be brought forward against the theory that we are combatting. Consequently, we can not reasonably accept the view that,—"a certain "cognition (of 'unreality' *f. i.*) is rejected merely by the "cognition of its negation (contrary), following upon its "appearing as the object of any denial,——the notion of such "denial presupposing the notion of all denials in accordance "with the theory of 'the sense-contact of universals.'"

[Here ends the Refutation of the theory of the 'sense-contact of universals'].

———:o:———

Question :—" In as much as all sensuous perceptions per-"tain to things in the *present*, how could perceptibility "be ascribed to the *unreality* of the shell-silver,—when such "*unreality* would consist in the character of being denied "with regard to the substratum in connection with which it "is cognised, *at all points of time*, past, present and future ?

"The Vēdānta view may be thus summed up—' What "happens in the case of the perception of shell-silver is "this: The piece before the Eye having, in the first instance, "been mistaken for *silver*, the man goes to pick it up, and "then finds that it is only a piece of shell—thus coming to "ascertain its character which is other than that of real "*silver*; and then on the basis of the presence of two contrary "characters (of shell and silver) in one and the same ob-"ject, we presume that the character of silver (previously "conceived) is entirely absent, and that *the appearance of* "*silver was an unreality*. And this negative conception is "quite compatible with the character of the *Witness* (the "cognising Self), who illumines, or manifests, or renders "cognisable, all things that may be related to him."

"But if such be the case, then, it would be possible for "this Witness, who can cognise things at all points of time, "to cognise the fact that the *Ākāsha*, that he sees now "directly before himself, will not be the object of negation "at any future time (and so the *Ākāsha* could not be regard-"ed as unreal)."

Answer:—As a matter of fact, what the Witness makes cognisable is only the thing existing at the present time; and as such he could not make cognisable any such thing as the *absence of negation* in the future. And secondly, the cognitions of the Witness are found to be correct as well as incorrect; and hence a fact that is otherwise proved to be true cannot be rightly rejected on the sole authority of his cognitions.

Objection:—"Whenever the Witness recognises the validity "of a certain cognition, he certainly recognises also the non-"sublatable (and hence *real*) character of the object cognis-"ed—the jar, for instance; as no cognition can ever be "regarded as valid, unless it is accompanied by a due con-"ception of the *reality* of its object."

Reply:—All that is necessary for the compatibility of the notion of validity of the cognition is that it should be accompanied by the notion of the reality of its object, *for all practical purposes* (and not *absolute* reality). And as such there need be no incompatibility between the recognition, by the Witness, of the validity of a cognition and his idea of the absence of *absolute reality* in its object. Because even when the cognition of the 'jar' tends to a coherent activity on the part of the agent (towards picking up the jar, for instance),—it is not a necessary condition in the validity of the cognition that its objective should be *absolutely* real, undeniable *at all points of time*; in fact all that is implied in its validity is, that it has a character different from that of such well-known misconceptions as that of the *shell-silver* and the like, and that it has for its objective a thing whose existence cannot be denied for the time being, for all practical purposes,—this latter character being such as belongs to all cognitions that have objectives whose practical existence can not be denied for the timebeing. And certainly this character would not be incompatible with that of being sublated at *some future time*. As regards the idea of the *future* deniability or undeniability of anything, it could not be rightly entertained by the Witness without sufficient proof; for he can perceive things only in the *present*, as we have already shown above.

Objection.—"If what you say were true, then we would "have to regard as true such cognitions as "that of the identity of the self with the body, "that of water being hot, and so forth,—all of which are true "for the time-being, for all practical purposes, their objec-"tives not being denied under ordinary practical conditions "of the world."

Page 26.

Reply.—These cognitions would be as true and in exactly the same condition, as the ordinary cognitions of the *jar* and such other things; as all such objects of ordinary cognition continue to be undeniable, until the attainment of the true knowledge of Brahman.

Objection.—"Even in a case where the objective of a certain "cognition is denied at some other time, does the denial refer "to the time at which the object was actually cognised? or to "some other time? In the former case, how could we attach "any validity to the cognition at all? (As even at the time its "object would be unreal; and yet the Vedāntin also admits "such validity at the time-being, for all practical purposes). "And in the latter case, all that the denial would mean would "be that the object cognised was transient (not eternal, having "existed at the time of cognition, and having ceased to exist, "subsequently),"

Reply.—What you say does not affect our position; as we never admit of any *validity*, in the shape of undeniability, in the ordinary cognitions of the phenomenal world; hence we hold that the *denial* does refer to the time at which the object was actually cognised. Then as for the validity that we do admit in the case, this would certainly belong to the ordinary cognition at the time that it appears; in as much as *during the entire process of worldly activity*, we do not find any such cognition to the contray as would invalidate the cognition in question.

Objection.—"According to the Vedāntin, the ordinary con-"ceptions of the *jar* and such other things, are *practically* "true, in contra-distinction to the misconceptions of the *shell-"silver* &c., which have only *apparent* reality; and from this "distinction he infers the *practical reality* of such objects "as the jar and the like. We can as reasonably go a step "farther, and deduce, from the said distinction, the *absolute "reality* of those objects."

Reply.—You can not do so; because the difference of the conceptions of the jar, &c., from the conceptions of merely apparent objects, lies only in the fact that, the former concep-tions are not set aside by any ordinary qualified or concrete cognition (being, as they are set aside only by the *unqualified* knowledge of Brahman); and certainly this could never prove the *absolute reality* of the objects cognised; as it could never prove any such reality in the case of the conception of the identity of the Body with the Self, and also in the case of the misconception immediately preceding the knowledge of Brahman (both of these not being set aside by any ordinary cognition, and yet their objectives not having any absolute reality, even according to the Logician, who also regards the Self to be different from the Body).

Objection:—"As a matter of fact, there does not ap-"pear to be any difference between the two conceptions "'the jar is real', and 'the shell-silver is unreal'; [as in the "former we have *reality* predicated of the *jar*, and in the latter "*unreality* predicated of the shell-silver.] How then should "we be justified in making any such distinction as that, 'the "jar is unreal' (*i. e.* the reality predicated of the jar is "*untrue*), and 'the *unreality* predicated of the *shell-silver* is "*true*'? This latter *unreality* cannot be regarded to be *untrue*; "as that whould imply the *reality* of the *shell-silver*".

Reply:—It is not so; because we have already shown above (in the section on 'unreality of unreality') that the unreality of unreality of anything—silver *f. i.*—cannot imply the *reality* of that thing.

A fresh objection is raised against the scriptural passages denying the absolute reality of ordinary things:—"As a mat-"ter of fact then, according to the Vedāntin, the *absolute* "*reality* of ordinary things is not perceptible by the senses; "well if that is so, the scriptural passages denying such "reality become open to the charge of striking in the air.—"denying something which can never be cognised."

Reply:—These scriptural passages refer to and deny the *duality* that is actually perceived by the eye and the other organs of perception. As a matter of fact however, even if they were to deny the absolute reality of duality, they would not be 'striking in the air'; because, even though such absolute reality be not perceptible directly by the senses, yet we could have indirect cognitions of it by other means. Then again, there can be nothing very incongruous in the denying of the improbable; as for instance, we have such denials in the Veda as 'the sacrificial fire should not be kindled in the sky'.

Objection:—"If there is no cognition, by the senses, of "*reality* in the *unreal* phenomenal world,—how could we "regard sense-cognition as providing wrong conceptions? "[It is only when we cognise a thing as what it is not, that "our cognition can be said to provide a wrong conception]. "Certainly, the sense-cognition could not be regarded as "wrong when representing the thing (phenomenal world) "as it actually is (that is, *not real*). [Consequently, in den-"ying the applicability of sensuous perception to *absolute* "*reality*, the Vēdāntin must admit the validity or truthful "character of such perception, which could be false or in-"valid, according to the Vēdāntin, only in case it represented "the world as *real*, which, according to him, it cannot.] And "we know it as a matter of fact that all men have distinct "cognitions of *reality* in the phenomenal world (and for "reasons just given, the validity of these cognitions cannot "be denied)."

Reply:—It is not so; because, according to us, a cognition is not valid, simply because it represents a thing as it actually is; nor is it invalid because it represents it otherwise; but it is valid only when its object is such as is not subsequently rejected (as unreal), and it is invalid when its object is thus rejected. And as a matter of fact, this validity can belong only to the knowledge of Brahman obtained by means of the scriptures, and not to any other cognitions; and it is Vedic Scripture alone that, as pointing out Brahman, can be regarded as providing the only *true* conception of reality. And thus there can be no incongruity in the invalidity of ordinary sense-perception, even though it does not provide the conception of the reality (of the phenomenal world). Then as regards the universally current idea of the reality of the phenomenal world, this may reasonably be regarded as indirect or inferential,—just like the idea of the presence in water of the power of allaying thirst (which is universally current, and is yet not got at directly through the senses); and thus it need not necessarily be regarded as 'direct' or 'sensuous.'

Thus then, in as much as the Opponent fails to explain the nature of such *reality* as may be directly perceptible by the senses, it is not right to assert that the Reasons brought forward above in favour of the 'Unreality' (of the phenomenal world) are not compatible with facts of direct sense-perception. Because, no kind of sense-perception,—either ordinary, or that of 'Universals', or that of the nature of the 'Witness',—contradicts (or sets aside the) Reasons pointing to 'Unreality.'

Thus ends Section (12) wherein it is shown that the Vedanta Arguments against the Reality of the world are not set aside by any fact of Sense-perception.

Section (13).

[There is no absolute validity in Sense perception; so it cannot set aside the validity of Inferential or Scriptural Knowledge.]

P. 27.

Just as in the case of the misconception, 'this is silver', in regard to the piece of shell, the notion of '*this*' is real (though that does not make the whole conception true),—so, in the same manner, in the conception 'the jar is real', (though the conception as a whole is not true, yet) the notion of 'real' is true; but the substratum of this 'reality' is Brahman Itself (not the *jar*).

Question:—"How could Brahman, being without colour "and other perceptible qualities, appear in cognitions "obtained by means of the Eye and the other organs of per-"ception?"

Answer:—We have already shown above that, though devoid of colour etc. Brahman can appear in such cognitions, exactly as we have the notion of Time (which also is colourless, odourless etc.) along with our ordinary cognitions.

Says the *Opponent*:—"If it be as you say, then, in the "case of all such conceptions as—'the jar is blue', 'the "silver is false', 'the man's horse is non-existent', and the "like—the notions of 'blue', 'false' and 'non-existent' also "should have for their substratum Brahman. It might be "argued that the *blue colour* subsists in the jar, while *Reality* "does not (and as such there can be no similarity between "the two conceptions, 'the jar is real' and 'the jar is "blue'). But then, the fact of 'reality' not subsisting "in the jar you know only after you have recognised the fact "of its being *imposed* upon it; and as such you involve your-"self in a vicious circle. If you do not regard the facts of "the 'reality' not subsisting in the jar and its having some-"thing else for its substratum, to be based upon the idea of "its being *imposed* upon it, (and in that case the said facts "could be based upon the very nature of Reality itself),—"then, in the case of the conception 'Brahman is real, conscious-"ness etc.' also, 'reality' will have to be regarded as having "something else for its substratum."

It is not so; as a matter of fact the case of the conception 'the jar is real' is different from that of 'Brahman is real' or 'exists'; because in the former we find that the notion of the co-extensiveness of 'existence' with the 'jar' is actually rejected by subsequent knowledge. For instance, the said notion of *co-extensiveness* could be based only upon one of the following three conditions:—(1) the manifestation or cognition of the universal form of 'existence' (produced by the word 'real' in the phrase 'the jar exists'); or (2) the actual existence of the jar itself; or (3) the fact of the notion not being sublatable at any point of time, past, present or future.

As regards (1), the Logician also denies the manifestation of any *universal form* in the case of the cognition of *Negations*; and as the notion of '*sat*' or 'being' is present in the case of Negations also, we could not admit the manifestation of any 'universal form' in the case in question also. It might be argued that—"in the case of the existence of negations, the 'existence' is cognised only as bearing an indirect relationship to the negation, while in the case of the conception of the existence of the jar, it is cognised as in direct relationship to the jar (and as such the two cognitions of '*sat*' cannot be regarded as similar)." But then, as a matter of fact, we could not have the cognition of 'existence' in the same form in the two cases, if there were any such difference in the character of the relationships borne by it And if you had no such cognition in the same form, then it would not be necessary to postulate the distinct relationships (the assumption whereof is necessitated only by the sameness of the notion of 'existence' with regard to a Negation and the Jar).

Then as regards the *second* of the three alternatives, as a matter of fact we find that in the case of the conception of the 'existence of a negation', we cannot regard the notion of 'existence' in its own real form; because if the notion of 'existence' were always based upon the existence of the particular thing concerned, then we could have no conception of any such generic entity as 'existence', including all *existing things*; and if we were to have common or generic notions without such generic entity, then there would be absolutely no ground for postulating any 'Class' or '*Jāṭi*' at all. For this reason, in all cases, we cannot explain the notion of 'existence' as necessarily based upon the actual existence of each particular thing concerned; specially as the postulating of a single generic entity in the form of 'existence' would explain all our notions of 'existence'; and as such there could be no ground for assuming an indefinite number of 'existences' for each thing concerned.

The *third* alternative also is not tenable; as we have already pointed out that the fact of any notion being unsublatable at *all* periods of time is not perceptible by the Eye and the other organs of perception; and also because this *unsublatability* we do not find in the case of the conception 'this silver exists' (with regard to a piece of shell),—[Though in this also we have the notion of 'existence,' and yet it is rejected by the recognition of the true character of the thing].

For these reasons, it is right to hold that what really *exists* is *one* only, and this is the substratum of all (notions of 'existence').

As regards the conception of the 'blue jar,' however, we find that there is nothing to set aside or deny the co-extensiveness of the *blue colour* with the *jar*; nor could the *blue* ever be its own the substratum; firstly, because it did not exist before the jar was made; and secondly, because it would greatly complicate matters if, with regard to anything, we were to assume an endless number of *substrata*, in the form of each of the qualities belonging to it,—the *yellow*, and so forth; and *thirdly* because, the *colour* is exactly in the same predicament (as regards *absolute reality*) as the *jar* itself; while as a rule the existence of the substratum must be of a character different from that of what subsists in it.

Then as regards the conception 'the silver is false, 'the man's horn does not exist',—there cannot be even a suspicion of 'falsity' or 'non-existence' being the *substratum*. As any such assumption would mean Nihilism; and the absurdity of this doctrine we have already shown, and will show further later on.

Further, it has been said that if such be the case, then in the conception 'Brahman is real' also, we should have to regard something else as the substratum of 'reality.' But this could never be the case. Because, in Brahman, 'reality' does not subsist throuh Its relationship with 'existence',—but the 'reality' forms Its very essence. So that the aforesaid arguments would not apply in this case. Nor could the reality be said to form the 'essence' in the case of the jar &c. also; because that this is not the case, we have already shown above.

Sense-perception, as a matter of fact, can set aside other kinds of cognition, only when its own validity has been fully established. And in the case of the reality of the world, we find that the validity of the ordinary facts of sense-perception put forward in support of such reality, cannot be regarded as fully established,—because they are in direct contradiction to scriptural declarations, and to inferential conclusions; and because it still remains to be seen whether or not they will be sublated by future cognitions.

Says the *Opponent* :—" As a matter of fact Sense-percep-
P. 28. " tion is stronger (more authoritative) than " verbal or inferential cognitions; and as such "it should set aside these latter, and should never be sublated " by them. As in the latter case, the validity of Verbal and " Inferential Cognitions would depend upon the invalidity of " Sense-perception, (which, by reason of its invalidity, would " not be a potent contradictory), and on the other hand, the " invalidity of Sense-perception would be dependent upon " the validity of Inferential and Verbal Cognitions, (which, " by reason of their validity, would be potent contradictories); " and this would lead to a vicious circle. This vicious circle " we avoid by admitting the validity of Sense-perception; " as the validity of this latter is inherent and does not depend " upon anything else."

Answer :—As a matter of fact, we find that in the case of our perception of the size of the moon and the stars, we always regard such *perception* to be invalid, solely on the ground of its being opposed to scriptural evidence and inferential knowledge (both of which point to a size different from what we actually *see*). Hence for the validity of Sense-perception also, it is absolutely necessary that it should not be opposed to other forms of knowledge. And thus the 'vicious circle' would apply as much in the case of Sense-perception as in that of Inference &c. And in a case where we find Sense-ception opposed to scriptural evidence, there arises a doubt in our mind as to which of the two is valid ; and then when we come to consider the character of the Scriptures, we find that they have not been compiled by any untrustworthy author ; and as we have the firm conviction that it is only the word of an untrustworthy person that gives wrong information, we naturally conclude that the Scriptures are true and valid; as regards Sense-perception on the other hand, we find that there is every likelihood of there being discrepancies in its very means; consequently the validity of this latter being doubtful, we reject it in favour of scriptural evidence. In this manner then, where is there a 'vicious circle' in our theory ? Then again, if Sense-perception could never be sublated by scriptural and inferential eviednce, then, inasmuch as we always *perceive* the Self to be identical with the body, we could never establish the fact of the two being different by any amount of scriptural texts or inferential arguments (and this would not be desirable for the Logician either).

Opponent :—" As a matter of fact, Sense-perception is, by its very nature, possessed of a stronger validity than that of scriptural or inferential cognitions. Otherwise, how could we account for the rejection of the inferential cognition of *fire as cool*, by the *perception* of its heat ? It might be argued that in this case the Inferential Cognition is one that is actually based on Sense-perception, and as such it is only natural that the latter should be more powerful and therefore able to sublate the former. But as a matter of fact we find that the object concerned (*i.e.* the Fire) is seen by the Eye, and as such the inferential cognition is question cannot be said to be *based upon* the Sense-perception by which it is sublated,—this Sense-perception being through the organ of Touch (and not through the Eye). Then again, Sense-perception must be regarded as more authoritative than others, because "it apprehends the detailed features of objects and such "others things which are not apprehended by means of "Inference and the rest, and also because it serves to set aside "such misconceptions as those with regard to the direc-"tions,—misconceptions which Inference and the rest fail to "remove."

Answer:—As regards the inference of the *coolness of fire*, it cannot but be regarded as based upon *tactile perception*, and as such rejectible by it; because even though the object, fire, may be such as is perceptible by the Eye (and not by the organ of touch), yet it cannot be denied that the *predicate, coolness*, is one which can never be perceived except through the organ of touch. Consequently then, we have no evidence for regarding any form of cognition as authoritative *in itself* (by its very nature). Nor is it right to regard Sense-perception as more authoritative than Inference and the rest, simply because it apprehends things not apprehended by these latter. Because in that case the mediate means of knowledge—Inference and the rest,—would have to be regarded as the more authoritative, as they apprehend many such *imperceptible* things as *Dharma* and the like. Lastly, we cannot regard Sense-perception as the most authoritative, merely on the ground of its rejecting misconceptions with regard to directions, which are not set aside by Inference &c. Because all that this fact shows is that the latter are of a character different from Sense-perception; and certainly this does not prove that this latter is the most authoritative of all the forms of knowledge. If it were as you say, then, as the Organ of Touch does not set aside the misconception of the *Vamshoraga* (the 'bamboo-serpent'), which is set aside by the Organ of Vision,—this latter would have to regarded as a more authoritative means of knowledge than the former organ; and hence the *Visual* perception of *solidity* in a picture could not be regarded as wrong simply because the picture does not feel *solid* to the *touch*!

As a matter of fact, it is Scriptural evidence that has been declared to be the most authoritative, in the following passage :— 'From among the three (Sense-perception, Inferential Knowledge and Knowledge obtained from Scriptures) it is the last that is, by its very nature, the most authoritative.' It might be argued that this declaration refers to the Veda. But then, the Knowledge of Non-duality also is obtained from the Veda. As for the declaration—"in certain cases, Inferential and Scriptural Cognitions are set aside by Sense-perception"—this refers to such perceptions as have their validity fully ascertained.

Objection :—" Sense-perception is such that its contradic-" tory does not appear (at the time), and as such it must be " regarded as authoritative, in accordance with the maxim of " the '*Upakrama*', in connection with which it is thus " declared :—' Inasmuch as the contradictory of the *Arthavāda* " passage does not appear, it must be regarded as true in the " form that it is found (*i. e.* in its direct signification) ; and it " is only in regard to the Injunctive Object that we should " have recourse to indirect significations.' "

Reply :—In the case of *Arthavādas* that you bring forward in support of your contention, what happens is this :—In the beginning of a certain section we have the words '*Ṛik*', '*Yajush*' etc., used in the sense of the *complete* Vedas ; and then towards the close of the section the same words are found to be used in the sense of the *mantras* contained in those Vedas (in regard to which particular methods of reciting are enjoined) ; consequently, in as much as the two sentences may be regarded as forming a single sentence, and as such standing in need of mutual help,—it is only right that in view of the sense expressed at the *beginning*, the subsequently appearing words should be taken in the same sense (and not in any other sense). In the case in question however, the matter does not stand in exactly the same position ; and as such the said maxim cannot apply.

Because in this case Sense-perception,—with reference to which it is still to be ascertained that it is not a mis-conception—is much weaker in its validity than the Scripture whose validity is firmly established. If it were not so, and if all Sense-perception were regarded as equally valid, then the sensuous perception 'this is silver' (with reference to a piece of shell) would be more valid than the trustworthy assertion with regard to it, that 'this is a piece of shell'.

This same process of reasoning serves to reject the following argument:—"Just as Direct Assertion "is more authoritative than Indirect Implication, on the ground of the former being quicker in its "operation than the latter,—so, for the same reason, Sense-"perception is more authoritative than the other forms of "cognition. As has been well declared in the following "passage.—'Just as in the case of ordinary worldly cogni-"tions, Sense-perception, being quicker in its operation, is "more authoritative than Inference, which is much slower, "so for the same reason, is Direct Assertion more authorita-"tive than Indirect Implication'."

P. 29.

This is not true; because even though one process may be slower than another, the former may be more authoritative, when it has its validity fully ascertained (while that of the other is doubtful).

Objection:—"In the case of the two Vedic declarations—"*yadāhavanīyē juhoti*' (Pour the offering into the *Āha-"vanīya* fire), and '*Padē juhoti*' (Pour the offering at the "foot-print'—we find that, because of the former referring to "fire *in general*, while the latter refers to a *particular* point "near the fire, the latter is regarded as the more authoritative "of the two; and in the same manner, the scriptural passage "denying the reality of *Duality* would deny *Duality in "general*, while the Sense-perception of the jar is found to "point to the *reality of the one particular* substance; and so "the latter must be regarded as the more authoritative of "the two."

Reply:—The rule that the Particular is more authoritative than the General applies only in cases where both have their validity equally well established. Otherwise, the *particular* assertion '*this* cow is a horse' would be more authoritative than the general assertion 'a cow is not a horse'!

Objection:—"In the case of the too sentences—'*yatkinchit* "*prāchīnamagnīṣṭomīyāt, tēna upāmshu charati*' and '*yāvatyā* "*vāchā kāmayīta tāvatyā dīkṣaṇīyāyām anubrūyāt*,'—we find "that the former makes a General Statement, refering, by "means of the expression *yatkinchit*, to every one of the sacri- "fices under consideration; while the latter refers to one parti- "cular sacrifice, the *Dīkṣaṇīyā* only; so that, even though we "admit the authority of the latter, the former does not become "wholly rejected; as it still applies to the sacrifices other "than the *Dīkṣaṇīyā*; while on the other hand, if we lay "stress upon the absolute authority of the former, then there "is no room left for the latter, which would in that case, "have to be rejected altogether; hence in order to keep "both, we decide to curtail the scope of the former, by "making it apply to all sacrifices *except the Dīkṣaṇīyā*,— "which leaves full scope for both sentences. In the "same manner, in the case of Sense-perception (of the reality "of ordinary things) and the Scriptural assertion (of the "unreality of all things), we could have scope for both if we "curtailed the scope of the latter, either by taking it as refering "to forms of existence other than the ordinary, or as refering "to things other than those ordinarily perceived."

Reply:—This would not be possible; for when it has been distinctly ascertained, in accordance with the maxims of '*Upakrama*' and the rest, which are the true indicators of the sense of Vedic passages, that these passages expressly deny the *reality of duality*, there would be absolutely no scope for these passages, if we were to accept the absolute reality of duality; while, on the other hand, even if we accept the denial of the *absolute* reality of duality, there would still be scope for Sense-perception, as this may be regarded as pertaining to the *practical* reality of things. And as between two mutually contradictory cognitions—*viz*: the Sense-perception in the form 'I am a man', and the Scriptural assertion 'the Self is all-pervading and eternal like Ākāsha'—both can never be regarded as absolutely true, it becomes necessary for us to regard the one as *absolutely*, and the other as only *practically*, valid; specially as it would not be right to regard either as absolutely *invalid*. Under the circumstances, if we could possibly regard the Scriptural passages laying down absolute non-duality as only *practically* valid, then alone could we regard ordinary Sense-perception as *absolutely* valid. As a matter of fact however, we cannot attribute mere *practical* validity to the said Scriptural passages (as for *practical* purposes, the reality of duality cannot be denied); and so we are forced to the conclusion that the said passages are *absolutely* valid, and the Sense-perceptions in question are only *practically* so. This is a conclusion which we leave to the intelligent and the learned to judge.

Says the *Opponent*:—"In the case of the *Panchadasha-*"*rātra* sacrifice (a sacrifice extending over fifteen days), we "find that in view of the first day's sacrifice, which is called "'*Angiṣṭuṭ*', the *Subrahmaṇyā* verse to be employed "is the *Āgnēyī*, which is indicated by the name '*Agniṣṭuṭ*' "(this name containing the word 'Agni' indicates the verse "whose name is '*Āgnēyī*', which is derived from the word "'*Agni*'); but as regards the sacrifices of the other fourteen "days, we find it directly laid down that the *Subrahmaṇyā* to "be employed is the *Aindrī*; and under the circumstances, "what we do is that, as regards these latter sacrifices we reject the authority of the former *indication by the name* of "the '*Agniṣṭuṭ*', and admit the '*Aindrī*',—on the ground, "that while the former applies to the single sacrifice "of the *Agniṣṭuṭ*, the latter applies to fourteen sacrifices, "and it is certainly the more reasonable course to sacrifice the "authority of the lesser number to that of the larger. By "exactly the same process of reasoning, we find that it is "only right that we should sacrifice the authority of the "direct signification of the Vedic passages declaring Non-"duality, in favour of so many cognitions as—(1) the Sense-"perception of Duality, (2) the Inferential Cognitions based "upon this Perception, (3) the Vedic passages laying down "sacrifices and other rites, and (4) the passages laying "down the worshipping of *qualified* deities (both of these "latter passages presupposing Duality). In connection with "this we have the following declaration:—'When *one* "cognition is found to be contrary to *many* cognitions, it "is regarded as invalid; as we find in the case of the "*perception* of the *shell-silver* and the like.'"

This is not possible, we reply; because in the example that you bring forward (of the *Panchadaharātra* sacrifice), we have the authority of one (which applies to only one case) sacrificed in favour of another *which applies to many cases*, while in the case in question, you seek to reject the validity of *one* in favour of the *many* (and not of that which *applies to many*); hence the two cases are not analogous; as a matter of fact we find that in the case of the notion of the identity of the Self with the Body (a notion regarded as wrong, by the Logician also), even though this notion is supported by the authority of ordinary Sense-perceptions, Inferences and Verbal Cognitions (though from unauthoritative sources), yet the means of knowledge pointing to the Self being something different from the Body is accepted as the more authoritative; and the reason for this is that these latter could not be applied to anything else. Exactly in the same manner, finding that the passages speaking of *Non-duality* cannot be applied to anything else, we shall be fully justified in regarding them as more authoritative than Ordinary Sense-perception, &c. Specially as in reality, there is no contradiction between the two sets of cognitions; because *firstly* the passages declaring Non-duality pertain to the final stage of True Knowledge, while ordinary Sense-perception, &c., pertain to the Illusory Stage;—and secondly while the former are for the *Knowing* or *Wise* person, the latter are for the *Ignorant*.

Objection:—"Even though, in view of the above arguments, greater authority might not attach to Sense-perception, by its very nature, yet it cannot be denied that it forms the very basis of Inferential and Verbal Cognitions, and as such is possessed of greater authority. What is meant by Sense-perception being such a basis is that it apprehends, sometimes directly and sometimes indirectly, all that is needed by Inferential and Verbal Cognitions. In fact, we have many instances where a means of cognition, apprehending only a part of what is needed by another cognition, is regarded as its basis, rejecting it in case it happen to be contrary to itself; for instance,—(1) the inference of the omnipresence of the jar is based upon the organ of vision (in so far as unless we see the jar we can have no inferences with regard to it), and yet inasmuch as we actually see the jar to have a limited existence, the said inferential cognition is rejected (though the Eye perceives only one factor of the Inference); (2) the inference of the cleanliness of the human skull is rejected by the Scriptural cognition of its uncleanliness, though this latter cognition pertains to only one factor of the Inference—*viz*: the Major Term; (3) the inference of the omnipresence of the Mind is rejected by another inferential cognition that we have of the substratum in which the Mind is contained. Thus when we find that inferential cognitions are rejected by other cognitions, even when these latter appertain to only a few of the factors needed by the former,—then it is no wonder that they should be set aside by those contrary cognitions that apprehend all that is needed by them. Then as regards the Eye and the other Sense-organs, and the Witness or Perceiving Soul presiding over them, though it is quite true that they do not apprehend

Page 30.

"either Words, or Verbal Cognitions or the validity of these,—
"yet these also must be regarded as the basis of Verbal Cog-
"nition; inasmuch as they belong to the same category as
"the Ear (which apprehends the words) and the Witness
"(who has the Cognition and the notion of validity). Just as
"we find that the scriptural cognition of the uncleanliness of
"the human skull is more authoritative than, and rejects, the
"inferential cognition of its cleanliness,—this latter cogni-
"tion being based upon (supposed) Scriptures pointing to
"such cleanliness; and this is the case because of the Scriptural
"cognition of uncleanliness belonging to the same category
"(of 'Scriptural cognition') as the latter Scriptural cognition
"(of cleanliness). It might be argued that the sense-organs
"also are cognisable by Inference only; and hence there is a
"mutual inter-dependence between Inferential and Sensuous
"Cognitions. But the aid of Inference is not needed for the
"actual appearance of Sense-perception, at least in the form in
"which there is no cognition of the organ of that perception.
"Whereas it is for the very appearence of Inferential and
"Verbal Cognitions that the aid of Sense-perception is
"necessary."

Reply:—There is no actual incongruity between the authoritative character of the Sense-perception, and the fact of its being rejected by the Inferential or Verbal Cognition based upon it. That is to say, the Inferential or Verbal Cognition does not reject that form of the Sense-perception upon which it is based;—inasmuch as what they reject is the *essential* reality of Sense-perception, while what they are based upon is its *practical* reality; as certainly the essential reality of the perception of *smoke* does not form an essential factor in the circumstantial causes leading to the inference of fire. This has been thus declared in the following verse:—
'Both of us (the Vēdāntin and the Logician) are agreed that the origin of Inference consists in a previous conception of the relationship of invariable concomitance; and as for the question of the *actual reality* of this origin,—which is not an

essential element in its character,—any discussion as to that would be profitless, (*Khaṇḍanakhaṇḍakhādya*).

Then again, if the mere fact of one cognition apprehending what the other stands in need of were to make the former the *basis* of the latter, and were, on this ground, to reject this latter,——then, in the case of the misconception 'this is silver', and its rejection by the notion 'this is not silver', we would find that for the appearance of the latter,—*i. e.* in order that the latter may reject the *silver*,—the previous conception of silver is necessary; and as such the said misconception would be regarded as the *basis* of the subsequent cognition rejecting it; and being the *basis* of this latter, it would (according to you) be capable of setting aside that of which it is the basis; and as such how could there ever arise any such cognition as 'this is not silver'?

Says the *Opponent*:—" Even though the cognition 'this " is silver' pertains to an object that is denied by the subsequent cognition, and as such may be regarded as forming " the basis of this latter, yet it is not the *validity* of that " cognition that can be regarded as forming such basis. " Specially as the cognition of a negative entity need not " originate in a *valid* cognition of its counter-entity; as any " such origination would lead to much confusion; and also " because, as a matter of fact, we often find cognitions of " negations appearing from mere *misconceptions* of their " counter-entities. Hence it must be admitted that it is " much simpler to regard the cognition of the negative entity " as proceeding from the *cognition* of its counter-entity. And " thus there would be nothing to stop the appearance of the " cognition ('this is not silver') contrary to the previous " cognition ('this is silver')."

Reply:—The same reasoning may be applied to the case in question: That is to say, the inferential cognition has its origin in the mere cognition (sensuous) of the 'Subject', and this origination does not necessarily involve the *validity* of this latter cognition.

Objection:—"As a matter of fact, one cognition can be "regarded as the basis of another, only when the validity "of this latter depends upon that of the former, both for its "own accomplishment and for the rejection of its contraries; "as we find in the case of Cognition and Remembrance. In "the case of the misconception of silver and its subsequent "denial, we do not find this to be the case; and as such in "this case, one could not be regarded as the basis of the "other."

Reply:—If such were the conditions for one cognition being the basis of another, then the cognition of 'invariable concomitance' would not be the basis of Inferential Cognitions. As it often happens that though the existence of fire is *inferred* from a misconception of *smoke* (while what is actually present is a mere *fog*), yet, by chance, fire is present in the place.

Objection:—" In reality, one thing must be regarded as the "*basis* of another, when the two are so related that the latter "can never appear without the former. And thus the "misconception of silver in the shell would certainly be the "*basis* of the subsequent right conception 'this is not silver'; "but this does not imply necessarily that the misconception "is more trustworthy than the subsequent conception. "Because the mere fact of being the *basis* does not make "any conception non-trustworthy; the trustworthy character "of a conception depends upon its being able to stand the "test of examination; and this examination consists first, "in finding out if the conception in question is compatible "with other conceptions, and if, in the resultant activity, "it is in actual agreement with the real state of things— "and secondly in ascertaining that it is absolutely free "from any sort of disagreement from other conceptions "or resultant activities. These two conditions we do not "find present in the case of the misconception of shell-silver.

"In the case in question however we find that these conditions
P. 31. "are fulfilled by Sense-perception, which there-
"fore must be regarded as trustworthy. We have
"the conception, 'the jar is'; and this is actually found to
"be followed by activities pertaining to the jar (and thus the
"first condition of the aforesaid test is duly fulfilled); and
"we also find that it is absolutely free from such sources of
"mistake as extreme distance and the like (and thus the
"second test is also fulfilled). In the same manner, in regard
"to the Scriptural text speaking of the identity of the *Jīva*
"and *God*, we find that it is incompatible with other Scriptural
"texts speaking of the two being different; and also with the
"actual direct cognition of the cognising Selves,—this latter
"cognition being such as is found on examination to be free
"from discrepancies, and as such not to be rejected, And
"even on finding after examination a certain cognition to be
"free from discrepancies,—if we were to have no trust in it,
"then there could be no trusting any conception at all; for
"instance, we would have no trust in any of the following:—
"(1) the conception that the Veda is not the work of a
"human author; (2) the idea that the inferential argument
"put forward by the Vedantin is free from fallacies because
"of our not finding any such etc. etc.; (3) every one of the
"conceptions put forward in the various *adhikaraṇas* of
"*Vedānta-Sūtra-bhāṣya*; (4) the idea that a certain concep-
"tion or statement is in keeping with the premises with
"which the discussion was started. And under such circum-
"stances, we could not come to any definite conclusion with
"regard to the validity or invalidity of any Cognition at
"all."

Reply.—The 'test' or 'examination' of a certain cognition consists in its being found to be in conformity with the resulting activity, and in its being free from all incongruities of such activity, as also from other discrepancies; and what this 'test' proves with regard to the validity of the cognition is that it is absolutely incapable of being rejected (or negatived) with regard to the object cognised *at that particular time and place* ; just as smoke proves the existence of fire at the time and place that it is perceived. Consequently, all that your examination and test would prove would be that like all other ordinary conceptions, the conception of the identify of the Self with the body is valid and incapable of being denied, *during the time that we are dealing with the mere practicol reality of things in the world* ; and under the circumstances, why should this stand in the way of the inferential and scriptural cognition of the *absolute unrejectibility* (*i.e.*, reality) of things? For these reasons, we conclude that our theory affords the necessary explanation for all ordinary beliefs, and ordinary cognitions, true as well as false, as also of the popular conception of difference between God and the Jīva, and so forth—all of which appertain to the region of practical existence. And thus it is only reasonable that the universe should be regarded as *unreal* (in the absolute sense of the term].

Objection:—"If Sense-perception be rejected as invalid, "then the knowledge of invariable concomitance (necessary "for all inferential knowledge) would have to be rejected; "and this would set aside the reality of all inferred things, "and reject the validity of all Inferential cognitions; because "the validity or invalidity of the subject of inferential cogni- "tion is dependent upon the character of the cognition of con- comitance, and that of the inferential cognition. If it were "not so (*i. e.* if the validity and invalidity of the inferred "thing did not depend upon those of the premises and the "conclusion) then, there would be a likelihood of the following "absurdities:—(1) The absolute or the practical reality of "Fire would be proved by means of Smoke misconceived with "regard to fog, and thus having a merely *apparent* reality; "(2) the absolute reality of fire would be proved by means "of the Smoke that has merely an *apparent* reality; (3) "the absolute reality of the Universe would be proved by "reason of its not being rejected as unreal. with regard to "the *practical* state of things; and (4) the absolute reality "of the difference between God and Jīva would be proved by "reason of the two being possessed of mutually contradic- "tory properties."

Reply:—Up to this point all that your objection means is that the conception of a certain invariable concomitance (*i. e.* of the premises) proves the conclusion with regard to the Subject, the character of whose existence (in the point of Reality or Unreality) is similar to that of the concomitance itself. And this is what we also accept by all means; as there is nothing except Brahman that is absolutely beyond rejection. As a matter of fact, however, in the case of Inferential Cognitions, it is not necessary that the character of the Subject of the conclusion should be similar to that of the invariable concomitance or premises. Because we find many instances, where correct inferential cognitions are brought about, in regard to the Subject qualified by the Probandum, by a wrong or invalid *Probans*; as for instance,—(1) according to the Mīmānsaka, true verbal cognitions are produced by Letters, which however are unreal, in so far as they are conceived of as qualified by *shortness and length* which in reality belong to the *Sounds*, and *not* to *Letters*, which are eternal and all-pervading;—and conversely (2) in the case of the jar, in which the odour is yet to appear (after baking), we *infer* the existence of the odour (which, for the time, must be regarded as unreal), from the premiss based upon the fact of the jar being of the Earth,—a premiss that is quite true and real; (3) the *unreal* reflection leads to the inference of the *real* reflected object. It might be argued that, in the last case, the premiss that we have is real—being as it is, in the form that 'there can be no reflection without a reflected object.' But if we were to admit of such 'concomitances', then the Ākāsha would also have to be regarded as invariably concomitant with the Universe, as there can be no Ākāsha without the Universe; and certainly this would not be admissible.

Says the Opponent,—"In the case of the reflection, what "we infer is the fact of its being *preceded* by the reflected "object; and this is inferred from the fact of the reflection "being an object of such negation as is due to the "negation of the Reflected Object; and certainly "this is a *Probans* as devoid of mere *apparent reality* as the "Object itself."

Page 32.

But what do you mean by one negation being *due* to another? It cannot mean that it produces, or is produced by, this latter; because there can be no such causal relationship between two negations. So all that it can mean is that one is invariably concomitant with the other; and thus the Probans of your inference would consist in the fact of the reflection being the object of negation with which the negation of the reflected object is invariably concomitant; and this reason has already been shown to be faulty and inconclusive, with reference to *Ākāsha*, &c. Hence it must be admitted that the existence of the reflected object is inferred from the *Reflection* itself. Specially as it has been shown above that it is not necessary for the existence of the Subject of the inference to be of the same character as that of the Probans or Reason leading to that inference.

The above reasoning also serves to set aside the following theory:—"In the case of verbal cognitions also the existence "of the denotation of the word must be of the same character "as that of its *capability* (to be construed along with the "sentence in which it occurs); specially because it is abso- "lutely necessary that the existence of this *capability* must "be of the same character as the meaning of the sentence "(and the meaning of the sentence is only that which is made "up of the meanings of the component words). Under "the circumstances, when the *capability* of words would be "rejected as *unreal*, how could there be any *reality* in the "meanings of the Vēḍānṭa texts (composed of those words)?"

This reasoning has no force; because in the case of the Vēḍānṭa texts, there is no rejection (as *unreal*) of the *capability* of the sentence,—this *capability* only consisting in the non-rejection of the meaning of the sentence regarded as one corporate whole.

Says the Opponent:—"Even then, according to you, the "Vēdānta text, the cognition derived therefrom, and its "validity, being all unreal,—how could you establish the absolutely *real Non-duality*?"

Answer:—For the reality of the object denoted by a word, it is not a necessary condition that the word and the cognition derived therefrom should be real. As in the case of the assertion 'this is silver' (with regard to a piece of shell) made by an untrustworthy person, you also hold that there is *reality* in the assertion (Verbal) and also in the misconception produced by it,—and yet you regard the object expressed by the assertion to be *unreal*. Then again, even though the validity of the cognition may be unreal, it does not necessarily follow that the object of that cognition is unreal.

Objection:—"The validity of the cognition being unreal, "the object cognised must also be unreal; as we find in the "case of the cognition of the shell-silver; similarly in the case "in question also the validity of the cognition (derived from "the Vēdānta texts) being unreal, the object therein spoken "of (*i. e.* Non-duality) should also be unreal."

Reply:—As a matter of fact, the unreality of the validity of a cognition cannot be regarded as the ground or reason for the unreality of the object cognised; because we have no rejection (as unreal) of any object in the case of Non-determinate cognitions, which are different in character from Misconceptions as well as Right Cognitions. [*I. e.* even though the non-determinate cognition be false, there is no falsity of the object, as there is no conception of any definite object in this case]. What is a sure indicator or reason of the unreality of an object cognised is that form of invalidity in the cognition which consists in its conceiving of the object as what it is not. And certainly there is no such contrary conception in the case of the Cognitions derived from the Vēdānta texts.

Says the *Opponent* :—"If there be an unreality in that "validity (of a cognition) which consists in the non-rejection "of its object, then certainly, this object itself would also be "unreal."

Reply :—In the case of the Vēḍānṭa texts, the Unreality of that validity which consists in the non-rejection of the objects spoken of by them, is not due to the rejection or denial of these objects;—because there is no possibility of any valid means of knowledge that would so deny them; specially as the object mentioned by the Vēḍānṭa texts consists of the denial of the reality of *all things*, [and we cannot conceive of any means of knowledge whereby we could reject this universal denial]. What the aforesaid 'Unreality' of validity is due to is the denial of the peculiar *relationship* of the objects as borne to the words denoting them. And hence even though there be an unreality of that validity which consists in the non-rejection of the objects,—this does not necessarily imply the unreality of the objects themselves. Because in the case of a qualified object, it is quite possible that while one section (the qualification *f. i.*) is unreal, the other is quite real; as for instance, in the case of the *man with a stick*, even though we may deny the existence of the stick, that does not imply the denial of the man.

End of section (13)—Wherein it is shown that no absolute validity belongs to Perception.

Section (14).

[Sense-perception is capable of being sublated by Inferential Cognition.]

In fact, an Inferential Cognition, which has the power of setting aside its contrary, becomes a sublator of even sense-perception (if this happens to be contrary to it).

"But," says the Opponent, "if direct Sense-perception "were to be set aside by Inferential Cognitions, then we "would have the whole elaborate system of interpretation "propounded in the Mīmānsā-shāsṭra rejected from its very "foundations. Because—(1) the direct cognition, afforded "by the Direct Assertion 'the priest should recite while "touching the Uḍumbara post', would be set aside by the "*Inference* of another Direct Vedic Assertion from the Smṛiti "declaration that 'the *whole* of the Uḍumbara post should be "covered up with cloth'; (2) the direct signification of the "Assertion 'the Gārhapaṭya fire should be worshipped with "the *Aindṛī* verse' would be set aside by the *Inference* "of the fact of the verse in question—'*Kaḍā cha nasta-* "*rīrasi nēndra suṣchasi ḍāṣukhē* '—pertaining to Indra "as indicated by the presence herein of the name of "Indra; and (3) the direct signification of the sentence 'the "sacred grass employed (at the Shyēna sacrifice) consists of "the *Shara*' would be set aside by the Inference of a Vedic "text laying down the use of the *Kusha* Grass,—this inference "being based upon the General Injunction (as to the use of "*Kusha* at *all* sacrifices)."

There would be no such thing; as the two cases are by no means analogous. What do you mean by bringing forward the case of these *Adhikaraṇas*? Do you mean that in these cases, the Inferential cognition, would set aside the sensuous Cognition *of the three Vedic* Sentences? Or, that they would set aside those Vedic sentences which are the objects of sensuous Perception? It could not be the former; because there being no actual opposition between the Inferences and the Sentences, any enquiry as to whether the one sets aside the other cannot rightly form the subject-matter of any serious dissertation. Nor do we admit of the existence of any such opposition [and it is only when the sensuous Perception is contrary to the Inferential cognition that the latter sets aside the former]. Consequently in this case your objection would be against something that we do not hold; and as such you would be open to the charge of *Niranuyojyānuyoja*, 'Objecting to what need not be objected to'.

For this same reason too the second interpretation of your position is not tenable. Because even though we have the support of the scriptures to the view that all Indirect Indications are set aside by Direct Asser-

P. 33.

tions found in the Veda,—yet these scriptures would not in any way be contradicted by the fact of such Indirect Indications (and Inferences based thereupon) setting aside sensuous Perception (as it is only the Vedic assertion that may never be set aside). And certainly the word or sentence (of the Veda) cannot be regarded as identical with the sensuous Perception that we may have of these; in fact as regards Verbal Cognition, we have already laid great stress upon its being the most authoritative form of cognition. Thus then, you will see that it was sheer foolishness or your part to have put forward the incompatibility of the aforesaid *Mīmānsā Adhikaraṇas* with our view.

Says the *Opponent*:—"If sensuous Perception were set "aside by Inferential Reasons, (and not *vice versa*), then the "inference of the *coolness of fire* could not be set aside by the "direct Sensuous Perception of its *heat*; nor would the "inference of the momentary character of the Self be set "aside by the direct recognition of its permanent character. "In fact in both these cases it would be the Inferences that "would set aside the direct cognitions."

In the case of the fire, the sensuous cognition (of fire being hot) is made stronger by reason of its being compatible with the nature of the effects produced by the fire; and in the case of the Self, the cognition of its permanence is supported by scriptural passages; hence being thus strengthened, the two cognitions in question are made capable of setting aside the inferential cognitions to the contrary. As a matter of fact, it is a sensuous Cognition that has not been duly tested which is weaker, or less valid, than a thoroughly tested inferential cognition; as for instance, the cognition of the sky as *blue* (as *seen* by the Eye) is less valid than the inferential cognition of the sky being *colourless*. Hence there can be no likelihood of a hopeless confusion as to all means of knowledge becoming mixed up with the *Sāmānyatodriṣṭa* form of Inference.

Objection:—"If Inferential Cognition were more valid "than Sense-perception then, whenever we would see an "animal, it would be right and correct to regard it as *horned* "also, as notwithstanding the fact of our *seeing* no horns, the "presence of horns would be inferred from the presence of "the *animal-character*; as it would be very much simpler to "regard the *presence of horns* as invariably concomitant with "the *animal-character*, than to regard it as concomitant with "such indefinite characters as those of the Cow, the Deer and "such other horned animals; because we can form no all-com-"prehensive conception of all such animals. And this reasoning "lending special support to the inference of the *presence of* "*horns*, this Inference would become more valid than the "sensuous cognition (whereby the horns are found to be "absent). This greater validity would be due to the fact that "the only strength or force that the validity of an inferential "cognition has consists in its being supported by corroborative "reasonings, as we find in the case in question. And in this "manner, in all cases we could go on inferring the presence "of certain characteristics from the presence of some general "property and character; as in all such cases the inference "would have the support of some reasoning or other bearing "testimony to its simplicity and validity. And it is only this "testimony which, according to you, makes the Inferential "Cognition capable of setting aside sensuous Perception. "Thus there would be no fixity even to the *practical* "state of things. As the only objection that there is to reject-"ing the *practical* reality of things is that such rejection "would be contrary to a fact of Sense-perception. [Hence "when the rejection of Sense-perception would be only desir-"able, there would be no objection to the rejecting of the "*practical* reality of things also]."

Reply:—Not so; because any inference of the *presence of horns*, which, by the very nature of the animal concerned, would be an impossibility, could never reject the Sensuous Perception (of the absence of horns); and as for the reasoning pointing to the concomitance of the *horn* with the *animal-character*, it will be shown by yourself that it is fallacious; and so it is quite possible for both of us to admit of a restriction or limit (under which alone would sensuous Perception be rightly regarded as sublated by Inferential Cognition). No person for a moment holds that any validity attaches to an Inference that is supported by fallacious reasonings. Thus it is only right to hold that a sensuous Perception is sublated by an Inferential Cognition which is supported by sound and valid reasonings.

End of Sec. (14).—wherein it is shown that Perception may be sublated by Inference.

Section (15).

[Perception may be sublated by Verbal Cognition also.]

In fact Sensuous Perception is also set aside by such Verbal Cognition as has its validity fully tested and established.

"But", says the Opponent,—"if Sensuous Perception were "sublatable by Verbal Cognition, then it would not be "right for Jaimini to have regarded the *Arṭhavāḍa* pass-"age—'therefore during the day smoke alone is seen of "fire',—and the Manṭra 'Aḍiṭi is heaven, &c.'—as contrary "to facts of Sensuous Perception, and then to have taken "them, on this same ground of contradiction, as indirect or "figurative descriptions, and as such not objectionable. Nor "again, would it be considered right for him to have taken "the words '*prasṭaraḥ*' and the like, in the sentences "'*yajamānaḥ prasṭaraḥ*' &c. &c., in their indirect figurative "signification, under the *Sūṭra* '*Ṭaṭsiḍḍhijāṭi-sārūpya* &c. &c.' "(*Mīmānsasūṭra* I—iv—Aḍhikaraṇas 12 to 17). [As in these "cases also it is only the incompatibility of the direct signi-"fications of the words with Sensuous Perception that makes "us take them in their indirect significations.] Thirdly, "the Vēḍānṭin also takes the words '*ṭaṭ*' and '*ṭvam*' (in the "sentence '*ṭaṭṭvamasi*') in the indirect figurative sense, "simply for the sake of making the interpretation compatible with well-recognised facts of Sense-perception; and "there would be no need for this if Sensuous Perception "were set aside by Verbal Cognition, which therefore would "be more authoritative, and as such would not need the said "compatibility; in reality the fact of the Sensuous Perception "being contrary to the signification of the sentence would "deprive the said Perception of all validity.

"It might be argued that,—'in the case of the sentence "'*taṭṭvamasi*', in the interpretation that we have adopted, there "is no abandoning of the direct primary meaning; as the "meaning that we accept is the one that is indicated by the "presence of many marks indicative of the sense of the sentence "—these marks being in the form of such peculiarities of the "context as the *beginning* and the *end* of the section in which "the sentence occurs. [And so in this case there is no "abandoning of the direct signification in view of any fact "of Sense-perception.']

"But if it is so in the case of the Vedantic interpretation "of the Vedic sentences, then in the case of the sentence "'*yajamānaḥ prasṭaraḥ*' &c., also, we find such marks indicative of the sense as the *apūrvaṭva*.* And a single mark "being rightly indicative of the sense of a sentence, the other "marks would be regarded as merely descriptive (and as such "having no direct bearing upon the sense of the sentence). "So for instance, according to the Vedāntin, if the *non-difference* "(of all things from Brahman) were proved by Sense-perception, the scriptural passages pointing to such non-difference should be regarded as merely descriptive. This "is enough for you; and there is no use for multiplying "further arguments."

Reply:—In the case of the Arṭhavāḍa passages— (1) 'During the day, the smoke alone &c.' (2) 'Adiṭi
P. 34.
is heaven', and (3) '*Yajamānaḥ prasṭaraḥ*' &c.—the greater validity of Sensuous Perception is established by

* *i. e.* the fact of the identity of the *yajamāna* with the *prasṭara* not being cognisable by any other means of knowledge.

the fact of its having been fully tested and found to have such supports as those of (1) *vākyashēṣa*, the subsequent words of the sentence, (2) the corroboration of other means of knowledge, and (3) the fulfilment of useful purposes; and hence as regards the *practical* state of things, the passages in question, being found to have their direct significations contradicted by the said facts of sensuous Perception, come to be taken in their indirect meanings. But though this is so in the case of the Arthavāda passages cited, yet, as regards the Vedanta passages speaking of Non-duality, these are never found to have their meanings contrary to any well-tested form of cognition; and as such these latter are quite capable of being taken in their direct significations. All that the testing of Sensuous Perception and such other forms of cognition does is to establish their truth *as regards the practical state of things*; and certainly this merely *practical* truth is not set aside by any Vedanta scriptures. What these scriptures do set aside is the *absolute* validity of such ordinary cognitions; and certainly these cognitions are never found, on testing, to have any such *absolute* validity; so that there is no incongruity. In the case of the aforesaid Arthavāda passages, on the other hand, it is the *practical* validity of sensuous Perception that is set at nought by their direct significations; and hence on account of this incongruity they have to be taken in their indirect significations. Thus there is a difference between the case of the Vedanta texts and the Arthavāda passages cited above.

Then again, it has been asserted that—"if validity attached to Sensuous Perception, then the Vedantin could not be led, by the contradiction of such Perception, to take the words '*tat*' and '*tvam*' in their indirect significations." But this is not right; because in the case of the sentence '*tattvamasi*', we have recourse to indirect signification, not because of its incongruity to any Sensuous Perception, but for the following reasons:—(1) As a matter of fact we find that the import of the sentence is one impartite whole, as indicated by the six * 'indicatives of import', and also by the analogy of other Vedanta passages; and such an import we find impossible to get at unless we have recourse to the indirect significations of some of the words. (2) We know that God (denoted by the word '*ṭaṭ*') is omniscient, and the Jīva (denoted by the word '*ṭvam*') is limited; and under the circumstances to speak of the two as identical would be absurd, unless we took the words as having meanings other than those directly signified. And thus we find that recourse is had to the indirect signification, solely for the purpose of getting at the one indivisible fact that forms the import of the sentence. In fact in all cases of indirect interpretation we find that the chief motive that leads men to have recourse to it, is to get at the true import of the sentence.

Says the *Opponent*:—"In that case the Vedanta text would come to be taken in its secondary signification."

What do you mean by a sentence being taken in its secondary sense? (1) Does it mean that its expressed meaning is abandoned and another meaning accepted? or (2) that it is taken in a sense not expressible by it at all? In the case in question the former explanation would not apply; because we do not renounce the idea of the identity of the Paramāṭmā and the Jīva, at any rate so far as co-extensiveness is concerned,—and it is this idea alone that is expressed (by the sentence '*taṭṭvamasi*'). Nor would the second explanation be applicable; because the form of indirect signification that we admit of in the sentence in question is that which renounces, and at the same time does not renounce entirely, the direct primary signification; and hence even though we do abandon one part of the directly expressed meaning, yet it is only another part of this same meaning that is accepted as forming the import; exactly as we have in the case of the

* These six 'indicatives of import' are (1) *Upakrama*, Beginning (2) *Upasamhāra*, End (3)—*Abhyāsa*, Repetition (4) *Apūrvaṭā*, Newness, (4) *Phala*, Result (5) *Arthavāda*, Praise or Dispraise and (6) *Upapaṭṭi*, Reasoning.

sentence '*So' yandēvadattaḥ*' 'this is the same Devadatta.' In fact in the case in question all that is meant by the signification being 'secondary' or 'indirect' is that out of the qualified thing that is directly denoted, the qualification is rejected, and the thing by itself alone is accepted as forming the denotation. This has been thus declared by Vāchaspati Mishra: "The sentences, '*Yajamānaḥ prastaraḥ*' &c. are taken as expressive of their secondary meaning, because they are all subordinate to other sentences;—as regards the Vedanta texts describing non-duality, they are not subordinate to any other sentences, and as such their signification must be non-secondary or primary." In the '*Shabara-Bhāṣya* also it has been thus declared:—"In an Injunction, the signification of words cannot be said to be *secondary*." We shall show later on how the sentences '*Yajamānaḥ prastaraḥ*' and the like cannot be taken in their direct significations, on account of such reasons as *Apūrvatva* and the like which point to their true import.

Says the *Opponent*:—"What leads a certain sentence to "be taken in its secondary signification is not the fact of "its being subordinate to another sentence, but the fact "of its being opposed to other forms of right knowledge; "and so also what makes a sentence to be taken in its primary "signification is the fact of its not being opposed to the "other forms of right knowledge, and not the fact of its not "being subordinate to something else. Because as a matter "of fact, we find—in the case of such ordinary sentences as "'this cow giving a large quality of milk should be purchas-"ed', and in the Vedic sentence 'Prajāpati wept, and "from the weeping was produced silver, &c. &c.'—that even "though the sentences are subordinate to other sentences, "yet they are taken in their primary signification, simply "because they are not found to be opposed to any other forms "of right knowledge; and we do not have recourse to any "indirect meanings, as we have in the case of the sentences

" *yajamānaḥ prasṭaraḥ*' and the like. And conversely, we " find, in the case of the sentence ' one should sacrifice " with the Soma-juice,' that even though it is not " opposed to any other form of right cognition, yet we " do not accept it in its primary meaning,—*firstly* because if " we do not accept the two words '*somēna*' and '*yajēṭa*' to " be co-ordinate (*i. e.* if we do not interpret the two words as " '*Somēna yāgēna*'), then we make the interpretation open " to the fault of ' threefold contradiction'; and *secondly*, if " we do accept the two as co-ordinate, then the meaning " becomes opposed to a fact of Sense-perception (as the *Soma* " is not actually seen to be the *sacrifice* itself); and conse- " quently, in order to guard against these absurdities, we accept " the secondary signification of the word '*Somēna*', taking it to " mean ' *Somavaṭā* '—the sacrifice *at which Soma is employed.*

" Similarly, in the case of the Sūṭra—'Now then there " should be an enquiry into the nature of Brahman'—wherein " we have an injunction for the enquiry,—as also in the Shruṭi " sentence ' seek to know That,'—we accept the word '*Jijñāsā*' " to indirectly indicate the *enquiry*, in order to establish the " syntactical connection of the injunction, without contra- " dicting any other forms of right knowledge; and so also " in the case of the sentence 'all this is Brahmaṇ' &c., we " admit of the secondary signification (for the sake of avoid- " ing the contradiction of other forms of right knowledge). " And as the whole of this sentence is accepted as indirectly " indicating *Brahman* only, which is not directly expressible " by all the words,—it would not be right to deny the indirect " secondary signification. There are two circumstances that " justify our having recourse to the secondary or indirect signi- " fication of sentences—*viz.* (*a*) if the direct signification " makes the syntactical connection impossible, or (*b*) if the " direct meaning of words fails to give the required import " of the sentence; and these conditions are fulfilled in both " cases—*i. e.* when the sentence in question contains an " injunction, as well as when it does not.

"As for the sentence quoted from the *Shabara-Bhāṣya*, "what it means is that there can be no indirect signification "in the case of an Injunction, only for lending predominance "to the Arṭhavāḍa passage.

"For these reasons, Sensuous Perception cannot be held "to be sublatble by Verbal Cognition."

To the above the following reply is made:——The Opponent apparently does not understand things: What Page 35. is meant by a sentence being taken in its primary signification is that it expresses a meaning that directly forms its import,—and not that it expresses what is directly denotable by it; and similarly what is meant by its being taken in the secondary signification is that it has an import other than what is expressed by the words,—and not that its meaning is got at by what is called the Indicative Process (of *Lakṣaṇā*). Thus then, in the case of the Vedānta passages, even though we have recourse to the indirect indicative process of signification, for the purpose of bringing about the due comprehension of what forms their true import,—yet this does not mean that the direct primary meaning of the passages has been renounced; as we have already explained. Similarly, in the case of the sentence 'one should sacrifice with the Soma-juice', its true import of the qualified injunction (that of the *sacrifice with the Soma-juice*) does not rest in the qualification (*Soma-juice*) alone; and hence even though we have recourse to the Possessive Indication (taking '*Somēna yajēṭa*' as equivalent to '*Somavāṭā yāgēna etc.*'), yet, as the primary meaning is not *wholly* abandoned, the sentence cannot be regarded as being taken in its *secondary* meaning.

Then, as regards the word '*Jijñāsā*' (in the Sūṭra '*aṭhāṭo Brahmajijñāsā*'), some people hold that the *knowledge as desired* is indirectly indicated by the root '*jñā*'; while others deny this fact; but even though there is this difference of opinion, yet when we come to consider the signification of the desiderative affix '*san*', the upholders of both opinions are equally obliged to admit of an *indirect* indication in which a certain factor of the *direct* signification is renounced. And thus though there is a renouncing of the direct signification, yet as the desired sense of 'Injunction' is accomplished all the same, we do not regard the expression as taken in its secondary meaning. Then again, even though we may have recourse to indirect indication in the case of a word,—this recourse being necessitated by the fact that without such indication the comprehension of the sentence in which that word occurs would not be got at,—yet that does not mean that the whole sentence is thereby taken in its secondary signification. Because the meaning of the sentence thus comprehended, not being subordinate to anything else, cannot but be accepted as *primary*. In a case however, where the meaning of the sentence is comprehended as subordinate to something else, the sentence would certainly be accepted as taken in its secondary signification.

Then again, the *import* of the *sentence* is something wholly different from that of the *word*. As for instance, in such sentences as '*saindhavamānaya*,' ('*gangāyām vasati*') and the like, though the import of the *sentence* is one only (that of *bringing something*), yet the imports of the words are diverse (the word '*saindhava*' being at one time taken as denoting *salt*, and at another, a particular kind of *horse*, and so forth); and conversely, in the sentence '*viṣam bhuṅkṣva*', even though the import of the words is one only (the *eating of poison*), yet the import of the sentence is diverse (the sense of the sentence when addressed by a friend being wholly opposed to that when it is addressed by an enemy).

Thus then, in the sentences—(1) 'the cow giving much milk should be purchased', (2) 'Prajāpaṭi wept &c.', (3) 'all this is Brahman',—we have recourse to secondary signification; because the *first* sentence is subordinate to the Injunction that *the cow must be purchased*, and as such it cannot but be taken as indirectly indicating the *excellence* of the cow;—the *second* sentence is found to be subordinate to the Injunction that *silver should not be placed on the grass, and the sacrificial gift should be given in gold*, and so the sentence is taken as indicating the *excellence* of gold indirectly through the deprecation of silver;—and the *third* sentence being found to be subordinate to the Injunction of *calmness* contained in the sentence '*tajjalāniṭi shānṭa upāsīṭa*', and so it is taken as indirectly indicating that form of *excellence* of the worship which consists in its being very easily accomplished.

Thus then, we have set aside the view that we have recourse to the indirect or secondary signification only when the direct or primary signification is contrary to other forms of right cognition. Because we do not find any such contradiction in the above-explained case of the sentence, 'the cow giving much milk &c.', where however we have the indirect indication of *excellence*. And we conclude that in all Arṭhavāḍa passages, we have recourse to the indirect signification, only for the purpose of bringing about the due comprehension of its real import. But the only difference is this : if that comprehension of the *Arṭhavāḍa* passage which appears before the indication of the excellence of the allied Injunction happens to be contrary to a certain other valid form of cognition, then it is rejected (as false),—as in the case of the *Arṭhavāḍa*, 'Prajāpati cut out his own fat &c.'; and it is for this reason that such Arṭhavāḍa passages are regarded as having some sort of an indirect or secondary signification. In a case however where the *Arṭhavāḍa* is found to express something already known by other means of knowledge, it is regarded as merely *descriptive* (and not as *Injunctive*)—as for instance, in the sentence 'Agni is the medicine for cold.' And in both these cases the Arṭhavāḍa passage is not regarded as authoritative or valid; because the *validity* of a cognition consists in its making known something that is not rejected by other cognitions, and which is not already known by other means of knowledge;

and this *validity* we have-seen is not present in the two kinds of Arṭhavāḍa just noticed. But there are many Arṭhavāḍa passages which neither contradict other forms of cognitions, nor have their subject-matter already known ; and as such passages fulfil the necessary conditions of *validity*, they are regarded as '*Bhūṭārṭhavāḍa*' ; as for example the sentence 'Indra raised his thundervolt against Vriṭṭra.' This is what has been explained under the *Ḍēvaṭāḍhikaraṇa* of the *Mīmānsāsūṭra*.

Says the *Opponent*:—"If such be the case, then, in the "case of such sentences as '*āḍiṭyo yūpaḥ*', and the like, as "the indirect Indication would be accepted only for the "purpose of the due comprehension of the meaning of the "sentence,—the meaning thus got at could not be regarded "as *secondary*."

Certainly, it could not be regarded as *secondary*, if the meaning of the sentence finally got at were that *the sacrificial post is like the sun*. As a matter of fact, however, the meaning of the sentence, though got at by indirect signification, is subordinate to the Injunction that the *Animal is*)*to be*
P. 36. *tethered to the post*; and hence the sentence '*āḍiṭyō yūpaḥ*' cannot but be regarded as indirectly indicating the mere *excellence* of the post ; and this indicated meaning would certainly be only *secondary*; but this *secondary* character of the meaning would not be due to any figurative use of the word '*āḍiṭiyaḥ*'. It is this that has been shown under the Mīmānsāsūṭra '*Ṭaṭsiḍḍhi &c.*' (I—iv— 12 *et, seq.*), where in connection with all the passages cited, the author has shown the various methods of secondary signification, to which recourse is had for the sake of the due comprehension of other sentences appearing among those cited. As for the indirect indication of the excellence of the sacrifice in connection with which the *Arṭhavāḍa* passage occurs, this indication is found in all *Arṭhavāḍa* passages ; and as such this indication is also present in the sentences cited under the Sūṭra '*Ṭaṭsiḍḍhi* &c. &c.' also. And thus we find that there can

be no incongruity in regarding these sentences as having *secondary* meanings. And consequently it follows that the case of these passages is by no means analogous to that of the Vedānta passages asserting *non-duality*.

———,,———

Then, the Opponent has quoted the authority of the *Shabara-Bhāṣya*, to the effect that we cannot have recourse to the secondary meaning of the Injunction, for the sake of getting at the primary meaning of the *Arṭhavāḍa*.

But this assertion of the *Shabara-Bhāṣya* is scarcely consistent; as we find that in the case of the Injunction. '*praṭigṛihṇīyāṭ*' 'one should accept'—occurring in connection with the *Ashvapraṭigraha Iṣṭi*—the word *praṭigṛihṇīyāṭ*' has been interpreted to mean '*praṭigrāhayēṭ*', ('should make to accept', *i. e.* 'should offer'); and this interpretation is possible only by assuming that the sense of the *causal* is got at by indirect indication, in accordance with the Arṭhavāḍa passage occurring in the context. In view of this the sentence quoted from the *Shabara-Bhāṣya* must be taken to mean that, in an Injunction, which is a sentence with a definite import, there is no other predominant factor save the meaning of the sentence that is comprehended.

———

Thus then, it is fully established that even though the Vedānta passages are taken in their indicated significations, yet the meanings thus got at are not necessarily *secondary*; and hence they are fully capable of setting aside sensuous Perceptions.

———

Section 16.

[Sensuous Perception is sublated by Inferential and Verbal Cognitions, because it the forerunner of these;—this being in accordance with the Apachchhēḍanyāya of the Mīmānsāsūṭra, by which that which follows is more powerful than that which goes before.]

Then again, Verbal Cognitions must be regarded as more authoritative than Sensuous Cognition, also in accordance with the *Apachchhēḍanyāya.* That is to say, in the *Adhikarana* of the Mīmānsā dealt with under the *Sūṭra*—'*paurvāparyē pūrvaḍaurbalyaṃ prakṛiṭivaṭ* (6-5-54), it has been shown that the sacrifice,—at which all the belongings of the sacrificer have to be given away, which is laid down as to be performed in expiation of the anomaly incurred in the line of priests passing out being broken by the Praṭiharṭṛi priest,—is set aside in favour of the sacrifice at which no gifts have to be given, and which is to be performed in expiation of a similar breaking of the line by the Uḍgāṭṛi priest; and the reason given for this is that the passing of the Uḍgāṭṛi *comes after* that of the Praṭiharṭṛi. In accordance with this law, it is only right that Sensuous cognition, which is the forerunner of all forms of cognition, should be sublated by Verbal Cognition.

Says the *Opponent* :—" When the breaking of the line by " the Praṭiharṭṛi occurs after that by the Uḍgāṭṛi, it is only " right that the sacrifice with all gifts laid down for the " former should make room for the sacrifice without gifts " laid down for the latter; and the reason for this is very " simple:—whether the breaking be done by the Praṭiharṭṛi " alone, or by both the *Praṭiharṭṛi* and the *Uḍgāṭṛi*, occurring " either simultaneously or one after the other,—there is " always room for the performance of rites in connection " with the passing of the Praṭiharṭṛi, even after the perform- " ance of that in connection with the Uḍgāṭṛi. Otherwise " (*i. e.* if the prior performance of the sacrifices in connection " with the Uḍgāṭṛi did not mean the mere postponement "of the other), we would be rejecting the authority of the "Vedic injunction that, 'if the Praṭihartṛi should break the "line one should give away all his belongings.' It is for "this reason that in the *Adhikaraṇa* under the *Sūtra*— "'*vipratiṣēdhād vikalpaḥ syāt*'—it has been said that "if the breaking of the line should be by the two priests "simultaneously, then there should be an option (as to "the performance of the expiatory rites in connection "with the one or the other). Then again, in the *Adhikaraṇa* "dealing with the passage—*Yadyudgāṭā jaghanyaḥ syāṭ* "*punaryajñē sarvāvēdasandadyāt, athetarasmin*, &c.' it has "been said that in case the breaking by the Udgāṭṛi should "occur after that by the Praṭihartṛi, the sacrificer should, "at first, perform the rites without gift in connection with "the former; and then during the second course of the "Jyotisthoma that he has to perform, the gift that he gives "in accordance with the Injunction 'he should give what he "was going to give during the first course,' is not in the "form of the 1,200 gold pieces ordinarily given at the *Jyotish-* "*toma* sacrifice, but in the shape of *all his belongings*; because "it was this form of gift that he was going to make during "the first course, in consideration of the breaking of the line "by the Praṭihartṛi; and the reason for this course is that "the desire that had arisen in his mind for giving away all "this in connection with the breaking by the Praṭihartṛi has "not been removed from his mind; and thus we find that the "performance of the expiatory rites in connection with the "break by the Praṭihartṛi is not set aside absolutely, but "only temporarily postponed, to be done in another course "of the sacrifices. In this connection, we find the state- "ment in the *Tuptīkā* that 'the performance comes in during "the other course.' Then again, in a case where the two "breaks occur in their natural order, the performance "of the sacrifice without gifts being performed before that at "which all one's belongings have to be given away, there is "no incongruity at all; just as in the case of the berry, there "is no incongruity in the appearance of the two colours, *green* "and *red*, in their natural order of sequence. It has been "said under the *Apachhēḍāḍhikarana* (in the *Shāstrāḍipikā*) "that—'all that is meant by a conditional injunction is that, "even though the main sacrifice should have been otherwise "performed, prior to the appearance of the stated con- "ditions, it should, on the appearance of those conditions, "be performed in accordance with that conditional injunction. "For these reasons we conclude that the law of the *Apachhēḍa* "is applicable to only those actions for the performance "whereof there is always some room left.

"If however we were to apply this law to the case in "question, then, all Sensuous cognitions being "sublated by the Vedanta scriptures, there would be "no room at all for Sensuous Perception as a valid means of "knowledge."

Page 37.

To the above we make the following reply:—You say that in the case of there being no breaking by the Uḍgāṭri, or in that of the breaking by both the Uḍgāṭri and the Praṭihartṛi occurring simultaneously, and also in case of the breaking by the Praṭihartṛi coming after that by the Uḍgāṭri,—there is room for the performance of the sacrifice with all one's belongings as the sacrificial gift, during the second course of the *Jyoṭishtoma*;—well, in the same manner, for Sensuous Perception also there will be room for validity, in regard to the *practical* state of things. And just as in the case of the sacrifices there would be an incongruity if both were to be performed during the same course, so, in the same manner, in the case in question also, Sensuous Perception and the Vedanta texts could not both be valid and true with regard to the *absolutely real* state of things. It is for this reason that it has been rightly declared that, 'it is by the law of the *Apachchhēḍanyāya* that the texts describing Brahman as qualified and phenomenal are set aside by those speaking of It as unqualified and transcending all phenomena'. In this connection we have the following declaration by Ānandabodhāchārya :—'Like the assertion *this is not a snake*, the Vedic text as a means of cognition sets aside the preceding forms of cognition, (1) because it refers to the real state of things, (2) because it comes after the other forms of cognition, and (3) because it is free from discrepancies.'

Says the *Opponent* :—"(1) As regards the first of these "three reasons, in a case where the Vedic text would be "contrary to the other means of cognition, the fact of its "referring to the real state of things would not be admitted by "your Opponent, and as such the Reasoning would be *Asiddha*, "'unknown', 'not accepted'. (2) As regards the second rea- "son, it is found to *fail*, or to be 'proving the contrary', in a "case where a misconception follows after the right cognition "(where the mere fact of the misconception coming last "does not make it true). It fact we often meet with cases "where even that which has gone before sets aside that "which comes afterwards,—as for instance, the *Sūtra* "'*na ktvā sēt*' (Pāṇini) is set aside by the previous *Sūtra* "'*mṛiḍamṛidagudhakushaklisharadavasaḥ*. (3) Then as re- "gards the third reason—freedom from discrepancies—this "may be explained as being due to some meaning of the texts "other than the direct one held by the Vedantin. As a summ- "ing up of all these we have the following verse :—'(*a*) The "fact of the text referring to the real state of things is not "so recognised by all parties,—(*b*) the fact of its coming "afterwards fails to prove the conclusion,—and (*c*) freedom "from discrepancies is otherwise explicable; consequently "none of these reasons is capable of proving the superior "authority of the Vedic text'."

Reply :—(1) Inasmuch as the validity of Sense-perception and other forms of cognition is only *practical*, whereas that of the Vedic text is *absolute*,—and as such, there being no actual contradiction between the two,—it is easily proved that the Vedic text refers to the real state of things. (2) Further, what we mean by one cognition *appearing after* the other is such *appearance* as is not sublated by another cognition; this form of appearance is not possible in a case where the misconception appears after a right notion, as this misconception is always set aside by a subsequent cognition; so this reason does not fail to prove our desired conclusion. Then as regards the case of the two Sūras of Pāṇini that you have cited, even though in the actual reading of the text the Sūṭra '*na kṭvā sēt*' appears later, yet as a matter of fact this can not but be regarded as meant to precede the other Sūṭra; because until the *kṭvā*, which would come in as a matter of course, has not been precluded by the Sūtra '*na kṭvā sēt*', the reassertion of the *kṭva* that we have in the *Sūṭra* would be impossible and meaningless. Because when we have an exception to the exception to a general rule, it is the general rule that remains intact. (*c*) Similarly, the absence of discrepancies too is not otherwise explicable; as the validity of a text is accepted only with reference to its real import (and not to any and every sense that might be got out from it).

Thus we find that it was through sheer ignorance that the Opponent asserted that the case of the sublation of Sense-perception by Verbal Cognition is not amenable to the law of the *Apachchhēḍa-Nyāya*.

END OF SECTION (16).

Section (17).

[The Inferential Cognition of 'Unreality' cannot be relegated to the category of such apparently absurd notions as that of Fire being cool.]

Says the *Opponent*:—"If even such an Inference as has "been rejected by Sense-perception (and is thus open to the "fallacy of Bāḍha) were to be accepted as proving its con-"clusion, then we might also regard it as rightly proving "that *fire is not hot*; and thus there could never be any talk "of the fallacy of '*Kālāṭyayāpaḍiṣṭa* or *Annulment*.

"It might be argued that—'in this inference of the fire being *not hot*, we would have the fallacy of *Annulment* distinctly present, as the *Probandum* is the *negation of heat*, while this *heat* is universally known to reside in the *Subject*, Fire, in which the presence of that negation is desired to be proved.'

"But in this way, in the case of the inference of fire being not hot also, if the absence of heat or presence of coolness were regarded as being predicated of any *particular* fire, then there could be no *Annulment* in this case either; as there would be other fires, than the one of which the coolness would be predicated, in which the *heat* might reside without in any way vitiating our conclusion.

"Then again, it might be urged that—'we have the *Annulment* of an inference only in a case where the contrary Sense-perception is specially strong in its validity (as we have in the case of the *heat* of fire),—and not in case where it is not so strong,—as in the case of the *reality* of the world; and so in this case there could be no *annulment* of the Inference by Perception.

"But as a matter of fact, even in the case of the Inference of Unreality we find that we have exactly the same reasons for regarding the contrary Sense-perception to be specially strong, as we have in the regard to the Perception of the heat of fire; and the Inference of the Unreality of the world is exactly in the same position—open to the same arguments for and against—as that of the fire being not hot.

"It might be said that—'for the upholder of Unreality it is only desirable that the inference of Unreality should be similar to the Inference of the negation of heat, with reference to the particular substratum in regard to which it is cognised.' But even though this similarity might be granted, on account of *heat* and *absence of heat* being in the form of a positive and a negative entity respectively,—yet no such similarity would be admitted when the inference

"would be with regard to *coolness*; because *coolness* is not "mere *absence of heat*. Hence it becomes necessary for you "either to deny the fact of *Annulment* being a fal-
Page 38.
"lacy in Inference, or to point out what difference "there is between the Sense-perception of *reality* on the "one hand, and that of the *presence of heat*, or that of *the* "*character of not being the sacrificer*, on the other.

"It might be argued that—'the validity of the Percep- "tion of heat in fire is acknowledged, after due exami- "nation, by both parties, while that of the Percep- "tion of *reality* is not so admitted; and this makes a great "difference between the two cases.' But there is no reason "to deny the fact that the validity of the Perception of *reality* "also is universally admitted; specially as the possibility of "due examination is equally present in both cases."

To the above we make the following *reply*:—There is a great difference between the two cases, for in the case of the Perception of *heat* &c., the Verbal and Inferential cognitions are distinctly contrary to the sensuous cognition; for instance, the fact of a certain person not having the character of the sacrificer, and also of the presence of heat in fire, which are *perceived*, both are such as pertain to the *practical* state of things; and in the same manner, the Verbal cognition of a certain person having the character of the *sacrificer*, and also the Inferential cognition of the absence of heat in fire,—both of these also pertain to the *practical* state of things; and thus both sets of cognitions equally pertaining to only the *practical* state of things, it is but right that the two latter cognitions should be sublated by the two former sensuous cognitions. Such, however, is not the case with the Perception of *reality*; as this *reality* that is perceived is only *practical*; and the *Unreality* that is sought to be proved by Inference is not contrary to this *reality*, as what is meant by it is the denial of the *absolute reality* of things (and not mere *practical* reality);

and so the Inferential cognition of such Unreality cannot be regarded as sublated by the sensuous Perception of mere *practical* reality.

Says the *Opponent* :—" What do you mean by this? (1) " Do you mean that, inasmuch as the inferential cognition " of *Unreality* pertains to the actual *absolute reality* of things, " it can only sublate other cognitions, and can never itself " be sublated? (2) or, that the inferential cognition pertaining " to the *absolute* reality of things, while the sensuous cognition " pertains to their mere *practical* reality, the subject-matter of " the two cognitions is entirely different, and hence there being " no contradiction, one need not sublate the other? Then " again, in this latter case, (*a*) do you mean to say that the In- " ferential cognition apprehends the absence of the *absolute* " reality of things (which reality is not apprehended by the " sense-organs), without having apprehended their *practical* " reality, which *is* known by means of the Sense-organs? (*b*) " Or is it that the Inferential cognition apprehends the absence " of *absolute* reality, after the thing has been cognised, in its " *practical* reality, by the Sense-organs? You could not " hold to this last view (*b*); because it would not be right to " assert that the cognition that apprehends the negation of a " thing apprehended by another cognition does not sublate " this latter cognition. Nor again could you hold to the other " view (*a*); because if the Inferential cognition were to reject " something which has not been previously cognised by the " senses, then it would be open to the charge of containing " the absurdity of denying something that is not known, and " for which therefore there is no chance of being asserted; " *i. e.* it would be regarded as 'striking in the air'; " and also because this would impart a sort of an absolute " reality to the object of Sensuous cognition (which the Vedantin " will not allow). [This disposes of the *second* of the two " alternatives set forth in the beginning]. Then as regards " the *first* of those two alternatives, that too can be " maintained; because an Inferential Cognition, which would be "indirectly contrary to the Sensuous Cognition that forms its "very basis, could never be accepted as having an object that "has any *absolute* reality."

No weight attaches to the above arguments, we reply; as there is nothing objectionable in either of the two alternatives set forth. As regards the *first* view, it would not be impossible to accept the absolute reality of the object of Inferential cognition under the circumstances. Because in the case of the cognition of shell-silver, we find that the cognition 'this is silver' does not set aside the cognition that 'this is not silver'; and this leads us to the conclusion that it is only a well-tested cognition that can be accepted as setting aside another cognition; and the 'testing' too of a cognition consists, among other things, in finding out if it is compatible with the activity that it arouses in the perceiving agent; and such a testing would be impossible until we admitted the fact of the cognition (and its concomitants) not being absolutely rejected, at least as regards the *practical* state of things; and hence this cognition (sensuous or otherwise) could set aside only such other cognitions (inferential or verbal) as would seek to reject its validity *as regards the practical* state of things; and it could have nothing to say to the Vedanta texts declaring Non-duality (as these pertain to only the *absolutely* real state of things),—as we have already explained before.

Then as regards the second alternative set forth by the Opponent, the Inferential cognition could not be objected to on the ground of denying something that does not exist; because though there may not be a possibility, then and there, yet it may turn up at some distant point of time (and as such the denial of such a possibility would not be like striking in the air). Some people (Vedantins) seek to meet the objection in question by asserting that there is a possibility of the reality of all objects of sensuous cognition being asserted, on account of the fact of the absolute reality of the Self being well-known (and the Self is an object of sensuous cognition), [and so the sublating by the inferential cognition would not be open to the aforesaid charge]. But this is not right; as the '*prasakti*' or *possibility* of a certain thing being asserted does not consist in the mere cognition of the thing sought to be denied by the *pratiṣēdha* or *sublation*; in fact it consists in its being known as the substratum of denial; and as a matter of fact, the Self can never be the substratum of such denial. For this reason, what the Vedantin has to do is to show that there is a remote 'possibility' of the thing denied being asserted.

Or, even granting that there is no such 'possibility',— as a matter of fact, it is only in the perception of the negation or absence (of a certain thing) that this 'possibility' is necessary, for the purpose of imposing a relationship (pertaining to which would the negation be perceived); in the case of *verbal* and *inferential* cognitions, however, where would there be any necessity for such a 'possibility'? The denial would not be meaningless, in the absence of this 'possibility'. As there would always be present a definite purpose in the shape of the cessation or avoidance of evil.

Nor would there be any chance for an *absolute* reality attaching to the object of Sensuous cognition; as what the Inferential cognition (of Unreality) would apprehend would be the absence or negation of that absolute reality which would pertain to that object (which therefore could never be regarded as absolutely real).

Thus then, we find that there is nothing objectionable in our stand-point. Thus has this been summed up in the *Khaṇḍanakhaṇḍakhādya*:—'The scripture taking its refuge in *absolute* non-duality, does not fear any contradiction by Perception, upon which it might be based.'

Says the Opponent:—"Arguing analogously to your "argument, the *non-hot* character of fire may be
Page 39. "regarded as *absolutely* real; and hence the Inferen- "tial cognition of such character would not be sublated by the

"perception of the *hot* character, which would be only *practi-*
"*cally* real. And similarly in the case of the sentence—
"'the sacrificial post is the Sun,'—the solar character of
"the *post* being regarded as *absolutely* real, the direct mean-
"ing of the sentence would not fear any contradiction by
"the perception of its non-solar character (which would
"have only a *practical* reality)."

No such thing is possible. In the first place, what is the meaning of the assertion that the *non-hot* character of fire may be regarded as *absolutely* real? If you mean by this that there is, in *absolute* reality, no heat at all,—then this comes to be a mere statement of the Non-duality of things; and as such quite acceptable to us in all its bearings. If however, it be meant that there is no heat, even in the *practical* state of things,—then, inasmuch as this declaration would have a strong sublator in the form of the sensuous Perception of *heat*,—a Perception which is duly tested and found valid in view of the activities set up by it,—you could not establish the *absolute* reality of the said *non-hot* character.

Thus we have shown that the Inferential cognition of Unreality is by no means similar to the Inference of fire being cool.

The above argument may also be applied to the case of the *Sun* and the *Sacrificial post*,—the denial of the difference between the two being regarded as either absolutely or only practically real; as a matter of fact, we find that the passage in question is subordinate to another passage, and as such can not be taken as asserting the actual non-difference between the *Sun* and the *Post*; and specially as such an assertion would be contrary to a well-tested fact of Sense-perception, the sentence is taken in its indirect signification, as containing the mere praise of the *post*. This explanation serves to set aside the view that the case of the Vedanta texts is similar to that of the sentence 'the sacrificial post is the Sun,'—a view that has been just expressed by the Opponent, in the sentence "the solar character of the post being, &c. &c."

It might be argued that—"inasmuch as the Vedanta texts "would only point out what has already been established by "Inference, they would be merely *descriptive* or *repetitive* in "their character (and would not have the character of true "*means of knowledge*, which affords knowledge of something "not otherwise known); just like the Vedic sentence,—'fire "is an antidote for cold'—which is merely descriptive of the "fact of the existence in fire of the power of removing cold, "a fact already known by other means of knowledge."

But as a matter of fact, Inferential cognition depends upon the intellectual capacity of each man; and as such it never has an equal force of application for all men. Consequently the mere fact of a certain thing being apprehended by the Inferential cognition of such limited application, is not sufficient ground for regarding the Vedic text pointing to the same thing, as merely *descriptive*. This has been thus declared by Vāchaspati Mishra, under the Sūṭra '*Ṭarkāpratisthānāt*' (Brahma-Sūṭra 2-1-11):—'A certain fact proved by people clever at inferences is turned upside down by people who are cleverer than them.' As regards the Vedic sentence quoted as an example—'fire is the antidote for cold'—the fact of fire being an antidote for cold is universally known by two such means of knowledge as Sense-perception and Presumption; and as such the case of this sentence is in no way analogous to that of the Vedānta texts.

Thus it is established that the Inferential cognition of the *Unreality of the World* is in no way analogous to the Inference of fire being cool.

Section (18).

[Refutation of the argument that Perception cannot be sublated by Inferential reasonings.]

Then again, the greater validity of a cognition depends upon its being well-tested, and not either on its being the basis for other cognitions, or on its being direct or immediate; because we find that Sensuous Cognition (which is immediate, and which forms the basis of other forms of cognition) is actually amenable to rejection by Inferential and Verbal Cognitions. For instance, (1) the direct Sensuous Cognition of silver (in the shell) is set aside by Inferential Cognition, and also by the cognition afforded by the assertion of a trustworthy person; (2) the Sensuous Cognition of the sky as *blue* is set aside by the Inferential Cognition of the fact of the sky being colourless; (3) such sensuous (visual) cognitions as 'I am fair', 'I am in this house,' and also the cognition of the Moon having a disc of the size of about six inches, and so forth, are all set aside by scriptural texts and by Inferences; (4) the Cognition—'the conchshell is yellow', 'sugar is bitter' and the like are set aside by Inferences and Trustworthy Assertions.

Says the *Opponent*:—"As a matter of fact, it must be "admitted that a misconception pertaining to direct Sensuous "Cognition it set aside by the same kind of cognition only. "Otherwise if mediate (Inferential) Cognition were capable "of setting aside immediate (Sensuous) misconceptions, then "the attempt of the Vedantin to prove that the cognition "obtained from the Vedanta texts is immediate and direct, "would be absolutely unnecessary [as even when mediate, it "could set aside the immediate misconceptions with regard "to the reality of the world]."

To the above the following reply is made:—What occurs in the case of an ordinary misconception is this: A man sees something lying on the ground,—he *sees* that it is a snake—then he hears a trustworthy assertion 'this is not a snake'; now this assertion does not bring about the absolute cessation of the ignorance and its ramifications shrouding his mind; all that it does is to indicate that the conception of the snake was wrong, and thereby it sets aside the idea of that conception being right, and also the idea of the object of that conception being real; and it is in view of these facts only that the assertion 'this is not a snake' is regarded as *setting aside* the misconception. And as for the idea of the misconception being right and its object being real, its being mediate or direct,—this does not require an immediate or direct Cognition to reject it. Specially as no one ever has an *immediate* cognition of the *validity* of cognitions, which is implied either by its not being brought about by a defective instrument, or by its having its object not sublated by any subsequent cognition;—nor is the reality of the object of any cognition immediately perceptible; as such reality also would be implied by its not being negatived by any person, at any point of time or place. For this reason then, it is only proper that these (the validity of the cognition and the idea of its object being real), should be set aside by *mediate* or indirect cognitions. Thus then, being set aside, even though the misconception of the silver would be present in its own form, yet, as it would not be capable of accomplishing the work of a piece of silver, it would be regarded to be as good as non-existent, and would for this reason be spoken of as 'rejected'. And in this we see nothing objectionable.

Page 40.

Says the *Opponent*:—"(1) The misconception 'this is "silver' is set aside by a subsequent direct Perception got at "through (inferential) reasons, and not by these reasons "alone. (2) The misconception 'I am fair' is set aside by the "stronger sensuous cognition appearing in the form *the body* "*is mine* (where a distinction is made between the *I* and "the *Body*). (3) As regards the conception 'I am in the "house', this is not a wrong conception; as the *jīva* being "atomic in its nature, it is quite right to speak of it as *in the* "*house*. [And thus in none of the above cases do we find "an immediate cognition set aside by a mediate cognition]."

Reply:—So long as the *sensuous* cognition of the *silver* (with regard to the *shell*) and of the *Self* (with regard to the *Body*) is present in all its force before the mind, there would be no chance for the appearance of any sensuous cognition (to the contrary, that would set aside the previous misconception),—until a certain amount of reasoning had made it capable of being set aside.

It might be argued that—'in the case of the conception 'I am fair', the application of *fairness* to *I* is figurative, based upon the fact of the *body* being related to the *I*, and the *fairness* to the body; just as with regard to a piece of cloth besmeared with mud, we have the notion that the 'cloth is dirty' (the dirty colour belonging to the mud which is applied to the cloth).' But the two cases are not exactly similar; as in the case of the cloth we are distinctly cognisant of the cloth being something different from the mud, while there is no such definite idea of the *Self* being different from the *body*; in fact in this latter case what we have is a distinctly erroneous surmise of identity. Thus then, in the case of the conception 'the water is hot', if we have a definite 'idea of the distinction between the *water* and the *fire* (to which the heat belongs)'—as we have in the case of the *mud* and the *cloth*—then we must regard the expression as figurative; while if there is no such idea of distinction between the two—just as there is none in the case of the *Self* and the *body*—then, the expression must be regarded as an erroneous surmise of identity; and as such this should be quite capable of being set aside by *reasoning*. Hence the expression 'water is hot' would serve as an instance in support of our argument.

Lastly, it has been argued that the notion—'I am in the house'—is a right one (on account of the *Jīva* being atomic in its nature). But this also is not right. Because as a matter of fact the Self is all-pervading in its nature,—as asserted in the text 'He is all-pervading and eternal, like *Ākāsha*'; and then to speak of it as '*limited*,' as being within the limits of a house, can never be right. Nor is the *Jīva* atomic; because as a matter of fact we find that we can experience pleasures and pains in the head and in the foot at one and same time; and if the *Jīva* were atomic, it could not reside in two such remote localities as the head and the foot. Nor can we regard the simultaneous experiencing of pleasure and pain at the two places as a mere misconception. As we have no reasons for denying the truthfulness of a fact that is universally recognised as true. We shall explain all this in detail later on.

Says the *Opponent*:—" The Vedantin holds that the " *sensuous* cognition of the *sky as blue* is set aside by the " *inferential* cognition of the *sky as colourless*. But this is " not possible. Because there is no Reason that can " lead to the said *inferential* cognition. The fact of *the sky* " *being of the largest dimension*, and that of *its being non-produc-* " *tive of any substance* are regarded as such 'Reasons'. But " none of these facts is recognised by the Vedantin. Ano- " ther fact put forward as the 'Reason' is the fact of the sky " being *intangible*; but this is found in *Darkness* also; and as " such makes the Reason too wide. Another 'Reason' put " forward is the fact of the sky being a material substance " other than Earth, Water and Air; but this Reason would " be absolutely useless—not pointing to the Desired Conclu- " sion. Thus then it cannot but be asserted that the " idea of the sky being blue is set aside by the *Sensuous* " Cognition, by the Witnessing Self, of the *colourlessness* of " the sky. It might be argued against this that the " Self being incapable of cognising colour (which is cognised " by means of the Eye), It could never be cognisant of the " *absence* of colour. But as a matter of fact, we find that " though the Eye is incapable of perceiving the ghost, " yet it is quite capable of perceiving the *absence* of the ghost. " But apart from this, our Opponent also admits of the fact " of the *Witness* being cognisant of Darkness, which he regards " as coloured. Then again, even though the sky is " *invisible* (being cognisable only by the Ear, through Sound), " yet, as in the case of Air, its *colourlessness* can be perceived " by the Eye; and so in the case in question we have the "setting aside of a *sensuous* cognition by another *sensuous* "cognition (and not by an *inferential* one)."

Reply:—So long as the sensuous cognition that the *sky is blue* remains intact, any cognition of the *absence of colour* —either by the Eye or by the Witness—is absolutely impossible. Hence what sets aside the conception in this case is only a powerful chain of reasoning. Nor would there be a want of proper 'reason'; as we have the true reason in the following form:—'(The sky is colourless), because it is the object of a conception which is not qualified by any colour, and whose presence or absence is always in keeping with that of the Eye,—like the conception of Colour' (Colour itself being regarded as colourless). Nor would this 'reason' be open to the charge of being absolutely 'redundant'; Page 41. as it helps to establish the reasoning that—if the Sky were a *coloured* substance, it could never, in its *colourless* form, be the object of the conception whose presence or absence is dependent upon the Eye (*i.e.* visual perception). It might be argued that it would not matter at all, if the sky did not form such an object. But it is a universally recognised fact that the sky, at least that much of it as happens to be in close proximity to the observer, is absolutely without colour.

Even if the Sky be regarded as perceptible by the Witness, we cannot avoid regarding it as the object of a conception dependent upon the Eye; otherwise it would be perceptible by the blind also.

It may be urged that—"Inasmuch as, in accordance "with the theory of *quintiplication*, each and every subs- "tance is composed of particles with all the five qualities of "colour, taste &c., the sky also should have in its cons- "titution some particles with colour; and this fact would "certainly stand in the way of the inferential conclusion "with regard to its colourlessness." But this argument loses "all its force if we admit only the 'Triplicate' theory of the "composition of substances. But as a matter of fact, even "in the case of the 'Quintiplication' theory, all that is meant "by this theory is that when a certain primary element "comes to be used in the practical world it displays through "'quintiplication' only such qualities as it may have possessed "in its *non-quintiplicated* state. And this can not prove the "presence of colour in the sky.

Says the *Opponent*:—"Even in the case of the miscon-"ception of the snake being set aside by the words 'this is "not a snake', what actually sets aside the misconception "is not the *word*, but the sensuous cognition (of the thing "as something else). That this is so is shown by the fact "that when the man is told 'this is not a snake', the answer "that he gives is—'do you merely *say* so, or do you "actually *see* it to be so, looking upon it intently and "deliberately?'"

Reply:—In cases where we have such an answer, it is evident that doubts are entertained as to the validity of the verbal cognition due to the words 'this is not a snake'; and as such, *in such cases*, the verbal cognition, being extremely shaky, cannot serve to set aside the previous sensuous cognition. But in cases where there are no such doubts, it does certainly set aside the sensuous cognition. It is for this reason that there is no such answer as you refer to, in a case where the negativing words come from a trustworthy person—one's father for instance; in which case there is no doubt with regard to their truthfulness; in fact, in such cases the person at once admits the validity of the verbal cognition, and proceeds to shape his action accordingly.

There is yet another sensuous cognition—that of the unity of the burning flame—which is set aside by reasoning.

Objection:—"This cognition is distinctly found to be "set aside by another *sensuous* cognition; for instance, when "the flame is blown out, and lighted again, we actually *see* "that what has been appearing as one and the same flame "is only a series of several different flames continuously appear- "ing and disappearing. [And so this cannot be regarded as "a case of sensuous cognition set aside by *reasonings*.] And "so also in cases where the flame is not blown out, we find that "it is at times *high*, and at others *low*; and in this we actually "*see* the difference between the two flames; and so it is this "*visual* cognition that sets aside the notion of the flame being "one and the same."

Reply:—In cases other than that where the flame is blown out and lighted again we cannot rightly assert that we have any such visual cognition of the diversity of the flames, as that 'this is high and that is low'. Because the notion that people have with regard to the flame is that *the flame that a few moments ago appeared high is now appearing low*,—a notion wherein there is a distinct identification of what was high and what is low.

Thus the recognition of the flame as the *same* is also set aside (by reasoning).

As regards the sensuous cognition of the conch as yellow, by the man whose sight is affected by bile,—and also the cognition of the lunar disc being a few inches in extent,—we cannot find any cognition except mediate or indirect ones that could set these aside; and as such we cannot but regard these as instances of sensuous cognition being set aside by indirect cognition (reasoning).

Says the *Opponent*:—"In all these instances that you have "cited, the operation of the other means of knowledge (Infer- "ence and the rest) comes in only after the Sensuous Cognition "(sought to be set aside by them) has been proved to be "almost as good as false. That is to say, Cognitions are of "two kinds—(1) that pertaining to two alternatives (Doubt-

" ful Cognitions) and (2) that pertaining definitely to only " one alternative. This latter again is of two kinds—(a) " that which is tainted with the suspicion of invalidity " and (b) that which is not so tainted. Of these three " kinds of Cognitions those belonging to classes (1) and (a) " admit of the operation of all the means of knowledge,— " for the simple reason that these do not afford any definite " knowledge of their objects, and are open to the suspicion of " invalidity. A cognition becomes open to the suspicion of " invalidity in two ways—(1) when it is found to have " been brought about by faulty organs, and (2) when it is " found that in reality there is no such object as forms the " objective of the Cognition. For instance, in regard to " the trees on the top of the mountain, we have " found that they appear small by reason of their great " distance (which interferes with the true functioning " of the organ of vision); and this leads us to the conclusion " that the similar notion of smallness with regard to the " Moon, which is at a much greater distance than the tree, is " also due to a certain discrepancy in the functioning of the " organ of perception. In the same manner, we find that " the sky that is close to us is colourless; and this leads us " to conclude that the notion of colour with regard to the " distant sky is due to the great distance causing a discre- " pancy in the organ of perception; all this is ascertained " before the operation of any other means of knowledge. " In the case of the notion of the conch being yellow, we find " that in its very origin it is faulty; and from the moment " that it appears, it is open to the suspicion of invalidity,— " due to the absolute non-existence of the *yellowness*, proved " by the previous and well-ascertained sensuous cognition " that the *conch is not yellow*. The case of the perception of " the 'hole' in the solar orb, and such other things, may also " be explained in the same manner.

"Thus then we find that the notion of the smallness of "the moon is already set aside by the recognition "of the discrepancy due to the great distance,— "and the notion of the yellowness of the conch is also set "aside by a previous sensuous cognition to the contrary; "and it is *after* these have been thus set aside that there "appears any chance for the operation of Inference and "Verbal Assertion. And so we cannot regard any such "Inferential or Verbal Cognitions as setting aside the afore- "said notions. As a matter of fact, a cognition is set aside "only by that Cognition which shows that the former is a "misconception; and in the case in question we find that it is "no Verbal or Inferential Cognition that points to the fact of "the notion of the smallness of the moon being a miscon- "ception; specially as we have found that the Verbal Cogni- "tion appears only *after* the notions in question have already "been known to be misconceptions.

Page 42.

"As regards the Cognition that is not tainted by any "suspicion of invalidity, it affords a definite knowledge of "its objective, and as such is quite capable of bringing about "an activity of the agent with full confidence; to this class "belong the cognitions—'Fire is hot', 'the bedding is "something wholly different from the Master of the "Sacrifice', 'the jar is a real entity', and so forth. "These cognitions do not admit of the operation of any other "means of knowledge; nor are they capable of being "set aside by any other Cognitions; and the reason for this is "that in the case of these we have none of the conditions "that favour these contingencies; for instance, (1) there is "no previous knowledge of their being brought about by "organs tainted by the discrepancies of great distance, &c.; "(2) we have no previous idea of the absolute non-existence "of the objectives of these Cognitions; (3) nor have we any "Cognition of the opposite alternative.

"Then again, as a matter of fact, in the case of certain "Sensuous Cognitions, it may be found that they are set "aside by reasonings; this would only be in view of some "other and more valid Sensuous Cognitions. Just as in some "cases it may be that the implied indications of a word are "set aside by the indications of context,—but only when "this latter has the support of some Direct Assertion; just "as in some cases it may be that the authority of the King's "minister may be set aside by that of a lower functionary "supported by the King. Though all this may be possible, "yet even in these cases we cannot admit that the Sensuous "Cognition is set aside by Reasoning *alone*, or that the "Implied Indication is set aside by the indication of the "Context alone; as we find that in other cases, just as the "Context is supported by Direct Assertion, so also is the "Reasoning supported by other Sensuous Cognitions,—con-"ditions which cannot be present in *all cases* of contradiction "between Sensuous and Inferential Cognitions. For instance, "in regard to sacrificial performances, we have the *Smṛiti* "injunction—'*āchamēt upavīṭī*, &c.'—laying down such "*principals* as actions in the shape of *āchamana* and the "like, as to be performed in case the sacrificer happens to "sneeze; on the other hand, we have the Vedic Injunction—"'*Vēdam kriṭvā* &c.'—laying down the *secondary element* of "Order in which the *Vēdi* is to be built *immediately* after "the Veda has been got ready; now, it may so happen "that the sacrificer sneezes after having got ready the "Veda; and in this case, even though the action of *ācha-"mana*, &c., may come in before the making of the *Vēdī*, "yet this rejection of the Vedic by the Smriti Injunction "(for which in this case there are special reasons) would not "justify the conclusion that all *Vedic* Injunctions are set "aside by those of the *Smṛiṭi*; similarly with all Means "of Knowledge (any stray instance of the rejection of one by "the other cannot justify the general conclusion that it is "always so rejected)."

Reply:—Even in what you urge, what sets aside the sensuous cognition is *reasoning* pure and simple, which may be stated in the following way;—'The cognition of the smallness of distant things is wrong, being due to the discrepancy caused by the distance,—as we find in the case of the tree on the mountain-top; therefore the cognition of the smallness of the moon is also wrong.' And thus we find that the sensuous cognition of the smallness of the moon is set aside by *reasoning*, and not by another *sensuous* cognition. Thus then, while upholding such rejection, you still assert that *sensuous* cognition is not rejected by *Reasoning*; and though you may win your point by this, yet, O foolish man! this would be nothing better than an extremely shortsighted view of things!

In the same manner, the cognition of the yellowness of the conch cannot be said to be set aside by the previous sensuous cognition of the absence of yellowness; because this latter cognition is not present at the time of the rejection. Nor could the rejection be held to be by the remembrance of this previous cognition; because remembrance is always weaker than direct cognition; in fact, the remembrance is of use only in giving rise to the Reasoning. For these reasons it must be admitted that in all the cases under review we have the rejection of sensuous cognitions by Reasonings and Verbal cognitions.

It has been argued above that—"It is not right to infer "the rejectibility of sensuous cognitions by Reasoning, mere-"ly from a few instances of such rejection that we may meet "with; as such rejection may be due to the greater authority "of certain other sensuous cognitions upon which the Rea-"sonings may be based."

But this argument is like striking in the air (objecting to something that has not been asserted); as we have never said that the fact of Reasoning rejecting sensuous cognitions *in all cases* is to be inferred from a few instances of such rejection; all that we have said is that the sensuous Cognitions of the smallness of the Moon and the yellowness of the conch being found to be rejected by Reasoning and Verbal Cognition, whichsoever sensuous cognition should be found to fulfill the conditions present in the case of these, should be regarded as similarly rejectible. Nor is it necessary that in such cases there should always be a sensuous cognition as the basis of the Reasoning or the Verbal Cognition,—in view of which you may explain the rejection otherwise than in the manner held by us. Hence it must be admitted that the notion of the reality of the phenomenal world is as rejectible as the notion of the smallness of the Moon; and the rejection in both cases is by means of Reasonings and Verbal Cognitions based upon Scriptures.

Then again, in the case of the cognition of the smallness of the Moon, the idea of its being due to such discrepancies as those of distance and the like is not present from the very beginning; if such were the case, then, inasmuch as extreme proximity also causes discrepancies in sensuous cognitions, there would be no trustworthiness attaching to any cognition of dimension [as in all cases the knowledge of the presence of discrepancies would, according to you, be present from the very beginning]. In fact, the idea, that the cognition of the smallness of the Moon is due to the discrepancy caused by distance, appears only *after* the cognition has been rejected by reasoning and scriptures. Similarly in the case in question also, it is only *after* the notion of the reality of the world has been set aside by reasonings and scriptures,—and the world proved to be unreal—that we come to realise that the notion was due to the discrepancies caused by

Nescience. And thus the case of this is exactly similar to the case of the notion of the smallness of the Moon.

It has been urged above that the thing that is actually *seen* cannot be set aside by anything except by another more authoritative thing that also may be *seen*. But this is to be taken as denying the incapacity of such Reasonings and Scriptures as are weak in their authority.

Then, it has been declared in the *Vivaraṇa*—"It may be that in certain cases, without due consideration a certain cognition (though not actually sensuous) may in a hurry be regarded as *sensuous*; and such a cognition may be rejected by Reasoning and cast out of ordinary usage; but when we come to examine the comparative authority of such sensuous and inferential cognitions as have been found to be so after due deliberation, what we find is that no inferential cognition can ever prove the reality or falsity of a sensuous cognition."

But this declaration must be taken as referring to such words or scriptures as have their validity not duly ascertained, and to reasonings based upon such scriptures. Because when the validity of a cognition will have been duly ascertained in one place, there could be no occasion for enquiring after the greater or less validity of cognitions [For Real *Validity* is something absolute and not comparative].

END OF SECTION (18).

Section (19).

[The Sensuous Cognition of the reality of the world being sure to be rejected later on, it is best to discard it at the very outset.]

Thus then, it has been firmly established that Sensuous Cognition is to be discarded,—*also because of the certainty of its being rejected at some later time*, as we said before. It has been shown that just as the notion of the *smallness of the Moon*, which is not set aside in any other way, is set aside by the scriptural statements with regard to its real size

—so in the same manner, the sensuous cognition that *the jar is real* is set aside by such scriptural texts as speak of the Unreality of all phenomenal things.

This explanation serves to set aside the objection brought forward by the Opponent, on the basis of the doubt with regard to future rejections. As this is an objection against a view that has never been held by us. As a matter of fact however, even in consideration of the suspicion of future *rejectibility* attaching to Sensuous Cognitions, it is only right to deny the fact of its being capable of rejecting Verbal Cognitions. Specially as before the comparative validity of the Sensuous and Verbal cognitions has been duly examined, the doubt remains as to whether the Verbal cognition is indirect (and as such not fully valid), or that the Sensuous cognition is not quite valid; and so long as this doubt remains, it cannot be ascertained which is to set aside which; but then the import of the sentence and such other indicative reasons lead us to the conclusion that the verbal cognition is the direct one; and thus the suspicion as to its being indirect having been removed, its validity becomes established.

Says the *Opponent*:—"As a matter of fact, Words and "Inferential Reasons can not set aside a sensuous cognition; "as for any other sensuous cognition (that might set "aside the sensuous cognition in question), there is always "a doubt as to its validity; and as such this could not set it "aside; and thus there is a total absence of anything "that could reject the cognition; consequently it does "not appear to be right to raise any questions as to the "cognition being set aside."

But we have already proved above that Words and Inferential Reasons are quite capable of setting aside Sensuous cognitions. And as regards the idea of there being nothing to set aside a cognition,—even though it may be possible to know of the absence of certain cognitions capable of setting aside a particular cognition, yet it can never be possible to ascertain the limit of such cognitions (that there are only so many cognitions, and *no more*, that could set aside the cognition in question); and under the circumstances, a suspicion as to the setting aside would always remain. Then as for your assertion of the fact of Sensuous cognitions being invalid as a reason for the absence of suspicions with regard to the setting aside of the cognition,—such an assertion is simply absurd (as coming from you, who take your stand upon the superior validity of sensuous cognitions).

A fresh question is started by the Opponent :—" According to you then, all cognitions during the waking state " would be *false*; and there could be no rejection of " such well-known misconceptions as the cognitions during " dreams and the cognition of the shell-silver (which are " set aside only by subsequent waking cognitions); and as " it is only these misconceptions that you have put forward " to prove your conclusion (regarding the world being false), " your reasoning becomes open to the fallacy of the ' Absence " of Corroborative Instances.' "

In reply to the above it may be stated that the waking cognitions may be regarded as *true* in comparison to the dream-cognitions &c., on the ground (1) that the (empirical) reality of the former is a degree higher than the merely imposed (apparent) reality of the latter,—(2) or that the reality of the former is in no way lower in degree than that of the latter; and as such they could very well set aside these latter cognitions. It is in view of this explanation that we can reconcile and understand the following assertion of the *Vārṭika* against the Bauḍḍha :—' For us the cognitions of dream &c. would become false as soon as the waking cognition to the contrary has been comprehended;

for you however, on what ground could there be any distinction between the two kinds of cognition ?'

Says the *Opponent* :—" As a rule we find that a misconception is set aside only by such a cognition as has for " its objective something that is not the objective of direct " apprehension at the time of the misconception; and the " cognition setting aside the reality of the world would not " be of this kind (as there would be no time at which the " *whole world* would be directly imperceptible)."

But as a matter of fact, what sets aside a misconception is only the *true* knowledge of the substratum of that misconception; and as Brahman is the substratum of the misconception with regard to the world, the true knowledge of Brahman would be quite capable of setting aside such a misconception.

Question :—" A cognition that would set aside any conception would always be a qualified (determinate

Page 44.

" or concrete) one; how then could the knowledge " of Brahman, which is always free from qualifications, set " aside the conception of the world ?"

Answer :—It would confuse matters greatly if we were to regard the *qualified or concrete character* as a necessary factor in the cognition setting aside a conception; hence we cannot admit it as such.

Says the *Opponent* :—" It is absolutely necessary to " regard the concrete character as a necessary factor; as " it is only when the cognition appears in a form preclusive " of the misconceived form that it sets aside the misconcep- " tion (and this preclusive form would be possible only when " the cognition would be concrete). If it were not so, then " even a Cognition that has a form *inclusive* of the form " misconceived would come to be regarded as setting aside " the misconception; and this would be an absurdity."

It is quite true that it is only when appearing in a preclusive form that a cognition sets aside misconceptions. But for this it is not necessary for the cognition to have a well-defined concrete qualification. That is to say, there are two ways in which a cognition may have a preclusive form—(1) through an inherent property, and (2) through accidental qualification. In the case of the first of these it would of course be necessary for the cognition to be definitive and concrete. As regards the second however, in case the preclusion be from the accidental property attaching to a certain other definite character, it would be necessary for the cognition to be well-defined and concrete; but in case the preclusion be from the accidental property attaching to the thing itself, the cognition must be unqualified and abstract; as in this case no accidental property enters into the cognition; and as for the thing itself, it could not be regarded as defining or qualifying itself.

It might be argued that:—"as in the case of such Universal "terms as '*knowable*' and the like, we find that the term is "its own qualification,—so in the same manner, the thing "in itself would form its own qualification."

But you can find such a case only in the case of absolute universals (like 'knowable' &c.); and in these rare cases also, you can admit of this only because you find no other explanation; and such a rule cannot apply to all cases.

"There is no real difference between the *form* and the "*qualification* of a cognition; hence the mere fact of the "cognition of Brahman having the *form* of Brahman would "make the cognition a qualified one (Brahman itself being the "qualification)."

As a matter of fact we find that even though the qualified cognition has the *form* of the qualified thing, yet, this qualified thing does not form its qualification; and from this it is clear that the *form* is quite distinct from the *qualification*; and we shall show later on that the *form* of a thing rests in the *Vṛtti* being a certain distinctive property, whereby the thing may be used and spoken of as apart from other things. Consequently, just as in the case of the word '*Ākāsha*', all that is comprehended by means of the word is merely a certain object qualified by the character of being the substratum of Sound,—so, in the case of the word 'Brahman', there is the cognition of Brahman as qualified by the character of *being without a second*, and so forth; and this cognition is direct or immediate, serving to set aside all *duality*, which is exclusive in its character, while Brahman is all-inclusive. As to how such a cognition is possible from words, we shall explain later on.

Says the Opponent:—"As a matter of fact, we find that "Sublative Cognitions (that serve to set aside misconceptions) "as a rule, do not set aside the Perceiver, obsessed as he "is by the discrepancies of the misconception and the Nescience lying at the root of this misconception; how then "could we accept the fact of such a Perceiver being set "aside by the knowledge of Brahman?"

Answer:—In the case of dream-cognitions we find that on waking, when the man finds out that he has been dreaming, he presumes that during the dream the perceiving Soul was possessed of faulty instruments of Knowledge, and for this reason the cognitions have been all misconceptions; and in this case. we certainly find that the subsequent waking cognition sets aside all the factors of Misconception (including the defective Perceiver). Even in the case of waking cognitions we find that sometimes it so happens that we have before us the picture of a man, and the man also is standing there, and even though there is no consciousness in the picture and there is no mirror to reflect the image, yet we impose consciousness upon it, and say—'*this* (referring to the man in the picture) is looking upon his *reflection* (referring to the man standing before us)'; and this cognition in all its details is set aside by the subsequent realisation of the

fact that *the picture has no consciousness, and there is no reflecting mirror.* And thus we find that there is nothing uncommon in what we have asserted above. Then again, in the case of the conception of *shell-silver*, it may be that the subsequent cognition 'this is shell', appearing with reference to what was the substratum of the preceding misconception, may not set aside the erroneous conception with regard to the Perceiver, just as it does not set aside the notion of 'serpent' in the rope; but what is the reason for this? It is simply this, that in the conception 'this is shell', we have no direct cognition of the real substratum of the erroneous surmise with regard to the Perceiver. As regards the knowledge of Brahman however, it would unfailingly set aside all Misconceptions with regard to the Perceiver and his discrepancies, just in the same manner as it sets aside the Misconceptions with regard to *Ākāsha* and such other things of the phenomenal world. And the reason for this lies in the fact that in the knowledge of Brahman we have a direct cognition of the real nature of the substratum of *all* misconceptions. The mere fact of the cognition being sublative does not necessarily imply the non-rejection of the discrepancies &c.; but we have this non-rejection only in case the cognition is something other than the true knowledge of the real substratum of the misconception concerned.

Objection:—"In the particular instance you have cited, "inasmuch as the whole thing is merely presumed, there "may be a rejection; but how could there be any rejection "in the case in question?"

Reply:—Inasmuch as we regard everything save Brahman to have merely a *presumed* existence, it is a grand stumbling block indeed that you, foolish as you are, have put forward against us!

Says the *Opponent*:—"The sensuous cognition of the "Perceiver cannot be set aside as false,—because it does not "proceed from any defect (in the perceiving agency); "in fact, what can be so set aside is the conception of *Non-"duality* obtained from the scriptures,—because it proceeds "from such discrepancies as the misapprehension of the real "import of the words of the scriptural texts."

But this is not possible. Because even though, by itself, Consciousness does not proceed from the discrepancies, yet its determining factor, in the shape of the organic func-
Page 45. tioning of Nescience, is always found to originate from discrepancies; and it is only the Consciousness thus determined or limited (by the functioning of Nescience) that is called the 'Perceiver.' As for the comprehension of 'Non-duality' as the import of scriptural passages,—inasmuch as such comprehension is not incompatible with the sensuous and other forms of right knowledge, it can not but be regarded as *right knowledge*, totally free from discrepancies; and hence the notion of Non-duality cannot be regarded as *sublated*. Specially as the fact of a certain cognition proceeding from Misconception cannot necessarily make the *object* of that cognition rejected (as unreal).

Says the *Opponent*:—"As a matter of fact, we find that "the Sensuous Cognition of Duality (or Diversity) has the "support of certain scriptural passages that speak of the "reality of Duality; and as the authoritative validity of "these passages is in no way less than that of those that speak "of Non-duality, how could these latter invalidate the Sen-"suous Cognition?"

Answer:—The cognition of Duality is obtained by means of such ordinary means of knowledge as Sense-perception and the like; and as such the scriptural passages that speak of such Duality cannot but be regarded as merely descriptive (of what is otherwise known; and hence having no independent authority as a 'means of knowledge'). Hence these passages cannot be accepted as equal in authority to those other passages that speak of Non-duality, which serve the useful purpose of bringing about the knowledge of things not otherwise cognisable.

A fresh discussion is started :—

"Anything that forms the object of the subsequent "sublative cognition (the cognition rejecting a previous "misconception) cannot itself be sublated. And as a matter "of fact, we find that *diversity* forms the object of a sublative "cognition; as the very apprehension of the objective of "of this latter cognition involves diversity, in the shape "of the difference of that object from something else; as for "instance, the sublative cognition 'this is not silver' involves "the notion that the real object of this cognition (*viz*: the "shell) is something 'different' from silver. If the object "were comprehended, either as identical with, or as having "nothing to do with, the object of the previous misconception, "then the cognition would be the *sublator* of this misconcep-"tion."

Our answer to the above is that we cannot admit the general statement that the very comprehension of the sublative cognition involves *diversity*. And the reason for this is that in the case of the misconception of shell-silver the sublative cognition that appears is in the form 'this is shell,' and the notion 'this is not silver' is only a subsequent resultant from that sublative cognition. In fact, all that is necessary in a sublative cognition is that it should have a form preclusive of that which it is supposed to sublate. And this condition we find present even in the 'Knowledge of Brahman unqualified and absolute'; as in this knowledge also we have the indication of a certain specific character (which precludes everything else). And for this reason we cannot admit that it is *Diversity* that forms the object of all sublative cognitions.

Says the *Opponent*:—"If we were to entertain doubts with "regard to the truthfulness of even such cognitions as are "found, on due examination to have their objects of a "character other than that of dream-cognitions,—then "we might have doubts with regard to such things also as "the scriptural passages speaking of Non-duality, the percep-"tion of such passages, the validity of these passages and "so forth; and under the circumstances, there could be "no authoritative validity even for those scriptural pass-"ages that speak of *Non-duality*. Then again, if even with "regard to a sublative cognition we were to have doubts "as to its being liable to sublation after some time, then "we could never have any such sublative cognition as "would not be liable to such suspicion; specially as there "would be no incongruity between *Non-sublatibility* on the one "hand, and *liability to the suspicion of being sublated* on "the other. And then if you were to cast suspicion on the "sublatibility of such sublative cognition as is yet to come, "then you would be undoing your own work (as it is on "this future sublatibility that you base the invalidity of the "Sensuous and other cognitions). Then again, with regard "to the 'perception' of Doubts also you would have your "suspicions; and this would make even Doubts impossible. "And in this manner, there being suspicions with regard to "everything, you would be landed in utter confusion."

Reply:—It is not as you think; what we mean is that a suspicion arises even with regard to well-ascertained things, *whenever another means of knowledge turns up* (presenting a phase of things contrary to that previously ascertained), *and is found to be of a degree of validity equal to that of the previous cognition*; and we do not for a moment imagine that there is a suspicion with regard to *all* well-ascertained things. It is for this reason that our view is not incompatible with the following declaration made by Kumārila (in his *Shlokavārtika*, *Nirālambanavāda*, Shlo. 34) against the Bauḍḍha:—'It is only right that there should be a denial of the thing forming the object of a defective cognition; if there were to be a rejection of everything that is cognised, then no one could establish his own position either.' Because we have never held either that there is sublation of *everything* cognised, or that there are suspicions with regard to *every such thing.*

Says the *Opponent*:—"In the case of the sensuous cogni-"tion of the reality of things, so long as there are none of "the well-known discrepancies—in the form of extreme "distance &c.—wherefore could there arise any doubt as "to its validity? It cannot be reasonably argued that—'even "though there may be a certainty as to the absence "of the well-known discrepancies, there would always remain "room for the suspicion of discrepancies not so well-"known';—because if such were the case, then in regard "to the validity of the Veda also there would always remain "room for the suspicion of the presence of unknown discre-"pancies,—even though there be a certainty as to the "absence of the well-known discrepancy in the form of "defects in the speaker or writer. It might be argued "that—'in the case of dream-cognitions even though we "are sure of the absence of all such well-known discre-"pancies as extreme distance and the rest, yet we find them "to be invalid; and in the same manner we could have the "notion of invalidity in regard to the sensuous cognitions "in question also.' But then, we find that in regard to the "dreamlike scripture (of the Bauḍḍha) that *all is void*, even "though we are sure of the absence of any actual misconcep-"tion on the part of the propounder of the scripture, yet we "regard it as invalid; and from this analogy it would follow that "the Veda itself is invalid. As for our actual experience, "whereby we find the Veda totally unlike Dreams, this may "be urged with equal force in support of the other scriptures "also."

Reply :—As a matter of fact, both as regards the sensuous cognition of reality and the scriptural passages speaking of Non-duality, there is an absolute certainty with regard to the absence of any of the well-known discrepancies. But this certainty does not in any way stand in the way of the arising of doubts with regard to their validity. For example, in the case of two apparently valid but mutually contradictory reasonings, the mere certainty as to the absence of discrepancies in them does not stop the arising of the question—'what is the truth on this point ?' The fact is that what stops the arising of such doubt is the recognition of a certain fact (in the present instance, the absence of discrepancies) *appearing simultaneously with the non-perception of anything to the contrary.* Then again, as regards the sensuous cognition of the Perceiver, it has been asserted to have its source in certain discrepancies (in the cognitive agency), simply on account of the evanescent character of the *vṛiṭṭi* determining that cognition.

Page 46.

This reasoning serves to set aside the following argument of the Logicians :—" Only such doubts should
" be raised as do not involve, in the raising, any self-contra-
" diction or other such absurdities. Well has it been
" declared in the *Bhatta-Vārṭika* against the *Bauḍḍha* :—
" 'During this life the invalidity of none is possible ; as
" for those who have reached the stage of the Yogin,
" we do not know what will happen to them.' Then
" again, the validity of cognitions is self-produced and self-cog-
" nised ; and in the case of ordinary sensuous cognitions we
" find that there is no obstacle, in the shape of discrepancies, to
" the self-production of its validity ; nor have we any rejection
" of the cognition, which rejection would be an obstacle
" to the self-cognition of its validity. Then as for the
" raising of doubts without sufficient grounds, such raising
" would be suicidal, and hence no such doubts could

" reasonably arise. Thus the validity of Sensuous cognitions " remains wholly unaffected."

This position is not tenable, because we hold that the doubt is raised on the authority of the scriptures.

As regards the negation of silver in the conception 'this is not silver,' (appearing after the misconception 'this is silver'), we find that this negation is by no means incompatible with the scriptural passages declaring Non-duality; and as such it is not open to the suspicion of invalidity. Consequently our standpoint is not open to the charge that, while we are anxious for the growth of the tree of our philosophy, its very root has been struck off. Nor again is the position of the conception 'the jar is real' in any way analogous to the negativing conception 'this is not silver'; because while the latter is quite compatible with the scriptural passages declaring Non-duality, the former is directly contrary to it.

This same reasoning serves to set aside the following argument of the Opponent:—" As there is no validity attach-" ing to the conception of bliss during deep sleep, how could " the bliss-form of the Self be real? Specially as the scriptural " passages speaking of bliss may be taken as merely descrip-" tive of the unreal bliss experienced in ordinary life." This is untenable, because Bliss constituting the very nature of Brahman, there is no incompatibility between the scriptural passages speaking of Non-duality (and those describing the Bliss in question); and hence the conditions of invalidity not being present, the passages speaking of Bliss cannot be regarded as unauthoritative.

To this effect is the following declaration in the *Khaṇḍana* * :—' Even though a certain thing may be absolutely non-existing, yet the word expressive of it brings about an idea of it; and this idea is true when there is no rejection of it,—the truthful character of the idea being based

* The Kārikā quoted here is not found in the *Khaṇḍana-khaṇḍa-khādya*. The first half is found in the *Shlokavārtika*, Sū. 2, Shlo. 6.

firmly upon its self-sufficient validity'. So also in the *Vārṭika* of Surēshvara :—'The validity of the Veda rests upon the fact of its being expressive, upon the absence of defective origin and upon non-sublation,—this validity (as the means of right knowledge) being like that of the Eye &c.' It may be noted that the example of the 'Eye' has been cited only with a view to the *empirical* reality of the cognitions produced by it ; even though we do not admit the *absolute* reality of Sensuous Cognitions, we do not deny their *empirical* reality ; and as such our view does not involve any self-contradiction ; nor is it incompatible with such declarations of the *Smṛiṭis* as—'one desirous of pure Dharma should seek to know well, Sense-perception, Inference and the Scriptures with their several branches.' (Manu XII.)

Thus then, it has been proved that either on account of the certainty of their being set aside, or even by a suspicion as to their being sublatable, Sensuous and other such cognitions cannot be regarded as capable of counteracting the validity of the Scriptural passages and Inferential reasons pointing to *Non-duality*.

END OF SECTION (19).

Section (20).

[Refutation of Inferential Arguments in favour of the Reality of the phenomenal world].

REASONING [A].

I. Says the Opponent:—

"It may be that Sensuous Cognition does not reject the "Inferential Cognition of Absolute Unreality, because of the "fact of the objectives of the two cognitions being different, "and such other reasons; but we have many Inferential rea- "sons that will serve to reject the said Inferential Cognition. "For instance we have the following:—'*Everything be- "sides Brahman, or the thing under discussion, which is not "the substratum of unreality, by reason of its not being rejected "by any other right notion, save that of Brahman, or save the "knowledge obtained from the right apprehension of the true "import of the Vedānta scriptures, or save such knowledge as "brings about Liberation,—Every such thing besides Brahman "is real, or absolutely real, because not being the substratum of "merely apparent reality, it is totally different in character "from an Unreal thing,—like Brahman, or like the hare's "horn* (the latter being an example corroborating *per "contra*)".

Reply:—This reasoning is fallacious; because in accordance with your view, that which is only *apparently* real is unreal; and as such the qualification in the above premiss ('not being the substratum of mere apparent reality') is superfluous; (merely '*asadvilakṣaṇatvāt*' being enough); and this would make the reason open to the fallacy of '*Vyāpyatvāsiddhi*', a form of 'Undistributed Middle.' If however you put forward the reason in accordance with our view of things (whereby a distinction is made between an *absolute* and an *apparent* reality),—then, the reason would fail to prove the conclusion; as it would not apply to the identification of the Soul with the Body, which is not rejectable by anything save the Knowledge of Brahman ; because a thing Page 47. is called '*apparently* real' only when it is such as is set aside by the knowledge of Brahman (and your premiss excludes all such things). Then again, with the sole view of excluding from the 'Subject' of your syllogism, the *apparently* real things like the *shell-silver*,—you have introduced three alternative qualifications in the statement of your 'subject', (*by reason of its not being rejected by any other right actions. Such knowledge as brings about Liberation*'). The first of these qualifications ('not rejected by any other right notion save that of Brahman') is in accordance with the view that Brahman is pervaded over by '*Vṛitti*'; the second is introduced in accordance with the view which does not admit of such pervasion, and by which the right knowledge of the *import* is a necessary condition in all right Verbal Cognition; and the third is added in accordance with the view that the knowledge of import cannot be regarded as necessary in Verbal Cognition, as this would involve a vicious circle. Then again, in the very form in which you state your premiss, you admit that the *apparently real* is not 'the substratum of unreality'; otherwise, as the apparently real would have been precluded by the qualification of *not being the substratum of unreality*, the addition of the further qualification (of 'not being the substratum of apparent reality') for the same purpose would be altogether superfluous. If, again, you mean to include in your 'subject', the identity of the Body and the Self, then, the reasoning is altogether 'annulled'; and this annulment of the qualification of the 'subject' would leave your 'subject' incomplete, and make the reasoning open to the fallacy of 'Āshrayāsiḍḍha', 'Want of a due substratum for the Reason.' Nor would these fallacies be escaped from by introducing any of the following qualifications for the 'Subject'.—(*a*) 'That which is not the objective of that unrejectible cognition which sets it aside and which proceeds from a discrepancy in the cognitive agency'; or (*b*) 'That which is not the object of that unrejectible rejection or invalidation which is meant to be the rejector of the thing concerned; or (*c*) 'That which is not rejectible by that cognition which is coeval with the previous non-existence of the action co-extensive with the thing concerned'. Because none of these would save the reasoning from the objections to which it has been shown to be open, in regard to the conception of the identity of the Body and the Self.

Some people have urged against the reasoning the following objection:—"In case the *probandum* is stated "in the first form ('is real'),—then if it is meant to include "*practical reality*, the reasoning is 'superfluous' (such "reality being admitted by the Vedāntin). And if it be "stated in the second form ('is absolutely real'), then for "the propounder of the argument himself, the qualification "would be superfluous, as he does not make any distinction "between the *absolutely* and the *practically* real, and hence "there could be nothing that would be precluded by the "addition of the qualification".

But this objection is not right; as the first form of the *probandum* could be justified as being put forward by one who holds that what is meant by a thing being *practically real* is that it is only *regarded in ordinary usage* as real (and not that it has any reality); [and hence even when such *practical* reality would be admitted by the Vedantin he would not admit the thing to be *real*; and as this is the *probandum*, the reasoning would not be 'superfluous']. As for the second form of the *probandum* ('is absolutely real'), this has been put forward in accordance with the view that *practical reality* is something distinct from *absolute reality*. Nor is the qualification 'absolute' or 'actual' useless; as in all cases of inference 'for the sake of others', such qualifications (even though useless so far as the propounder of the argument is concerned) serve, with regard to the opponent to whom the reasoning is addressed, the distinctly useful purpose of saving the reasoning from the charge of 'superfluity' (on the ground of the *apparent* or *practical* reality of things being admitted by the opponent, Vedāntin). And further, the qualification in question may be regarded as merely explanatory (and not forming an integral factor of the reasoning), just like such universal qualifications as 'knowable' and the like; in fact such qualifications are often met with in course of argumentation; for instance in the *Tattvachintāmaṇi* in the section on 'Reasonings in support of God's existence', we find an argument stated in the form—'Such and such things are not produced by such actions *as have any beginning in time* &c. &c.'; and as this reasoning is averred against the Mīmānsaka, who does not admit of any actions except such as have beginning in time, the qualification does not serve any useful purpose, and yet it is introduced as an explanatory clause.

For the above reasons these objections against the Opponent's reasoning not being tenable, we hold to the objection that we have put forward before.

The *Probans* of the Opponent's reasoning is also open to the charge of having a useless qualification. It is quite true that both the Logician and the Vedantin admit the fact of even valid and true things forming the objects of negations; and as such both admit of the *apparent reality* of things,—this *apparent reality* consisting either in the thing having a mere assumed existence as acknowledged by both parties, or in its having a mere semblance of an existence; in fact, if it were not so, then in the case of the Vedantin also putting forward the reasoning in favour of *unreality*, it would be necessary for him to state as his 'subject' *everything except that which has apparent reality*; and this would be open to the same objection. Though all this is quite true, yet the introduction of the qualification '*having apparent reality*' in the *probans* is absolutely useless; specially because for the proving of the *absolute reality* of a thing it would be enough to state as the reason that, *not being a substratum, it is not the subtratum of reality.*

As regards the corroborative instance cited by the Opponent, it must be the *pure* Brahman that is meant; as if the *qualified* Brahman were meant, then the Instance would be wanting in the very thing that is sought to be proved (the *qualified* Brahman not having *absolute* reality); specially as the *reality* sought to be proved is that consisting of *freedom from rejection* (a negative factor); and as such it must be in the form of the substratum (of that reality), and not in that of a property; because it has already been explained that a negation can have no existence apart from a certain substance with properties.

Then again, it is true that in some cases,—such, for instance, as the inferential reasoning 'the eye is luminous in its nature, because *from among colour &c.* it brings about the cognition of colour only'—a certain qualifying clause, in this case '*from among colour &c.*', though added only with a view to guard against the fallacy of the Reasoning being 'unknown', still serves the useful purpose of helping in the apprehension of the invariable concomitance necessary for the inference, and thereby of saving the reasoning from the charge of being 'contradictory'; and for this latter purpose all that is necessary is that the qualification should help in the apprehension of invariable concomitance. Though all this is quite true, yet, just as in the argument—

'the Earth &c. are not created by a creator, because they are not created by a body' &c., the mention of 'body' is absolutely useless,—so, in the same manner, in the case in question, no useful purpose can be served by the qualification 'apparently real'; specially as (even without the qualification) in regard to the *unqualified* Brahman, the invariable concomitance between the *absolute reality* and *not being the substratum* could be apprehended, just in the same manner as in regard to *Ākāsha*, it is easy to apprehend the concomitance between *not being created* and *not being created by a creator*.

Page 48. Thus then, while seeking to avoid one kind of the fallacy of the 'unknown', you fall into another kind of the same fallacy. That is to say, you introduced the qualification for the purpose of avoiding the fallacy of the 'unknown' with regard to the invariable concomitance of the Probandum; as we have already shown that the qualification serves no useful purpose in regard to the apprehension of the necessary invariable concomitance.

Then again, inasmuch as all that is necessitated by your premiss would be fulfilled by the admitting of mere *practical* reality, the *Probandum* would be of no use as regards the desired conclusion (where you assert *absolute* reality). And further, your reasoning becomes set aside by the counter-reasoning that if everything were *absolutely* real, then there would be no possibility of the *rejection* of such reality of phenomenal things (the rejection that is spoken of in many scriptural passages).

The *Opponent* starts a fresh discussion (against the *Sachchidānanda* character of Brahman).

" In regard to Brahma, we find that it is only Its *absolute* " *reality* that forms the necessary condition in the preclusion " of *unreality* and *apparent reality*—which preclusion forms

" the reason (for absolute reality). As a matter of fact " too, we know that it is the 'character of the Earth'; which " is the necessary condition for the preclusion of the 'charac- " ter of 'Not-Earth'; and similarly for the preclusion of " *unreality* what we want is its direct contradictory—viz: " *reality*. 'Knowledge' and 'Bliss' however do not form " any necessary condition in the said preclusion; for the " simple reason that these two are not direct contradictories " of *unreality*; and that they are not present in the World " (which also is absolutely real). Hence it must be admitted " that the only necessary condition for the said preclusion is " *absolute reality* which is common to Brahman and the World. " It might be argued that—'The World being unreal, *absolute* " *reality*, just like Knowledge and Bliss, cannot be regarded " as common to Brahman and the World.' But this would " involve you in a vicious circle (the unreality of the World " resting upon the reason which would in its turn depend " upon the same *unreality*)."

This is not right; because the *preclusion of unreality* and that of *apparent reality*,—be they one or two—are equal, or similar, in the degree of their concomitance, and as such they could, on no account, be dependent upon one and the same necessary condition. But it must be asserted that Brahman is such a necessary condition for the preclusion of *apparent reality* as pertains in common to the World and to all that is unreal,—this assertion being necessary because there are some *unreal* things which have no *apparent reality*; and similarly also that Brahman is such a necessary condition for the preclusion of *Unreality* as pertains in common to the World and to all that has mere *apparent reality*;—this assertion also being necessary in view of the fact that there may be certain *apparently real* things which may not be *unreal*. Thus then, inasmuch as Brahman affords a fitting combination for the two necessary conditions, it becomes quite reasonable to hold that it is the ground for the preclusion of both (Unreality and Apparent Reality); and thus there can be no reason for assuming any other necessary condition for the said preclusion ; just as the *blue jar* affording a fitting ground for the two characters of 'blue' and 'jar', there is no necessity for assuming anything else.

This is a fact for the consideration of all intelligent people.

(I) Your reasoning is also open to the charge of having a vitiating condition in the shape of 'Eternality'; inasmuch, in the absolute nonentity and also in things that have merely apparent reality, we have the negation of 'eternality' as also that of your *probandum* (absolute reality). [II] For this same reason you cannot put forward, as your *probans*, the fact of the things in question forming the direct objectives of right cognition as something not be denied. Cognition is regarded as right either when it apprehends a thing as with the qualification that actually belongs to it, or when it apprehends the true state of things ; and if we accept the former explanation, then the character you put forward as the *probans* would be one that is altogether absent in the Instance (Brahman) ; as the absolutely real pure Brahman never forms the object of any *qualified* cognition ; and we have already said that the *qualified* Brahman can not form a right corroborative Instance,—the reason for this being that such Brahman forms part of the 'Subject' under discussion, and as such can not be regarded as universally recognised to possess the *probandum* (a character necessary for the Corroborative Instance). If however you accept the second definition of *right cognition*, then, inasmuch as the character of *apprehending the true state of things* would be the same as the character of *unrejectibility*, it would be identical with the *probandum* ; and if such a *probans* would be one that is already accepted by both parties the reasoning would b 'Superfluous'; and if it be not recognised by both parties, the reasoning would be open to the fallacy of the 'Unknown.'

Against the *probans* under discussion, some people have brought forward the following objection:—"Inasmuch as the absolute reality of things would be sufficiently proved by the fact of their forming objects of right cognition, the qualifications added to the reason (*as undeniable* and *direct*) are absolutely superfluous."

But this is not right; as without the qualification 'direct' the character put forward as the *probans* would apply to the object of the representative cognition 'I know the object before me as silver,' which cognition (in the *representative* form) is right, though the object as such has a merely *apparent* reality; and this undesirable extension of the probans is avoided by the addition of 'direct' (as the Silver does not form the *direct* object of the representative Cognition) and the qualification 'as undeniable' serves a like purpose with regard to the silver (misconceived in the shell) which would be the *direct object of the right cognition*, 'the silver is unreal' (and the silver could not be regarded as having an absolute reality); and as the silver is not 'undeniable,' the undesirable contingency is avoided by the addition of the said qualification. Nor can the possibility of the aforesaid representative cognition and the right cognition of unreality be denied.

Nor again would it be right to bring forward as the *probans* or reason for the absolute reality of things, the fact of their being *undeniable objects of the direct or immediate perception of God*. Because until you have proved their reality the *undeniability* of things cannot be accepted; and thus your reasoning would be involved in a vicious circle (*reality* depending upon *undeniability* and *vice versa*) Nor can it be argued that if the world, which forms the object of God's cognition, be unreal, then God will have to be regarded as mistaken in His cognitions. Because God knows the unreal world, but knows *it as unreal*; just like the magician does with regard to his performances ; and as such He cannot be regarded as mistaken. If we were not to accept the above, then there would be no possibility of any person being regarded as mistaken, in regard to any misconception that may have an object (as the object would be there all right).

It might be argued that if God knew the world as *deniable*, He could not act towards the sustaining Page 49 of it. But the action of God in this respect can be explained as similar to that of the magician (who knows his tricks to be false and yet keeps them up).

Another reason likely to be put forward is the fact that all things while being unrejectible along with their qualifications, are such as bring about distinct effects. But this also will not be right; because as a matter of fact we find that we often dream of bathing or of meeting our loved ones; and these dreams are such as are not rejected along with their qualifications by any waking cognitions, and also bring about distinct effects (in the shape of pleasure at the time),—though the dreams are regarded as false ; and thus the reason under consideration would be applicable to the objects of these dreams also. It might be argued that—"what causes pleasure in this case is the *cognition* (during the dream) ; and certainly the cognition as such is not rejectible." But this will not be right ; because mere *cognition* by itself is not capable of bringing about any pleasure, the causality of this pleasure must be attributed to the cognition as qualified or characterised by a certain thing ; and for a cognition there can be no qualification save in the form of its object ; as has been asserted in the following words of *Uḍayanāchārya* :—

'Cognitions, by themselves formless, are specified only by their objects. That is to say, the objects are the only specifications of Cognitions.'

Thus then, if you admit the fact of the cognition specified by an unreal object being the cause of certain effects, then it would be necessary to admit the capability of the Unreal object also of being such a cause; and thus the *probans* applying to such objects also would become "too wide." This has been thus declared in the *Shāsṭradīpikā*, as against the *Bauḍḍha*—"The argument of the Bauḍḍha being that, in case the experiencing of pleasure alone be the useful effect, then the concomitance is all right, as without pleasure there is never any experiencing of it,—the answer is that though this may be quite true, yet it would not be right to infer from this the validity of the preceding cognition; because we find that even such invalid cognitions as those of the meeting of loved ones, &c., during dreams bring about pleasure."

Objection:—"We grant that it is only such a cognition as is specified by an object that can be the cause (of pleasure); but how does it follow from this that the causal efficiency belongs to the *object* (and not to the *cognition*)?'

Reply: (If the causal efficiency be not attributed to the *object*, then) the *object* could not in any way serve as the distinctive factor in the cognition,—a factor that would be necessary for having a cognition that would be comprehensive and yet not too wide; because if each cognition were taken by itself, we could not have any comprehensive cognition; and if (in order to avoid this) we were to take the whole class 'Cognition', then that would apply to all cognitions, and thus become too wide.

Objection:—"It is not possible for the Object to serve "as the distinctive qualification of the Cognition; because "in the case of such pleasure as is brought about by the "(prospective) cognition of something yet to come, the "Object (which is yet to come) could not be regarded as "being the cause; as for a cause it is necessary to have an "existence prior to the effect that it is to bring about."

Reply:—As a matter of fact we often find that the action of a certain thing brings about an effect, even when the thing has ceased to exist; and in this case the thing, though not-existing, is regarded as the cause of that effect. In the same manner the Object, though not existing at the time, can very well be regarded as the cause of that which is brought about by its cognition; specially as an object that has either ceased to exist or is yet to come is admitted to be the substratum of the property of *non-existence*. (And as such it cannot be regarded as an absolute non-entity). If such a substratum be denied, then we could have no substratum for such characters as—(1) that of the objects of destruction and prior non-existence, (2) that of the object of cognition, and so forth. Then if in such cases, the causal efficiency be admitted on the strength of sound evidence, the same may be said with regard to the case in question also.

Then again, it is not possible to assert that dream-cognition is true; because (its object is always negatived subsequently, and) whenever the object of a cognition is negatived, the denial or rejection of the cognition itself follows as a necessary consequence; specially as a matter of fact we know that any Cognition that is not itself deniable is such as has its Object undeniable also.

And further, the reasoning based upon the *probans* under discussion would have a vitiating condition in the shape of '*beginninglessness*' whose concomitance (with the *probans* and the *probandum*) is not uniform.

The following argument might be here brought forward:—"In the case of Brahman it has been found that the "necessary condition for really effective or useful action is "Its *absolute reality*; and hence the *probans* in question "(*being unrejectible along with qualifications and bringing "about distinct effects*) would be invariably concomitant with "the *probandum* (*absolute reality*),—specially in view of the "reasoning negativing the contrary conclusion based upon "the impossibility of any effect being produced without a "cause; and yet the vitiating condition that you have "pointed out (*beginninglessness*) is not one with which the "*probandum* would be invariably concomitant; and as such "what you have put forward would not be a true vitiating "condition (for which it is necessary to be such that while "the *probandum* is invariably concomitant with it, the "*probans* is not so concomitant)."

But this is not so; because what is the necessary condition for effective action is not *absolute reality*, but only a reality *during the time of cognition*; and this condition, while precluding all *absolute non-entities*, is yet found to be present in things that have mere *apparent* reality; as we find in the case of such action present in the *apparent* snake perceived in the rope, which produces actual effects in the shape of fear and the consequent trembling and the like. If effective action be denied in regard to things having mere apparent reality,—then there would be absolutely no use for the qualification '*unrejectible along with qualifications*' in your *probans* (as what is *not* merely apparently real is never rejectible in any way). Because *absolute reality* consists in the character of being *unrejectible or undeniable by any person at any time and at any place*, and certainly in comparison to introducing such a reality, it would be for simpler to accept '*reality during the time of cognition*' (which would include *absolute* as well as *apparent* reality).

Then again, *pure Brahman* is absolutely without any action; and hence the *probans* fails with regard to your *Instance*. And as for the qualified Brahman, inasmuch as it is included in the *Subject* itself, if this Brahman be meant to be the *instance*, then it would be such as is not universally recognised to be possessed of the *probandum* (as the proving of such presence would depend upon the reasoning under discussion).

Page 50.

Another form in which the *probans* may be put forward is this :—"*because it has unreality imposed upon it.*" But this too would not be a correct reason. If by a thing being 'imposed' you mean that it is merely apparent, then, according to your own view, your *probans* would not apply to the phenomenal world; because the recognition of the fact of unreality being *imposed* upon would depend upon the previous recognition of its *absolute* reality (and this recognition is sought to be brought forward by means of the reasoning in question). If however by a thing being imposed you mean that it has *practical reality*, then the *probans* would apply to the *shell-silver*, and as such would have an undesirable extension. [The unreality of the shell-silver *having practical reality*]. Lastly if it mean both *apparent* and *practical* reality, then too the *probans* becomes open to the last fallacy.

Another reason put forward in the reasoning under discussion is in the form—" because the things of the world are devoid of all impositions (free from all determining or qualifying elements)." This also is fallacious; firstly because it applies to the absolute non-entity also, and as such has an undue extension; and secondly because no such *freedom from imposition* is known in the way it is put forward.

Says the *Opponent* :—" The reason cannot be said to be *unknown* ; as the pure Brahman is 'free from impositions' for the simple reason that It is free from impurities ; the qualified Brahman also is free from impositions as It is itself *determined* ; and as such if It had something else for Its *determining element*, it would be necessary to assume such determination *ad infinitum*. And thus the corroborative Instance being all right, it must be admitted that absence of imposition in general is recognised in all cases of the absence of particular characters."

This cannot be accepted ; as the pure Brahman also can be shown to be an imposition, through the imposition of the beginningless Nescience. Because the character of the *determination* consists in the fact of its being—(1) either the substratum of the determination or (2) the object of determination, or (3) the illuminator or manifestor of that determination ; and every one of these characters being coeval and co-existent with the determination, there is nothing in any of them that could be incompatible with the purity (of Brahman). This has been thus declared in the following verse of the *Saṅkṣēpashārīraka* :—' The indivisible Consciousness alone is the substratum and object of Nescience; as everything else appearing after this Nescience could not be its substratum or object.' Then again, the character of the determination might very well belong to the qualified Brahman which is itself *imposed*. Nor would this lead to a *regressus ad infinitum* ; because the imposition of Nescience does not stand in need of any further imposition ; as this imposition is quite capable of accomplishing itself as well as other impositions ; and further, that which is itself not *imposed upon* cannot serve as 'imposition ;' as we find that it is only when a mirror is accompanied by a reflection imposed upon itself that it has the capability of imposing that image upon another mirror. This we shall explain in greater detail later on.

Thus we have refuted all the six Reasons put forward by the Opponent with a view to prove the absolute reality of the World. In the same manner all other reasons may be refuted.

REASONING [B.]

The Opponent brings forward another argument in the following manner :—"*The thing in question (the world) is not different from reality,—because it is different from absolute nonentity,—like the Self.*"

But this also is not correct reasoning; as it would be applicable to all such *apparently* real things as the shell-silver and the like. It might be argued that the *probans*—'difference from absolute non-entity'—does not apply to such things (as they are unreal). But if the shell-silver were not different from an absolute non-entity, it would never be the object of a direct sensuous cognition.

Says the Opponent—"In that case, if the shell-silver be different from an absolute non-entity, it could not possibly be different from a real entity; and thus this too being rightly included in the *probandum*, the *probans* would not be open to the fallacy of being *too wide*."

But to hold that the shell-silver is real is contrary to the universally admitted fact of such reality being rejected by subsequent cognitions. Then again, as a matter of fact we find that even though the elephant is different from the cow, it is yet different from the horse, which in its turn is different from the cow; and in the same manner, even though a thing may be *different from reality*, it would be quite possible for it to be *different from unreality* also; as we have already explained under the first definition of *unreality*.

REASONING [C.]

" The thing under discussion is not the product of the " Ignorance of Consciousness,—or, is not the objective of the " conception produced by that Ignorance,—or, is not possess- " ed of an essence or reality which is the product of that " Ignorance,—or is not possessed of a reality which is set " aside by the due knowledge of that Ignorance,—because even " while Consciousness is imperceptible, the thing in question " (the World) is directly cognised in a form that cannot be " denied,—as we find in all similar cases; for instance, while " the *jar* is imperceptible, the *cloth* appears directly in an " undeniable form; and this latter is not the product &c. of " the Ignorance of the jar. The contrary conclusion is set " aside by the fact that whenever we have the direct cogni- " tion of a certain thing, there is absolutely no chance for an " Ignorance of that thing. The *probans* of the above reason- " ing cannot be said to be open to the fallacy of the ' Un- " known'; because even at the present moment we have " direct cognition of Consciousness, as the substratum (of " Ignorance and other things) and also as the Witness or " Perceiver of pleasure &c."

The above reasoning too is not tenable. Because even though it is true that we have a direct cognition of Consciousness *in its general form*, yet the reasoning is ' too wide'; inasmuch as it applies to the shell-silver also; as (at the time of the misconception) the silver is *directly cognised in its undeniable form.*

If again you put forward your premiss in the following form,—" If one thing is directly cognised as undeniable on the cognition of another thing in its own exclusive form, then the former cannot be the product &c. of the ignorance of the latter thing",—then the Reason becomes ' Unknown'; because at the present time Consciousness

Page 51.

does not form the object of any direct cognition in that exclusive form which is held to be destructive of Misconceptions; as if It did form such an object, It could not be the substratum (of the cognition); and when It does form the object of such exclusive cognition, upon the appearance of the *Vritti* produced by the due comprehension of the Vedanta texts, then, there is not the slightest chance for the appearance of any direct cognition of the phenomenal World as an undeniable reality. Thus then, inasmuch as what is incompatible with Ignorance is only that knowledge or cognition of the thing in its own individual form which is *brought about by a valid means of knowledge*,—the mere fact of the thing being directly cognised cannot be held to remove the Ignorance with regard to it.

The following objection also has been put forward against the reasoning :—" If by 'Ignorance' is meant the *negation or* " *absence of knowledge*, then the argument becomes 'superfluous' (as no one holds the World to be the product of any " such negation); and if 'Ignorance' is something *inexplicable*, " then it is as good as the 'skyflower' (*i.e.* an absolute non- " nentity), and its counter-entity (*knowledge*) would be an " impossibility."

But there is not much weight in this objection; as for one who admits a negation which has an absolute non-entity for its counter-entity (*i.e.* the negation of a non-entity), the said counter-entity would be possible, (for the purposes of argumentation), simply by reason of its being admitted by the Opponent (even though for the propounder of the argument himself, the counter-entity has no existence at all).

REASONING [D].

" The World is not imposed upon the Self,—because, it " forms the objective of the activity of persons who have " direct cognition of the Self,—as for instance, the jar, which " is the objective of the activity of persons who have the

" direct cognition of the *Cloth*, is not imposed upon the Cloth. " Nor is the reason open to the fallacy of the 'Unknown'; " because as a matter of fact we find that even though God " has the direct cognition of the Self, yet He engages " Himself in the *Sustaining*, &c, of the World, and, though " the person who has become liberated during life has the " direct cognition of the Self, yet he engages himself in such " actions as the begging for food and the like. Nor would " the Reason apply to the case of the misconception of the " conch as yellow; because the *yellowness* that is imposed upon " the conch never forms the objective of the activity of the " person who has the direct cognition of *whiteness*."

This Reason has an undesirable application to the case of reflections; because the reflection of the face is imposed upon the face, and forms the objective of the activity of the person who has the direct cognition of the identity of the reflection with the face.

The Reasoning is also subject to the 'vitiating condition' in the shape of the character of *being perceived apart from the Self* (which while covering all cases of the *probandum*, does not cover all those of the *probans*).

REASONINGS [E] AND [F]

Other two reasonings brought forward by the Opponent are:—(E) " The world is not the product of illusion cast " by God,—because it is directly perceptible to Him,—as " for instance, the jar, which is directly perceptible by " Chaiṭra, is not the product of any illusion cast by " him. (F) The world is not the product of illusion cast " by the Jīva (Individualised Consciousness),—because it " continues to exist even when he is in deep sleep,—like " the Self. Nor is this latter Reason 'unknown', as the " World is actually recognised by the man to be the same "(when he wakes up); and it is not possible, in the absence "of any unseen agencies, for the World to have been pro- "duced over again on the man's waking."

The former of these two reasons (E) has an 'undue extension,' inasmuch as it applies to the case of the magician, who perceives all the things he produces by his magic; and yet these things are the product of the illusion cast by him. Then again, Illusion being the same as Nescience, the Reason would apply to the case of the misconception of the identity of the body and the Self. And as regards the other argument (F), it is distinctly open to the fallacy of the 'unknown' (the world perceived after sleep not being precisely the same as the one perceived before it). Nor could this fallacy be avoided by the fact that the World is recognised to be the same; because we shall show, under the section on '*Dṛiṣṭisṛiṣṭi*', that no such Recognition can prove the existence of the World during the time that the person is in deep sleep. And it is quite possible for the World to appear over again (on the man's waking); as there is every possibility of there being causes at work in the shape of certain *unseen* forces.

REASONING [G].

"Unreality does not belong to *all* things save the Self,— "because it subsists only in such things as are unreal,— "like the character of shell-silver"—This is another argument put forth by the Opponent. But this also is not right; because it is open to a 'vitiating condition' in the shape of *the character of subsisting in things other than unreality.* Then again, what is *Unreality*? (1) Is it a character different from that of entity and non-entity? (2) Or, is it only that which is different from that of the entity? In the former case the argument becomes 'superfluous' (the conclusion being acceptable to all parties),—inasmuch as such an unreality would not (even according to the Vedantin) belong to the *non-entity*, which also would be included in 'all things save the Self'. In the latter case, inasmuch as in the premiss as put forward the word 'Unreal' has been used in the sense of 'different from the character of the Entity and the Non-entity', the Reason [in the case of the word 'Unreal' being regarded as equivalent to 'different from the character of the entity'] would be open to the fallacy of being 'Unknown' in its true form. Because the character of the 'Subject' of the argument,—'Unreality' in the shape of 'difference from the character of the entity'—belonging also to the absolute nonentity, it could not be concomitant with the *probans*,—'non-subsistence in things other than those that are different in character from the entity and the nonentity.' If in order to avoid this, the word 'unreality' in the premiss also be regarded as equivalent to 'difference from the character of the entity',—then the reason becomes 'doubtful', and thence 'inconclusive'; as it would be doubtful whether or not the *probans* is concomitant with the *absence of the probandum*, as conceived in different selves (diversity of selves being held by the propounder of the argument). And lastly, all the fallacies of the 'Ineffective' and the like that we have shown above (in connection with the previous reasonings) are all applicable to the present reasoning also.

REASONING [H]

"The Self is something different from the absolutely real "entity,—because it is a thing or category (of thought),—like "the Not-self. It might be argued that the reasoning is open "to the fallacy of 'proving something else', inasmuch as the "difference' sought to be proved might be that pertaining "to the assumed (and not to the real) Self. But in that "case, the Vedantic reasoning for Unreality also could be open "to the fallacy of 'superfluousness,' inasmuch as the 'unre-"ality' sought to be proved might be such as is *assumed* (and "not actual)."

This reasoning too is not tenable; because there would be 'superfluity' in the reasoning, by taking into account only such things as have only *practical* reality. Nor would any fallacy, on these lines, be shown to be applicable to our argument for 'Unreality.' And further, the reasoning in question is open to the 'vitiating condition' in the shape of the *character of bliss*.

Page 52.

REASONING [I.]

"The Self has in it the Not-self permeating all forms, "—or, it has in it the Not-self in the shape of a positive "entity permeating all forms,—(3) or, it has in it the Not-self "that is not rejectible by a knowledge of the Self—(4) or, it "has in it a Not-self in the shape of a positive entity, "which is not rejectible by the Knowledge of Self,—because "it is a thing or category of thought,—or, because it is a "positive entity,—like the jar and such other things. We "have added the expression *in the shape of positive entity*, in "order to guard against the charge of 'Superfluity' that might "otherwise be brought against our reasoning, in accordance "with the view that Nescience is a fifth kind of things, the "cessation whereof would be admitted by both parties."

There is not much force in this argument either; for what do you mean by 'permeating *all forms*'? If it mean *any* form, then (as we do not deny this) your argument would be 'superfluous.' If however it mean the form *of the Self*, then the *probandum* comes to be of a character that is absolutely 'unknown'; as nobody knows of any such Not-self as *permeates all forms of the Self*; for if such Not-self were known, there would be no use for any such reasoning as the one under consideration.

Says the Opponent:—"The word 'form' always refers "to that along with which it is compounded; consequently, "at the time of the comprehension of the major Premiss, it "would refer to the *form* of that which is brought forward as "the Corroborative Instance; and at that of the comprehension "of the Minor Premiss, it would refer to the *form* of the Self. "And thus the reasoning cannot be open to the fallacy of the "'Unknown *Probandum*.'"

This is not right; as the bringing forward of the peculiar nature *of words* can serve no useful purpose in regard to *Inferential* reasoning.

The above objections also apply to the case of the word "*Sva*' as appearing in the expression '*Svajñānabādhya*' (in the third and fourth of the four alternative conclusions).

REASONING [J.]

For the above reasons we also reject the following reasoning:—"The *cessation of bondage* in question (1) is coeval or co-existent with the Not-self, which is not rejectible by the knowledge of its counter-entity,—or (2) it is coeval with the Not-self in the form of a positive entity, which is not rejectible by the said knowledge,—because it is the cessation of bondage—like the bondage of chains."

In this reasoning the denotation of the word 'bondage', as used in the premisses, and in the instance, is not the same; and hence it becomes open to the one or the other of the fallacies of—(1) the 'Unknown Probans' and—(2) the 'Absence of the Probans' (in the Instance). And the use of the word 'Sva' again makes it open to the aforesaid fallacy of the 'Unknown *Probandum*.' Then again, as regards the *Probans*, there being no useful purpose served by the addition of the qualifying word 'bondage', the reasoning becomes open to the fallacy of the 'Unknown Concomitance of the Probans.' And lastly, if what is meant to be proved is the said coevality of *all cessation*, then, inasmuch as we always find some cessation or other to be coeval with Not-self, the reasoning becomes 'futile'; just as it would be if the coevality of only *the cessation of pain* were meant to be proved; because of the fact that we find the cessation of ordinary pain during the wordly state to be coeval with the previous non-existence of the pain coexistent with that cessation.

REASONING [K].

Says the Opponent:—"The general reasonings having "been refuted in the above manner, we can put forward the "following specific reasonings:—*The notion of Self is not "rejectible by any notion of which the objective is the same as "that of the former notion,—because it is a notion,—like the "notion of the Shell.*"

This reasoning is altogether childish, as it is subject to the vitiating condition' in the form of *the character of not having for its objective that which is contrary to itself.* And further, the Probans becomes 'too wide', inasmuch as we find that in the case of the assertion—'this blind person has the knowledge of colour'—the knowledge or notion that is assumed as having colour for its objective is such as is not comprehensible by the blind; and hence this affords an instance of a notion 'being rejected by a notion of which the objective is the same as that of the former notion'. It might be argued that in this case the notion in question is *assumed*, and hence rejectible. But then, in the case in question also, the '*Vritti*' (necessary for all forms of cognition) is *assumed*, and as such equally rejectible. And if (in order to avoid this,) the word 'notion' be taken as equivalent to mere 'Consciousness', then the reasoning becomes partly 'Superfluous'

REASONING [L].

"The source of the misconception of which Self is the "substratum cannot be set aside by a knowledge of the "substratum of that misconception proceeding from that "source,—because it is the source of misconception,—like "the Eye-disease which is the source of the misconception "of which the shell is the substratum."

This reasoning also is not correct; as it is subject to two 'vitiating conditions'—(1) *the character of not extending up to the knowledge of a substratum in its exclusive form*, and (2) *the character of not being imposed upon the substratum of the misconception proceeding from the source in question.* Further, the Probans becomes 'too wide', in view of the following fact:—Seeing a piece of stone from a distance, we presume a certain degree of brightness in it; and just as in the case of the shell, so here also, this presumed brightness leads us to regard the stone as silver; and when we come to know the real substratum (the stone), we find that this knowledge sets aside the brightness as well as the silver.

REASONING [M].

"Anything other than Brahman, when beginningless, is an "absolutely real entity,—because it is beginningless,—like "Brahman."

This reasoning is subject to the 'vitiating condition' in the shape of *the character of not being the object of absolute destruction.*

REASONING [N].

"Brahman cannot subsist without being related to (and "conditioned by) place and time,—because It is a category "of thought (or thing),—like the jar."

This reasoning too is not sound; because all that the conclusion—'Brahman, cannot &c.'—means is that

Page 53.

'whenever there is Brahman, there is always the relationship of time',—which involves an invariable concomitance that is (at any rate, partly) accepted by the Vedantin; and thus, to that extent, the reasoning becomes 'Superfluous'. Because as a matter of fact, *at the time* that Brahman exists; It does not exist without a relationship to time. Then again, a similar invariable concomitance with regard *to place* also, in the form—'Wherever the Self is there is relationship with place',—makes the reasoning 'superfluous.' Because the relationship to Time and Place never ceases to exist (so long as Time and Place exist); during Absolute Deliverance however there is no Time or Place; and thus the aforesaid 'Superfluity' cannot be denied as a fallacy in the reasoning under consideration.

REASONING [O].

"Such things besides Brahman as Dharma and the like, "which are cognisable by means of the Veda only, are abso-"lutely real,—because they form objects of the import of the "scriptures,—like Brahman."

This also is untenable; as it is subject to a 'vitiating' condition in the shape of *the character of being spoken of in the scriptures as absolutely real.*

REASONING [P].

"Pleasure and such other things, cognisable by the "Perceiver, are absolutely real,—because they form undeni-"able direct objects of such cognitions as do not proceed "from any deficiency in the cognitive agency,—like the "Self."

This also is not tenable; as the Probans would be 'too wide', in view of such cases as that of the *shell-silver*; as such things form the objects of *Vṛttis* proceeding from deficiencies, and yet they are the objects for the Perceiver who does not originate from any deficiencies. Then again, inasmuch as the *Pure* Self is not regarded as the object of any *Vṛtti*, your *Instance* becomes such that the *Probans* does not subsist in it. If however it be meant that the Self (herein introduced as the Instance) is one that does not form the object of cognitions proceeding from deficiencies, then the Probans itself becomes 'Unknown'. Because the *Vṛtti of Nescience,* which is the distinguishing feature of the Perceiver, has its source in deficiencies. And further, the reasoning is " too wide ", in view of the fact that it applies to the non-entity, the definition whereof being made by the verbal cognition which has a non-existent objection, has its source in deficiencies. In accordance with the view that the Self is an objective of *Vṛittis*,—inasmuch as such *Vṛittis* have for their basis the mistaken notion of identity between the Body and the Self, the Instance becomes such as is totally devoid of the *Probans*. In case however, such character of the Self be not accepted,—inasmuch as the necessary absolute reality of a thing could be proved by the mere fact of its not being an objective (like the Self), there would be absolutely no use for the additional qualification '*of cognitions proceeding from deficiencies*'; and thus the *Probans* comes to be such as is not known to be invariably concomitant with the '*Subject*'; and this also constitutes another fallacy,—that of the 'unknown Subject'. This we have explained in detail elsewhere.

REASONING [Q].

" The thing in question is absolutely real,—because " it has an existence prior to its own cognition,—like the " Self. "

This reason is subject to the fallacy of 'Unknown Probans', in accordance with the theory of '*Dṛiṣtisṛiṣti*'; and it is also subject to a 'vitiating condition' in the shape of *beginninglessness*, the concomitance whereof is not of the same character as that needed for the reasoning.

REASONING [R].

" The character of the negation of this jar as inhering " in this jar;—[this negation being other than mutual " negation]—cannot be co-eval or co-existent with this jar,— " because such character can subsist only in the negation of " this jar as inhering in this jar, this negation being other "than mutual negation;—like the character of the prior "negation of this jar. In accordance with the view that "the Probans must be entirely free from all properties that "are incompatible with the *Probandum*, we should add the "qualification 'not qualified by any such incompatible "properties'. What this reasoning proves (for the jar) "is that kind of reality which consists in the thing not "being capable of any such absolute negation as is co-eval or "co-existent with it."

This reasoning also is not correct; as it is subject to the 'vitiating condition' in the shape of *the character of subsisting either in the product only, or in the cause only, of this jar,—this product and this cause being such as has* this jar *for its counter-entity*; this character having for its invariable concomitant the *Probandum* as qualified by the *Probans*.

It might be argued that, "it is uncertain whether this "character is not concomitant with the *Probans*; because "we cannot be sure if the property that forms part of the "*Subject* subsists in absolute negation. [And as such the "character put forward cannot be regarded as a true 'vitiat-"ing condition'.]"

But as a matter of fact we know that even a doubtful 'vitiating condition' serves to vitiate a reasoning, so long as there does not appear another reasoning rejecting the conclusion contrary to that sought to be proved by means of the former reasoning. Further, the reasoning is 'too wide', inasmuch as it is applicable to the character of the absolute negation of the jar. As in a place where the jar resides *by the relation of conjunction* (*i. e.*, wherewith the jar is in contact), there is an *absolute negation* of the jar *by the relation of Inherence, i. e.* (the jar does not inhere in, or form part of, the place wherewith it is in contact); and thus we have the *Probans* subsisting in a place where the *Probandum* is absent.

END OF SECTION 20.

Section (21).

Specific Inferential Reasonings proving the Unreality of the phenomenal World.

Reasoning [*A*].

The character of not being the substratum of the negation of things other than Brahman, which are not rejectible by anything except the Knowledge of Brahman, cannot subsist in the substratum of absolute reality,—because it does not subsist in Brahman,—like the character of shell-silver, and like the difference from absolute reality.

[B] The thing under discussion is unreal,—because it is something other than Brahman,—like the shell-silver.

[C] Absolute reality cannot subsist in anything that is the object of a mutual negation subsisting in itself,—because it never subsists in anything but an absolutely real entity,—like the character of Brahman.

P. 54.

[D]. The character of absolute reality is invariably concomitant with the character of Brahman, or with Unity,—because these two characters are co-existent with reality,—like the character of being different from unreality.

[E]. The Jar and other things having a pervasive existence (extending over the whole of themselves) are the objects of only such negation as is co-existent with its substratum and is other than those that are produced (and not external),—because they are the objects of negation,—like *nameability.* According to the Logician, *Nameability* being a purely universal term, this character can be the object of mutual negation only. In accordance with our view however, it is unreal; and hence the character of the *probandum* cannot be said to be absent in the Instance.

[F]. Absolute negation subsists in the whole of its object,—because it is eternal negation,—like mutual negation.

[G]. The character of absolute *negation* subsists only in that which resides in the substratum of all that forms the object of that negation,—or it subsists in that which resides in all the objects of the negation,—because the negation is an eternal one,—like *mutual negation.*

[H]. The character of the absolute negation of the jar subsists in that which is co-existent with the negation, this negation being the Prior Negation of the Object that is productive of the object of that negation,—because it subsists in the negation of a certain jar which is coeval with a certain piece of the jar,—like the character of *cognisability.*

[I]. The piece of the jar is the substratum of the absolute negation of that jar,—because it forms its receptacle,—like the jar.

[J]. The character of Brahman cannot belong to any object of mutual negation subsisting in an absolutely real thing,—because it belong, to Brahman,—like the character of being different from Unreality.

[K]. Any distinction from, or negation of, the absolutely real thing cannot subsist in any absolutely real thing,—because it has for its object an absolutely real thing,—like the negation that has for its object all things having absolute reality.

[L]. All differentiation (or negation) must belong either to an object other than the real, or to the substratum of such an object,—because it is a negation,—like the negation of the shell-silver.

[M]. The differentiation (or negation) residing in the absolutely real thing cannot have that thing for its object,—because it resides in an absolutely real thing,—like the negation of the shell-silver.

[N]. Unreality is unvariably concomitant with all things except Brahman and the absolute non-entity,—because it belongs to all unreal things,—or because it is not the object of that absolute negation which is co-existent with unreality,—like the character of *perceptibility.*

[O]. Perceptibility cannot belong to the absolutely real thing,—because it resides only in nameable things,—like the character of the shell-silver.

[P]. Perceptibility is invariably concomitant with the character of differing from the absolutely real thing,—because it is a character not residing in things than other perceptible,—like the character of apparent reality.

[Q]. That which, according to both disputants, is not unreal can never form the substratum of any character that is not co-existent with unreality,—because it is its receptacle,—like the shell-silver.

[R]. That point in space which is characterised (or occupied) by an object is the substratum of the absolute negation (of that object),—because it is its receptacle,—like Time.

[S]. Anything endowed with the character of the Self is devoid of that negation which has for its object something possessed of absolute reality,—because it is absolutely real,—like all things possessed of absolute reality. Even in accordance with those who hold that one absolutely real thing may be different from another absolutely real thing,—

the difference or negation cannot be regarded as subsisting in *all things* endowed with absolute reality; in fact it must be regarded as subsisting only in such things as are endowed with the character of the jar and the like.

[T]. The shell-silver does not in any way differ from the world, in point of unreality,—because it forms the object of ordinary activity,—like Brahman. As a rule, the probandum can belong to or exist in another thing in the following three ways:—(1) It may be that the Subject in which the *probandum* is sought to be proved is not unreal; (2) or that both the subject and the probandum are unreal; (3) or that both of these are not unreal. The last of these alternatives is not possible; so the probandum could be proved to exist in the Subject, in accordance with the second alternative; while the same probandum can belong to the Instance in accordance with the first alternative. This distinction has to be borne in mind.

[U]. The thing under discussion is unreal,—because while not being the object of that knowledge which leads to deliverance, it is something other than an absolute non-entity,—like the shell-silver.

[V]. The character of being the object of that knowledge which leads to deliverance is such that absolute reality is invariably concomitant with it,—because it is co-existent with absolute reality,—like the character of being spoken of in the scriptures as absolutely real.

[W]. The absolute negation of a certain piece of cloth is located in this *yarn*,—because it is the beginning-

Page 55.

less negation of the cloth,—like the mutual negation of the cloth. Inasmuch as the destruction of the cloth caused by the destruction of the yarn never resides in the yarn, we have introduced the word 'beginningless', in order to preclude the reason from applying to such destruction. But as regards the cloth whose destruction is brought about by the disruption of its substratum,—if the absolute negation of such a cloth be meant to be the 'subject' of the argument, then there is no need for the introduction of the word 'beginningless.' Then again, what is meant to be the 'subject' of the argument is *every one* of those absolute negations that have the particular cloth for their object; and hence it would not be right to bring forward against the reasoning the charge of 'superfluity' on the ground that any *particular kind* of the absolute negation of the cloth may be admitted by the Logician to reside in the yarn. And the reason is that what is sought to be proved is the *probandum* with reference to *all* those things that may have the character of the 'subject' as put forward. Or, we may have for our 'subject' that absolute negation of the cloth which is characterised by (*i. e.* resides in the cloth in) the relationship of inherence, and which is not characterised by any such character as is not co-existent with it. By the word 'yarn' again what is meant is the constituent or material cause of the cloth; and as in this we have the previous negation of the cloth, the reasoning cannot be said to be faulty with reference to that. Then lastly, as regards the objections of 'superfluity' and the rest based upon the conception of the identity of cause and effect,—these we have already refuted above in connection with the reasoning quoted from *Tattva-pradīpikā.*

Or, we may put forward the above reasoning in the following specified form:—That absolute negation of the Cloth which is characterised by the relationship of inherence resides in the yarn,—because it is the absolute negation of the Cloth,—like that absolute negation of the Cloth which is characterised by another kind of relationship.

[X]. That which is devoid of the character of having partial existence and which has the character of the 'subject' of the preceding reasoning, is the object of that absolute negation which is co-existent with itself,—because it is not-self,—like Conjunction. This reasoning could not apply to the absolute negation of the Universe; as if this were regarded to be of the form of the substratum of such negation (which could be none other than Brahman Itself), it would not be the not-self, and as such the *probans* could not apply to it; on the other hand, if it were held to be something different from that substratum, then, as it would be unreal, the character of being the object of absolute negation would be quite compatible with its nature; and as such the said *probandum* would be fully applicable to it. It might be argued that—"in the case of the absolute negation of an absolute negation, the reasoning would be open to the objection that we do not know of any such unreality as consists in the character of being the object of such an absolute negation." But this is not correct; because there can be no incongruity between the fact of a negation being the object of negation and that of a positive entity being the object of negation. Because as a matter of fact, it is universally known that even though prior negation is the object of absolute negation, yet the jar and other things are the objects of that negation. This we have fully explained above under the section on 'the Unreality of Unreality.'

In the above reasoning what is meant by *being devoid of the character of having partial existence* is that the Subject is meant to be such as does not exist over only a part of its substratum. And this clears the reasoning of the following objections:—"If what is meant be the character of being the object of such absolute negation as is co-existent with itself, then the reasoning becomes open to the fallacy of 'Bādha', 'Annulment'. And if what is meant be the character of not being the substratum of the character of not existing in mere parts, then, such objects as the jar and the like become precluded from the range of the *Subject*."

The *probans*—'being the not-self'—must be taken in the same sense as 'unconsciousness', and this is what lends support to the next reasoning.

[Y]. Everything besides eternal substances, which is not the subtratum of partial existence, and having the characteristics of the aforesaid *Subject*, is the object of such absolute negation as is not itself the object of such negation,—because it is a *thing*, a category of thought,—like the eternal substance. The particular corroborative Instance has been put forward in accordance with the view of the Opponent; in accordance with our own standpoint, the shell-silver would be the fittest instance.

Says the Opponent:—"When a thing is an object of "absolute negation, it becomes an absolute non-entity; as "there would be nothing that could distinguish the one from "the other (*i. e.* the *object of absolute negation* from the "*absolute non-entity*)."

But as a matter of fact, the anomaly of there being no such distinguishing feature is set aside by the fact of the *object of absolute negation* being such as is *produced* (brought into existence) or *destroyed* (neither of which can be said of the absolute non-entity).

[Z]. Any differentiation from the Self cannot have for its object an absolutely real thing,—because it has not the Self for its object,—like the differentiation of the shell-silver. Nor would the reason apply to the Conjunction of the jar and the cloth; because the mere presence of a doubt as to the presence of the *probandum* in an object other than the Subject cannot vitiate the argument; as we find in the case of the argument,—'the world has a cause,—because it is an effect—like the sprout',—that the sprout being known to be possessed of the *probans* (the character of being an effect), the mere presence of a doubt as to the presence therein of the *probandum* (the character of having a cause) does not in any way vitiate the argument.

In this manner may other reasonings be put forward by the learned.

Thus we have clearly shown that, for the establishing of our desired position, there are many and excellent reasons, while those for the Opponent are very few.

Later on we shall put forward reasonings corroborative of our main thesis; and then having examined the comparative strength of the *pros* and *cons*, we shall point out the weak points in the reasonings of our Opponents; on the present occasion, therefore, the student need not trouble his mind over that point.

Section (22)

Explanation of Vedic texts that appear to be opposed to the view that the world is unreal.

Page (56).

Says the opponent:—"The notion that the world is unreal may be regarded as rejected by scriptural passages, such as—(A) *Shruti*:—'The Universe is "real' [*Rigveda*-Aṣṭaka II], 'That which is regarded as "real is the false' [*Rigveda*-Aṣṭaka VIII],] 'For eternal "years. He created things in reality.' [*Īshopaniṣad*]; (B) "*Smriti*:—'They (the ill-guided) declare the world to be "unreal, unstable, and without God' [*Bhagavadgīṭā*]. Then "again, the author of the *Brahma-Sūṭras* also has proved the "reality of the world in such *Sūṭras* as—'There can be no "negation of the world because we actually perceive it' "[*Brahma-sūṭra* II—ii], and 'The perception of the "world cannot be regarded as a dream, as there is no similarity between the two [*Ibid.*]."

The sense of these passages is not as you take it to be. For the first passage you have cited is from the second *aṣṭaka* of the *Ṛigveḍa Samhiṭā*; and the meaning of it is as follows:—(1) 'O, Indra and Brahmanaspati! You who are rich (*magha*—wealth), or to whom sacrifices are offered (when we read *makha*)! All actions that are real, because they are good, or because they serve to bring about their results,—such actions are yours, verily!' That is to say,—'it is to you that all actions are offered! The all-pervading deities do not destroy or adversely affect your determination or action [*cha na*, though really two words, are read by traditional teachers and students as one word; the word *praminanṭi* is from the root *mi—to destroy*, of the *kri*-class]. In fact those deities support you in your actions! With a view to accepting our offerings of curds, cooked rice and cake &c., do come to the sacrifice, like two fleet steeds yoked to the chariot [the root *jigati—to-go* belongs to the *juhoṭyāḍi-class*]! Or, come towards our offering as horses run towards grains and grasses!' Or, another meaning of which the sentence is capable is as follows:—'O' Indra and Brahmaṇaspati! The world that appears to be real is yours! *i. e.* it has been created by you! Or, all the hymns and praises sung to you apply to you really or literally, and not only figuratively! The pervading deities, or the five elementary substances, Water and the rest, do not affect adversely your work of creating the world! May you two, who are so great, come over &c., &c.';—the rest as above. Thus we find that the passage is a hymn addressed in praise of a certain deity; and as such it cannot be taken as having its sense in the declaring of the reality of the World.

(2) As regards the second passage you have quoted, it is from the 8th *aṣṭaka* of the *Ṛigveḍa samhiṭā*; this also is a

hymn addressed in praise of Indra ; and as such it cannot be taken as declaring the reality of the World. What it really means is as follows :—'He (Indra) is, by his very power, capable of doing everything! That is, he does not stand in need of any help; and this for the very reason of his being *Indra*. He is like the beautifully coloured bird *that comes* (this sense of *coming* is got at from the *prefix* '*ā*'), grave and ancient, and *without a nest*. That is, at sacrifices Indra does not, like Agni, make a home for himself. What-
Page 57.
ever then such an Indra knows as fit for doing, is real, and not fruitless. He wins eminently desirable wealth from his enemies, and gives it to those that praise him.' In the words '*jēṭā*' and '*ḍāṭā*' we have the *ṭrin* affix; and this precludes the use of the Genitive, in accordance with Pāṇini's *Sūṭra*-'*nalokāvyayaniṣṭhākhalarṭhaṭrīṇām*].

Any other passage that might be quoted as declaring the reality of the world may be similarly explained (as having a sense other than that).

(3) The third passage quoted by you from the Īshopaniṣaḍ cannot be accepted as declaring the reality of the world, as what it means is that the God created the world in the same manner as on previous occasions; and it does not mean that the world or its creation, is real.

Even in the case of such passages as cannot be taken as addressed in mere praise to some deity, we cannot accept them as pointing to the reality of the world ; as all that they do is to describe things that are perceived in ordinary experience. For instance, the Vedic sentence—'Fire is the antidote for cold.'

Says the Opponent.—"In accordance with the Vēḍānṭa " view, it is only the essence of Brahman that manifests itself; " consequently anything else, in the form of the essence "of the jar and such other things, can never be cognised by "Sense-perception, as something not rejectible at any time; "hence no Vedic sentence can be accepted as pointing "to such perceived things, and as such being merely descrip- "tive of these."

As a matter of fact what occurs is that whenever the essence of Brahman manifest itself, it does so after having set aside all other essences; and it is only to the Essence of Brahman that we apply such words as 'real' and the like; and so the 'reality' of anything else cannot be accepted as the object of verbal cognition obtained through the Veda; and thus the descriptive character of such passages cannot be explained away in any way.

Says the *Opponent*:—"In the case of the assertion 'the "Earth is different from other substances,' we find that the "fact asserted is *partially* perceived in such ordinary things "as the jar and the like, and as such, though its predica- "bility in reference to that part (the jar) is already known, "yet this predicability of the whole extent of the *Earth* is "not equally known; and hence the assertion is not regard- "ed to be merely *descriptive*. In the same manner, in the "sentence 'no animals should be killed', even though "the *non-killing*, as predicated of a portion of the class "'animal', in the shape of the '*Brāhmaṇa*', is already "known from another sentence ('the Brāhmaṇa should not "be killed'),—yet, inasmuch as the non-killing with "regard to *all animals* is not known, we do not regard the "passage as merely descriptive. In the same manner, in "the case in question, inasmuch as the *reality* of the *whole* "universe has not been known by Sense-perception, the "passages quoted by us cannot be regarded as merely *des- "criptive* of that fact of perception."

This is not right. Because in the case of the passages you have cited, the *character of 'Earth'* and the *character* of '*slaughter*' are such as subsist in common among a number of substrates; and hence it being not possible for the whole of those substrates to be previously *known*, the passages cannot be regarded as purely descriptive. In the case in question however, there is no such single character as that of the '*Visva*,' 'Universe'; as the word '*Visva*' being a pronoun is merely indicative of every one of such things as the jar and the like, in their respective forms; and as in regard to each of these, 'reality' would be *known* (according to the Logician), how could you deny the fact of the sentence ('*Vishvam sat*') being merely *descriptive*; specially as there are not different kinds of *Sattva* or *reality*.

Says the Opponent:—"In the case of Vedic passages " we find that when the same injunctive passage with the " same meaning appears in two different Vedic 'texts,' in " neither of the two places is the passage regarded as " merely *descriptive*, in view of the sense being already got " at from the other texts; and in the same manner, the " assertion 'the world is real' could not be regarded as " merely descriptive, for the simple reason that the fact " herein declared is not *known* to the person who has been " put in doubt, as to the reality of the jar and other things, by the declarations and arguments put forward by the " other disputant."

If we were to accept such an explanation, then there would be no instance where any passage could be regarded as merely *descriptive*. It might be argued that we would have such instances in the shape of cases with regard to which all men are agreed. But then, it is absolutely impossible to ascertain any case with regard to which all men may be agreed. As regards the case of the same passage occurring in different Vedic 'texts', the fact is that a passage can be regarded as *descriptive* only when we have the idea that 'this has already been declared before'; and as no such idea is possible except when the two passages occur in the same 'text', it is only natural that the merely descriptive character should not be attributed to any of the passages occurring in different 'texts.'

Says the *Opponent*:—"In the Bhāṣya on the *Brihadāra-* " *ṇyaka Upaniṣad* we find that in regard to the passage 'it " should be perceived as existing', the author has raised the " question of its being merely descriptive, on the ground of " its describing what is known by Sense-perception, and has " then declared that it is not so, because there are differences " of opinion on the point. In the same manner, even though " the sentence 'the world is real' expresses only the " reality that is known by Sense-perception, yet, it cannot " be regarded as merely descriptive; because it serves the " useful purpose of setting aside the differences of opinion " on the point."

This argument is based upon a misunderstanding of the Bhāṣva referred to. What is meant by that passage is that, inasmuch as there is a difference of opinion among the disputants, the Self as apart from the body cannot be accepted as known by sensuous perception; as if it were so perceptible, no exception could be taken to its existence by the
P. 58. *Chārvākas*, who admit the validity of all Sensuous Perception; and the passage does not say anything as to whether or not the setting aside of the diverse opinions of disputants makes the words 'the Self exists' fully significant, and not merely descriptive. That such is the sense of the Bhāṣya is shown by the following sentence in it:—'It is the Scripture that has its bearing upon the fact of the existence of a Self related to lives more than one, and also on the matter of these being particular means for the obtaining, in future lives, of desirable, and the avoiding undesirable, things.'

Says the *Opponent*:—"In the case of the two middle "sections of the Chāturmāsya sacrifice, we find the passage "'he lays the fire at the two sections'; and this passage has "been taken as *enjoining* the *laying of fire* other than that "which has been enjoined by the original injunction (of the "Chāturmāsya). And in the same manner, we can take the "sentence 'the world is real' as directly *laying down* the *reality* "in the shape of *undesirability at all points of time*,—this "*reality* being something different from the mere *empirical* "reality which is perceived by the Senses."

This cannot be; as in that case, the passage in question would be contradictory to that which lays down the fact of the world being *desirable* at all points of time; and for this reason, the sentence 'the world is real' cannot be taken as laying down the fact of the world being *undesirable at all points of time*. It might be argued that,—"in view of the contradiction pointed out, the sentence 'the world is real' may be taken as laying down its undesirability at all points of time; and hence the other passage cannot be taken as denying such undesirability; nor is there any ground why we should accept the one or the other sentence as more authoritative". But as a matter of fact we do have ground for accepting the Vedantic interpretation of the two passages. For instance, in the first place, unless we accept that interpretation, we do not get at the true import of the sentences; and secondly, as all Vedic texts point to the reality of the One only, we cannot be justified in admitting any interpretation that would ascribe reality to other things.

All Vedic texts speaking of Non-duality are endowed with all the six marks, indicative of their true import. Three of these marks, establishing the Validity of the Cognitions obtained, pertain to the *meaning* of the texts; and these are—(1) the fact that what is mentioned in the text is such as is not already known by other means of knowledge; (2) the fact of this cognition not being sublated by any subsequent cognition; and (3) the fact of the cognition thus obtained being such as serves a useful purpose. The other three, pertaining to the *words*, serve to preclude the possibility of any incongruities in regard to the passage; and these are—(1) full agreement between the beginning and the end, (2) repetition, and (3) the presence of eulogistic passages. Now, with regard to these three verbal marks, there is no dispute; as all the Upaniṣaḍs proceed in this same manner. Then as regards the former three marks, we may point out the following facts:—(1) What is spoken of in the texts concerned is not known by any other means of knowledge, and thus the first condition is duly fulfilled. (3) Nor can there be any dispute with regard to the fulfilment of the third condition of *us-fulness*; as the texts pertain to such knowledge as leads to Final Deliverance. What remains doubtful then is the fulfilment of the second condition, of the cognition not being sublated &c.; but of this also we become assured by the fact that in no other way could the texts be explained, and also that such alone is the interpretation that could apply to all the texts in question. The idea of 'non-duality', which consists in the denying of the reality of all that is phenomenal, cannot be regarded as merely *empirical*; and hence the Validity of the texts pointing to it cannot be regarded as merely *empirical*; in fact their Validity must be accepted as *absolute*. On the other hand, the reality of Duality is at best only *empirical*; and so the Validity of any texts pointing to that could never be regarded as *absolute*. Specially as no absolute reality can be attributed to two mutually contradictory things; and there can be no optional alternatives with regard to the very nature of things.

Thus then, it is quite admisisble for us to take one set of passages as *absolutely* authoritative, and the other set as only *practically* so; and then as we have already shown that the passages speaking of the world as real are merely eulogistic in their character,—it is only right that these passages should be accepted otherwise than in their direct meanings.

[The author puts forward another explanation] There are four different kinds of co-ordination:—(1) Based upon Superimposition (*adhyāsa*),—as in the conception 'this is silver' (with reference to the shell); (2) subsisting in that which is subsequently denied or rejected,—as in the conception of 'man' with reference to the *pillar*; (3) based upon the relationship of the qualification and the qualified,—as in the idea of 'the blue lotus'; and (4) based upon the notion of identity,—as in the conception 'that thou art'. And in the case of the sentence 'the world is real', we find that the co-ordination expressed between the 'world' and 'reality' may be taken either as the one based upon 'superimposition', or as that which snbsists in that which is subsequently denied; consequently, the sentence cannot set aside those passages speaking of 'non-duality' which are fully equipped with the six 'indicatives' of their import.

Says the Opponent:—"If the Vedic declaration 'the world "is real' be regarded as merely *descriptive*, then in that "case those declarations in the Veda that speak of Brahman "as *bliss* would have to be regarded as merely descriptive "of such bliss as is perceptibly experienced by the Perceiver, "in all such instances as 'I have slept in great bliss'."

Not so; the bliss that the Perceiver experiences is something *adventitious* or ephemeral, whereas the bliss spoken of in the Vedic sentences referred to is the *pure* bliss unconditioned by any adventitious circumstances; hence the two cannot be regarded as identical; and hence the one cannot be regarded as *descriptive* of the other. Then again the bliss that is spoken of in such assertions as 'I have slept in bliss' is of the form of the ordinary experience; and we know the ordinary experience that the Perceiver has is always shrouded in ignorance.

Says the Opponent:—" The declaration that 'the world is " real' cannot be regarded as merely *descriptive* and hence " useless, because it may be taken as put forward for the pur- " pose of strengthening the notion of reality (which has been " already perceived),—just as in the following instances:— " (1) the nine repetitions of the declaration 'That thou " art'; (2) the rushing together of the various means of " knowledge pointing to the existence of water, for one who " is extremely thirsty; (3) the crowding together of the six " indicatives of 'import' pointing to the reality of the " One; (4) the declaration 'it was all darkness', following " upon the due perception by the person of the positive fact " of having known or perceived nothing."

This can not be right; because that which is cognised by

Page 59.

means of such Sensuous Perception as comprehends all the peculiarities of the thing concerned, does not stand in need of anything else for the *strengthening* of its conception. In the case of the thirsty man, it so happens that when he is told of the existence of water, this verbal cognition of his needs the corroboration of the actual perception of water; but when he has actually seen the water, he does not stand in need of any corroboration by words.

It might be argued that, " in that case, the assertion 'it " was all darkness' could not be regarded as corroborating " or lending strength to the notion of ignorance 'I know " nothing', got at by means of the sense-organs."

But the assertion 'it was all darkness' refers to absence of knowledge at a time prior to the beginning of creation; while the sensuous conception 'I know nothing' refers to the want of cognitions during the state of deep sleep; and as such the two conceptions have two distinct objects; consequently the former may be regarded as having an independent effective validity of its own, (apart from the mere corroboration of the latter conception).

Says the Opponent:—' In connection with the Ashvamēdha sacrifice, we find laid down, in the first instance, the "*mantra* '*ṣadvimshatirasya vaṅkrayaḥ &c.*'; a little further on "we find the use of this *Mantra* precluded by the specificatory mantra '*Chatustrimshad vājino dēvabandhoḥ*'; and "then lastly we have the usage of the former Mantra re-established by the direction '*Ṣadvimshatirityēva brūyāt*'. "In the same manner, in the case in question, we find that "the reality of the world is known in the first instance by "Sense-perception; and then it happens to be denied by the "scriptural passages speaking of the unreality of the world; "and under the circumstances we could very well take the "subsequent passage 'the world is real' as re-asserting "and re-establishing the previously-perceived reality".

This cannot be accepted; if you once admit the fact of the scriptural passage speaking of Unreality setting aside, and as such being more authoritative than, a fact of Sense-perception,—then the said passage becomes so powerful in its authority that the subsequent passage found to be contradicting it must be taken as meaning something else. And as the law of the *Dēvatādhikaraṇa* (Mim. Sūtra) is not applicable to the case in question, we cannot regard the passage as re-asserting or re-establishing what has been denied.

Says the Opponent:—"The authoritative validity of the "sensuous perception of 'reality' being established (before "everything else), the perception must be regarded as sublating all Vedic texts speaking of 'unreality', as also all "inferential and other means of cognition pointing to the "same. And these latter being thus invalidated, we cannot, "on the strength of these, regard the texts speaking of "*reality* as merely *descriptive*."

But even though the Sense-perception you speak of be absolutely valid, yet any text that speaks merely of the same fact cannot but be regarded as merely *descriptive*. Because what is meant by a passage being *descriptive* is, not that it lends additional validity to what has already been cognised by a valid means of knowledge; but that it is *behindhand* in the supplying of the knowledge of the thing concerned; and as this 'behindhand' character may be computed either from a valid or from an invalid means of knowledge, it does not make any difference (as regards the fact of the 'behindhand' means being merely *descriptive*).

The Opponent retorts—"Inasmuch as the *Shruṭi* is accepted by all parties to be authoritatively valid, it is absolutely "necessary that what it speaks of (affords the knowledge "of) must be of the right kind of things (that form the "objects of valid means of knowledge); and it is necessary "also that it be not merely *descriptive*; and for the sake of "these two facts, we must take the Shruṭi in question as "speaking of that *actual reality* which is not already known "by Sense-perception. And thus the Sense-perception not "being a valid means of knowing this reality, how can the "*Shruṭi* be regarded as merely *descriptive*?"

But as a matter of fact, we find that even though we may regard the *reality* as cognised by Sense-perception, yet the Shruṭi text speaking of such reality may be saved from being merely *descriptive* by being taken as affording the knowledge of something new, which is expressed by the correlation of the said reality with the Verb and the other factors occurring in the sentence; and hence for the sole purpose of saving the text from being merely *descriptive*, it is by no means necessary to assume that text to be expressive of that 'reality' of things, which would be opposed to the 'unreality' spoken of in the Vedānta texts. As regards the fact of *all* Vedic texts speaking of things that are *absolutely real*, this can be true only in so far as they all have their import pointing *eventually* to the pure Brahman. And as regards indirect or intervening import or meaning of the texts, this can only show that the things spoken of thus indirectly have a mere *practical* reality. This we shall show when we shall explain the validity of the Ritualistic Section of the Veda.

The Opponent might urge the following argument :— "Inasmuch as Sense-perception stands in need of corroboration by the Vedic texts, these texts could not be regarded as merely *descriptive*, on the ground of their expressing what is already known by that Perception. Otherwise, even such Vedantic texts as, 'Brahman is true knowledge, endless &c.', 'There is no diversity &c.', would also have to be regarded as merely descriptive; (1) as the essence of Brahman is already known in the world, (even without these texts), as being the ultimate substratum of all misconceptions; (2) the 'unreality' of the world is also known by means of Inferences based upon 'perceptibility' and such other characters; specially as all this is known even to people holding such Anti-Vedic theories as that the worldly process is an eternal flow, and that 'Ideas' are the only things that exist, and so forth. [And certainly the sayings of these people could not be based upon any Vedic texts]."

If even with regard to perceptible things, Sense-perception were to stand in need of the corroboration of Vedic texts, then, in a case where there would be no such texts, people could never, with any certainty, undertake any activity on the strength of mere perception. And further, even such texts as 'Fire is the antidote for cold' could not be regarded as merely descriptive. Nor could this be accepted as a contingency desirable for the Oppo-

nent. Because if even in the case of things already definitely known by means of such Sense-perception as has its validity based upon altogether independent sources, the merely *descriptive* character were not attributed to other means of knowledge pointing to the same things,—then there could be no talk of any 'descriptive character' at all.

Nor again could we rightly attribute descriptive character to such texts as 'Brahman is true &c.,' or 'There is no diversity' &c. &c. Because these cannot be regarded as descriptive of things already known by Sense-perception; as what the texts express is *existence* as co-existent with the character of 'Brahman'; and certainly this is not cognisable either by Sense-perception, or by Inference; as it has already been shown above that Inference cannot operate towards such things, because of the fact that Reasoning does not pertain to all men at all times and places, &c. &c. &c. Nor again could the texts be held to be merely descriptive of facts already known to those who hold the worldly process to be eternal, and 'Ideas' to be the only entities; because none of these theories could be regarded as *prior* to the Veda which is independent of all human agency.

Page 60.

Says the Opponent:—"The text speaking of the "'reality' (of the world) not standing in need of the "Sensuous perception of such reality, it can, in no "case, be regarded as *dependently-descriptive;* and as as "for being *independently-descriptive*, such descriptiveness can "not deprive it of its validity as an independent means of "knowledge; as this would be similar to the case of con-"tiguous cognitions appearing in a continuous series. This "has been thus declared in the *Nayavivēka*:—'When the "descriptiveness is dependent, there is no *right cognition*; "but such is not the case when the *description* is by mere "chance, as in the case of contiguous cognitions'."

As a matter of fact, however, it is much simpler to accept as the vitiator of the validity of a means of cognition, mere 'descriptiveness', than '*dependent* descriptiveness;' as the real validity of the means of cognition, which consists in its affording the knowledge of something not otherwise known, disappears even by its being merely *descriptive*.

It might be argued that. in that, case we would have to regard as invalid all contiguous cognitions appearing in a continuous series. But as each of such cognitions comprehends an object existing at the particular point of time at which the cognition itself appears, each of them would apprehend the object as qualified by the different points of time, so that none of these could be regarded as the mere repetition, and as such merely *descriptive*, of the other.

Then again, as a matter of fact all that is necessary for regarding a Vedic text as not having its import in the pointing out of a certain thing, is that that thing be already known (by other means of knowledge). For if it did point to such a thing, then it would be altogether superfluous; and as such it could not be included in the Injunction for Vedic study (which lays down the study of something that is *useful* to the learner). Then too, as regards the Vedic text speaking of 'reality', we find that it depends upon the Sensuous perception of such reality; and hence in reality it comes under the category of the '*dependently*-descriptive'. Specially as until we have the sensuous perception of 'reality', we could never use or comprehend any words, the use or comprehension whereof is based upon the due apprehension of the potencies of the word, and things denotable by it,—such apprehension being got through Sense-perception.

It is for this reason that the above view is in keeping with the following declaration of Vāchaspaṭi Mishra:—'In a case where we have one means of knowledge corroborated 'by another, the knowledge afforded by the latter is exactly 'of the same character as that afforded by *Arthavāḍa* passages; 'as in such cases the two would be pointing towards the same 'thing, independently of each other, like Sense-perception and 'Inference. But (even though such be the case) so far 'as the Cogniser is concerned, one 'means' cannot but be 'regarded as merely *descriptive* of the other. As the ordinary 'cogniser, being not very learned, cannot comprehend things 'by means of the Veda with the same facility that he can by 'means of Sense-perception and the other means of knowledge; 'as in the case of the former, a certain amount of learning is 'necessary'. What is distinctly stated herein is that the Veda (as a Means of Knowledge), depending upon learning, is dependent upon Sense-perception.

It might be argued that,—"the texts in question cannot "be regarded as '*needlessly*—descriptive'; inasmuch as they "serve the useful purpose of setting aside the different "opinions of disputants (with regard to the reality of the "world). Then, as for being *descriptive-with-a-purpose*, this "character is by no means incompatible with the fact of the "texts having their import in what they directly signify. "As for example, in the case of the text—'one who knowing "this performs the Paurṇamāsī sacrifice acquires what "people acquire by the Ukṭhya, and he who knowing this "performs the Amāvāsyā sacrifice acquires what they acquire "by the Aṭirāṭra',—we find that by reason of the sentence "serving the useful purpose of dividing the sacrifices into "two distinct groups (one group including all that go under "the name of '*Paurṇamāsa*', and the other including the "'*Ḍarsha*'), it is accepted as having its direct signification in "the *duality* that is already known (by means of the other "text '*Ḍarshapūrṇamāsābhyām yajēṭa*'), and of which there-"fore the former sentence is only *descriptive*. In fact, it is "for this very reason that the sentence (one who knowing "this &c.') *as a whole* is construed along with the whole of "sentence (*Darshapūrṇamāsābhyām yajēta*). Otherwise (*i. e.* "if the former sentence were taken as pointing to two such "groups as are not already mentioned in the other sentence, "then) it would be only *a few words* of the former sentence "(viz: those that speak of the *result*, 'acquires &c.') that "could be construed along with the other sentence [as in this "case the '*Paurṇamāsī*' and '*Amāvāsyā*' mentioned in the "former sentence would not be the '*Paurnamāsa*.' and the "*Darsha*' of the latter]."

But if even in the case of a thing known by Sense-perception, there were a need of other means of knowledge for the purpose of setting aside the different opinions of disputants,—and for this reason, this other means of knowledge were to be accepted as pointing to its own direct objective,—then even such texts as 'Fire is the antidote for cold' would be regarded as serving the same purpose, and as such having their import in what they directly signify. Consequently in the case of a thing known by Sense-perception, there can be no need for any other means of knowledge, for the purpose of setting aside the different opinions. Then, as regards the case of the two texts cited by the Opponent, what is aimed at by the second passage is to refer to the previously-mentioned sacrifices with a view to pointing out the fact of their constituting *two* sets; and as this could not be accomplished otherwise, it may be necessary, for that purpose, to take the passage in its own direct signification. It is this that is meant by the passage quoted above from the *Nayavivēka*.

The Opponent may say—"Even though a passage be "merely *descriptive*, all that we can say is that it is 'useless', "and not that it is 'invalid' as a means of knowledge. As "all that is meant by 'validity' is that the knowledge afford-"ed is that of a real state of things, and not that it be of such "a thing *as is not already known*."

But as a matter of fact, words have their validity as a means of knowledge only with regard to the thing wherein lies their import; as we have this view thus laid down in the declaration of a trustworthy person—'the denotation of a word consists in that wherein its import lies (*i. e.* with reference to which it is used).' Specially as if this were not so, the words could not be included in the injunction of 'Vedic study,' as we have already pointed out above (*Text* p. 60, *line* 12). And certainly the true import of a scriptural text cannot lie in a thing that has already been known by other means; and hence it can have no 'validity' with regard to that thing. This has been thus declared by Kumārila Bhatta—'The word is *useful* only with regard to the thing not already known.'

Page 61.

Says the Opponent:—"(Even granting that the passage " 'the world is real' is merely *descriptive*) this *description* is " not found to serve the purpose of mere *praise*, as we find in " the case of the sentence 'Vāyū is the eftest deity'. Nor can " this be regarded by the Vedantin as serving the purpose of " *enjoining* something else (other than the principal factor " in its denotation), as we have in the case of the sentence " 'Offers the libation of curd' (where it is the *curd* and " not the *offering* that is accepted as the object of injunction). " Because even though a certain thing may be only 'des- " cribed' (or 'repeated'), for the purpose of the enjoining " of something else, if the former thing happens to be " 'described' by a valid means of knowledge, then it cannot " but be accepted as real (and this would be unacceptable " to the Vedantin). For example, in the case of the sentence " 'the corn should be washed' (where the 'corn' already " known is 'described' for the purpose of the enjoining " of the *washing*), the idea of the *corn* that we have is not " that of the *imposed* or misconceived corn. Because if " the thing 'described' were not real, then there would be " no chance for the sentence to afford any meaning; as the " only meaning that it could afford would be in the shape of " a certain relationship between the thing 'described' (the "*corn*) and the predicate ('should be washed'); just as in "the case of Inferential cognition, the knowledge afforded "is in the form of the relationship between a thing and a "certain quality predicated of it. [And in the case in "question no such relationship would be possible if the *corn* "had no real existence]."

What we mean by the sentence being 'descriptive' is that it affords the knowledge of something other than what is not already known. Nor is it necessary that that which is subsequently *described* by a valid means of knowledge *must* be real. Because if such were the case then 'reality' would belong to *dreams* also which are *described* (or referred to) by those valid scriptural texts which speak of the results following from dreams (and which results not being known by any other means of knowledge, the texts cannot but be regarded as being quite valid *means of knowledge*). And similarly *reality* would belong to the misconceived silver in the shell, which is *described* in the subsequent valid cognition '*this* is not silver.'

It might be argued that, "in these cases the things are "*described* (in the subsequent cognitions) only *as objects of* "*misconception*, and hence *as something to be negatived*; and "as such on the strength of these cognitions alone no reality "could be attributed to them."

But then in the case in question also, the *description* or *reference* that we have of the *world* (in the sentence 'the world is real') is for the purpose of pointing out only that which is negatived in the sentence 'there is not anything that is diverse'; and hence merely on the ground of the former, no reality can be attributed to the world. Thus too the denotation of the sentence 'the world is real' does not cease to exist altogether; as the object of its real import (Brahman) remains a real entity.

It might be argued that—"all the description of, or reference to, the world that is necessary for its denial (by the sentence '*nēha nānā* &c.'), we have in the sentence itself, in the word '*kiñchana*'; and as such what would be the use of any further 'description' in another text?"

But the word 'Kiñchana' is only a general term, meaning 'anything'; and hence a reference to the particular thing—the world—is absolutely necessary.

Says the Opponent:—"As a matter of fact a negativing "assertion does not stand in need of the object of negation "being mentioned by another sentence. If there were such "a need, then for the negation 'one should not eat "the meat of an animal killed by a poisoned arrow', there "would be a necessity of some such assertion as that *one "should eat this meat*."

We do not mean to say that *all* negations stand in need of such assertion. What however we do mean is that, when such an assertion is available, as in the present case, we cannot ignore it. Specially as in the Veda we have instances where something that is asserted in one sentence is denied in another; as for instance, the sentences 'one should hold the *Ṣodashī* vessels at the *Atirātra* sacrifice', and 'one should not hold &c., &c., &c.'

The Opponent might argue that, as in the case of these sentences we admit of an *option* (regarding the holding of the vessels), so in the case in question also, (we may regard the reality of the world or its Unreality to be *optional*, in the face of the two contradictory texts)."

But as matter of fact, the nature of a thing cannot admit of an option. Then again, in the case of the sentences with regard to the *holding of the Vessels*, both sentences equally afford the knowledge of something not known by any other means of knowledge, and as such they are both of equal authority; on the other hand, in the case in question, the sentence 'the world is real' speaks of something already known (by means of Sense-perception), while the sentence 'the world is unreal' affords a knowledge not obtained by any other means; and as such both cannot be accepted to be of equal authority. It is for this reason that, the negativing sentence being more authoritative, it is in subordination to this that the other sentence has to be interpreted (as being merely *descriptive*).

Says the *Opponent*:—"Even if we admit the fact of a "text being merely *descriptive*, on the ground of its affording "knowledge of something other than what is not already "known,—the text 'the world is real' cannot be regarded "as *describing* the world only for the purpose of the *negation* "contained in the text 'not anything is diverse'; because the "said *reference* to the world may be for the purpose of the "*assertion* contained in such passages as 'Even the all-per- "vading deities know it to be real', which also speak of a "superphysical fact (not already known by any ordinary "means of knowledge)."

But the sentence that you quote has been explained as meaning something different from what you make it mean. [The sentence means 'the all-pervading deities do not harm &c. &c.',—this being a mere *praise* of the deities referred to.] (Text, *page* 56).

—:o:—

Says the *Opponent*:—"In all cases where something is "*described* or *referred to* for being negatived, we have the "expression '*yat...... tanna*' (*That this is so is not*). In the "case of the text in question however we do not find any "such expression; and hence we cannot accept it as merely "*descriptive*."

It is not so; because the mere absence of a few such expressions cannot prove the absence of that which may be indicated by them (specially when other indications are present).

"Well, in that case, such declarations as '*Taṭ satyam*' "(*That is real*, referring to Brahman) also may be taken as "merely *descriptive*, referring to *That* simply for the purpose "of denying its *reality* in the texts—'That is said to be "neither real nor unreal', 'In the beginning this was not', "and so forth; and the '*Taṭ*' in *Taṭ satyam* being *descriptive* "of that *being* or *reality* of Brahman which is apprehended in "such cognitions as 'the jar is real', 'the manifestation of "happiness is *real*', and so forth."

It is not so; firstly because *being* or *reality* as belonging to Brahman can never be known by means of Sense-perception and other ordinary means of knowledge (and a *description* could be possible only if the thing were already known by such other means); and secondly because, the denial of Brahman would land us in *Nihilism*. Then again, the 'indicative' that the Opponent seeks for is present in the text '*Iḍam sarvam yaḍayamāṭmā*'; and this would justify our regarding other texts (speaking of the *World* as real) to be merely *descriptive*.

In the same manner, texts speaking of 'bliss' cannot be

Page 62.

taken as *describing* or *referring* to the *bliss* or happiness cognised by Sense-perception, for the purposes of the negation (with regard to Brahman, of such *bliss*) contained in the texts—'*Aḍuḥkham asukham samam*' (It is without pleasure, without pain, calm). Because in this latter text the mention of 'pleasure' along with 'pain' distinctly shows that it is *material* pleasure that is meant; and certainly for the purpose of negativing *material* pleasure, there would be no need for *describing* or referring to that (*immaterial*) bliss which constitutes the nature of Brahman. All this has been fully explained in the *Vivaraṇa*, as follows:—'The texts *iḍam sarvam yaḍayam* &c.' and the like become co-ordinated or reconciled with those other texts that speak of the Self as *not phenomenal*, *not-gross*, and so forth, only by being taken as pointing out what is negated in these latter; specially as *freedom from all that is phenomenal* is distinctly cognised during deep sleep as being a desirable end.'

A fresh objection is raised :—" *Freedom from all that is* "*phenomenal* can not be a desirable end; as we have this " freedom in a swoon; and a swoon is not regarded as desir- " able. It cannot be said that what we have in a swoon is " only the *absence of all knowledge of phenomenal things*, and " not the *freedom* from these. As the same may be said of " deep sleep also."

It is not so; because in a swoon we have no *manifestation* (or appearance) as such of Consciousness in the form of bliss. To this effect, we have the following *Sūtra* :—'When the Cogniser is in a swoon, there is only half-bliss, because of the remnant (of the organs of actions, even though those of Sensation cease to exist).' On the other hand, in the *freedom from things phenomenal* that we have during Deep Sleep, and also in the state of Deliverance, there is present a distinct consciousness, of *bliss as such*; and hence this is regarded as a desirable end. Says the Scripture:—' Fear arises from a second.'

It might be argued on the strength of such texts as ' a man who is *alone* is not happy ' that *connection with phenomenal things* also is a desirable end. But it is not so; because such connection is a source of pain; and as such can never be regarded as desirable; and also because like the Ritualistic Section of the Veda, all such texts are to be taken as being meant for people who have not attained true wisdom.

" In the text—' Having come to know the separate self " as the propeller, becoming attached to this, one reaches " immortality ' (Shvēṭāshvaṭara Upaniṣaḍ I—6)—we find the " knowledge of diversity spoken of as the means of Deliver- " ance. And in view of this how can we deny the desirable " character of *connection with phenomenal things?*"

According to us also, the cognition of such difference (between the supreme and human selves) is quite desirable, *until the attainment of True Knowledge*; as, like the knowledge of Brahman-with-attributes, the knowledge of Brahman as the 'propeller' serves the purpose of indirectly helping in the attainment of Deliverance; but that which helps to accomplish this *directly*, is only the knowledge of *non-difference*; as is implied in the text.—'It should be known *as one* only'. (*Bṛihaḍāraṇyaka Upa*—iv—20). It is for this reason that the cognition of Brahman as the 'propeller' has been spoken of, in the text cited above, as the cause of 'attachment'; and hence also subsequently to this passage, we have in the same Upaniṣaḍ, the following—'Persons learned in the Veda having known and becoming merged in Brahman, and being identified with it, become liberated, and it is this Essence of Self which man, on knowing, becomes one and happy, free from all troubles' (Shvēṭāshvatara Upa. II—14); and in this we have *unity* distinctly laid down. And hence the knowledge of diversity cannot be accepted as a means of Deliverance.

The above explanation also supplies the answer to the following question:—"Why cannot we regard the text "'*nēha nānāsṭi &c.*' as merely *describing* or referring to the "denial of the reality of the world by the Idealist,—for the "purpose of the negation of this denial and the consequent "assertion of the undesirable character of such reality, con- "tained in the text, 'this world is real?" Because even though both *existence* and *non-existence* are equally the negation of each other, yet the cognition of *existence* being self-sufficient does not stand in need of the cognition of *non-existence*; the cognition of *non-existence*, on the other hand, is not possible without a corresponding cognition of its counter-entity (*existence*), and hence it stands in need of this latter. Consequently it is the negativing text '*nēṭi nēṭi*' that stands in need of another text descriptive of the reality (that is negatived in the former); and the text asserting the reality does not need any text negativing it. If it were not so, then we would have a most objectionable interdependence

Says the Opponent :—" To the case in question we may " apply the 'Law of the General and the Particular'. That " is to say, we find that even though the text 'one should " not kill any animals', does not speak of any particular " *killing*, yet, inasmuch as the *killing* in general here nega- " tived is already known by Sense-perception, &c., the said " text does not, for this purpose, stand in need of any text " where any particular killing is asserted;—as for instance, " the text, 'one should kill the animal dedicated to Agni- " Soma'; And in the same manner, even though the text " '*nēṭi nēṭi*' does not speak of the negation of the reality of " any particular thing, yet, inasmuch the reality sought to " be negatived by it is known by Sense-perception and other " ordinary means of knowledge, it cannot stand in need of any " such other text as '*Vishvam saṭyan*' which speaks of the imperceptible reality of such things as *Dharma* and
P. 63. *Aḍharma*. In a case however, where what is sought to " be negatived is not known by any other means of knowledge, " there is certainly a need of some other text pointing out " that thing; as we find in the case of the passages speaking " of the *holding* and *not-holding* of the *Ṣodashī* vessels. If " even in a case where the object to be negatived is already " known by other means of knowledge, it were necessary to " have a text speaking of that object, then the killing of the " animal dedicated to Agni-Soma would be taken as men- " tioned in the text, simply for the purpose of being nega- " tived in the general prohibition of *killing*; and as such it " would have to be regarded as *sinful*."

The two cases are not analogous. (1) Because the sentence 'one should kill *the animal dedicated to Agni-Soma*' has its application less extensive than that of the corresponding negative sentence ('one should not kill *any animal*)'; and (2) not being subordinated to any other sentence, it must be regarded as having its import in what it itself directly signifies; for these reasons it cannot be taken as only pointing out something that is to be negatived by the negative sentence; and as such it cannot be regarded as subservient to any such negative sentence. In the case of the sentence 'the world is real', on the other hand, we find that its application is equal in its extention to that of the negativing sentence ('*nēṭi nēṭi &c.*'); and having no import in what it itself signifies directly, it is only right that it should be taken only as pointing out something to be negatived by the other sentence; and hence it must be regarded as subservient to this latter. And (even though the reality of such ordinary things as the jar and the like is known by Sense-perception; and hence for the pointing out of this object for negation by the negativing sentence, the sentence 'the world is real' would not be needed, yet) for the said reason of the sentence pointing out the object to be negatived, we take it as serving the useful purpose of including such imperceptible things as *Ḍharma* and the like, the reality of which latter also is negatived by '*nēṭi* &c'; and we have also shown that its case is analogous to that of the sentence laying down the killing of the animal dedicated to Agni-Soma; as while the latter has its import in what it directly signifies, this is not the case with the former. For these reasons we conclude that even with regard to such imperceptible things as Ḍharma and the like, the arguments based upon '*Ḍrishyaṭva*' &c. are not rejected by the text 'the world is real.'

Or, we can take the text 'the world is real' as speaking of *practical or empirical* reality. Nor can it be said that, there being no difference of opinion as to the *practical* reality of the world, it would be entirely superfluous for the Veda to assert such reality. Because in the case of the texts speaking of Heaven and Hell, we find that even though they might have been propounded under special circumstances (*i. e.* for those people who deny the existence of Heaven &c.), yet they serve the useful purpose of leading to such activity or cessation from activity as lead to the attaining of Heaven and the avoiding of Hell. [In the same manner the sentence 'The world is real' serves the purpose of denying the fact of the world being an absolute non-entity]. This *practical* character of the reality of the world consists in its *being not sublated by anything except the knowledge of Brahman*, and not in its being not sublated at all; as this latter would be directly contradictory to the text speaking of the 'Unreality' of the world. Nor would it be right to assert that, "in this case, inasmuch as the text 'the world is real' would be affording an entirely erroneous conception, it could not be regarded as *valid* (*i. e.* as a means *of right* knowledge)." Because the validity of the sentence would be like that of those that describe dreams (which are unreal); with only this difference that while the reality of dreams is only *apparent* that of the world is *practical or empirical.*

Says the Opponent:—"The text speaking of the Unreality "of the world is taken (by the Vedāntin) as indicating, by "indirect implication, the reality of the pure indivisible "Consciousness; and certainly this need not be irreconcil-"able with the reality of the world (*i. e.* both can be real, "the text in question not being regarded as denoting the "unreality of the world)."

It is not so; because the comprehension of the Indivisible Entity is got at through the recognition of the fact of there being no *second*; and as such this can never be compatible with the reality of the world (or of any other thing except that entity). Nor would this imply the utter invalidity of those texts that speak of the reality of the world;

because as for the view that some texts, when taken in a certain limited sense, do not express what is absolutely true,—this view is quite acceptable to us; but in their ultimate sense, all texts are equally true and valid. Then again, with regard to the world it cannot be denied that, as it is possessed of a certain *practical* reality, as apart from mere *apparent* reality, the notion of such reality would be a *true* notion—being the notion of a certain character with regard to a thing in which that character is really present; and so far, the validity of these texts (even in this sense) remains unshaken.

Nor would it be right to take the text 'That is real' as referring to the *practical* reality of Brahman, in view of the declaration 'In the beginning this was unreal' (which appears to deny the *absolute* reality of Brahman). Because as a matter of fact, Brahman is beyond the reach of all thought and action (and hence beyond all that is *empirical*). And if Brahman were not absolutely real, then there would be no substratum for reality, and we would be landed in pure Nihilism. Nor would this denial of all reality be reasonable; as no denial of *reality* would be possible without admitting something as *real*.*

The above reasonings also set aside the view that, "inasmuch as the texts speaking of the unreality of the world are not reconcilable with those that speak of its reality, we must regard the former as meaning something else." Because the texts speaking of unreality are fully endowed with all the six 'indicatives of import', all which indicate that it cannot mean anything else except what it directly signifies; and as such it is superior, in this respect, to the texts speaking of reality

* Whenever the cognition of one thing sublates the cognition of another thing, the reality of the former thing is always of a higher grade; and so when we would deny the absolute reality of *all things* there would be nothing absolutely real, the cognition of which would sublate the cognition of the other things.—Comm.

(and hence it is that these latter have their import altered in view of the former). Specially as it being admitted on all hands that that which forms the object of the true import of Vedic texts is real,—the 'indicatives' also of such import must be regarded as ultimately pointing to the reality of those things. On the other hand, as regards the texts speaking of the reality of the world, the words of these texts are found to signify something wholly different (from their direct denotation); and as such there could be no question as to these being endowed with any 'indicatives of import' pointing to the reality of the world.

Says the Opponent:—"If the text speaking of *reality* "were to be regarded as not having its true import in what "it directly signifies, because of this latter being already "known by Sense-perception,—then the text speaking of "*unreality* also could not be accepted as having its true im- "port in what it signifies directly, because this latter is "directly contrary to what is known by Sense-perception. "Specially as in the case of both we have one of the reasons "for not accepting the real import to lie in what is directly "signified,—the only two reasons for this being, (1) the "fact of its being already known, and (2) the fact of its "being contrary to what is already known."

But as a matter of fact we find in the case of the size of the moon, that the scriptural texts speaking of its large size are more authoritative in their validity than the Sense-perception of its smaller size; and in the same manner, the text speaking of the *unreality* of the world is more authoritative in its validity than the contrary Sense-perception, and also than the text which merely repeats the *reality* that is already known by Sense-perception. If we do not admit of some such explanation both the texts will have to be rejected as invalid. This has been thus declared in the *Sankṣēpashārīraka*:—'The text that has not its true import in what it directly signifies, when contradictory to other texts that have their true import in what they signify, must be taken indirectly or figuratively (as indicating something that it does not signify directly)'.

It is for this reason of its being contrary to the text speaking of *unreality*,—which text is not subordinate in its signification to any other texts,—that the text speaking of the *reality* of the world cannot be taken as signifying that *reality* which consists in not being sublated at any time, and which is not cognisable by Sense-perception. What make the text speaking of *unreality* more authoritative in its validity are—(1) the fact of its not being capable of any other interpretation, and (2) the fact of its being a *negative* sentence; and hence there can be no strength in the following argument of the Opponent:—" If the text in question were more " authoritative simply by reason of its being a negative sen- " tence, then the *Sūtra* '*Kniti cha*' (Pāṇini), which precludes " in a general way all *Guṇa* and *Vṛiḍḍi* forms, would have to " be regarded as more authoritative than the *Sūtra* '*Kiti* " *cha*' (Pāṇini) which lays down the *Vṛiḍḍhi* form in all such " nominal affixes as end in 'K'. (And hence we could not " have such words as '*Gāṇapaṭam*' and the like); and (2) " the text prohibiting animal-slaughter would be more " authoritative than the text laying down the killing of the " *Agnīṣomiya* animal; (3) the text that prohibits the holding " of the *Ṣodashī* vessels would be more authoritative than " that which lays down their holding; and (4) the negative " sentence 'all this was *not* in the beginning' than the " affirmative passage 'Brahman is truth, knowledge &c. &c.' " (and none of these contingencies would be acceptable to the Vedāntin)."

All these arguments lose their force because of the reason mentioned above; and also because the comparative strength or weakness of the validity of different texts depends upon the fact of their being incapable or capable of other interpretations or applications,—a fact which is determined by the general or particular character of the texts concerned (and not by their negative or affirmative form). As regards the text 'the world is real' we have already shown that it refers to *practical* reality; and as such it is subordinate to other means of knowledge; and hence capable of other interpretations (than its direct one). Consequently the text declaring the *Unreality* of the world cannot be said to be contrary to the text speaking of its *reality.*

Nor is it contrary to such *Smṛiṭi* texts as—'These people regard the world as unreal and unstable, without a God,—and taking their stand upon this view they destroy their selves' (*Bhagavaḍgīṭā*). Because for me, who hold the world to be something *different from 'real'*, and hence accept also the fact of its being different from 'unreal', there is no congruity in any text that speaks of the world as being *unreal.*

Says the Opponent:—"Your present position is not reconcilable with that taken up in the two Sūtras (*a*) 'There "is no absence (of the world) because it is perceived' "and (*b*) 'It cannot be regarded as a dream, because of its "not being similar to it' (Brahma-Sūṭra II—i), where we "have the *absolute* reality of the world distinctly declared. "Nor can it be said that, 'these two Sūtrās being meant to "refute the theory of Nihilism, all that they prove is the fact "of the world being *different from an absolute non-entity*; and "this is not incompatible with the Vedantic stand-point.' "Because even in accordance with the theory of Nihilism, "the world is admitted to be different from a Non-entity, "this difference consisting in its being capable of effective "action; and hence the Sūtras could not be taken as meant "to refute that view; and as regards that '*difference from* "*non-entity*' which consists in *not being sublated*, this, m "regard to the world, is denied by you also. And further, "if the Sūtras were meant only for proving the fact of the "world being *different from non-entity*, then there would be "no sense in the declaration of the world being different "from a dream; specially as in regard to the world, that "*difference from dreams* which consists merely in its having a "*practical* reality, is admitted by the Bauḍḍha also; as has "been thus declared by them—'The Buḍḍhas teach Dharma "through two kinds of reality'."

Reply:—This is not so; as you have evidently not understood the sense of the *Sūṭras* you have quoted. These have to be explained in the following manner:—The Vedantin has shown that the trend of all Vedanta texts is towards the declaring of the fact of the World having originated from Brahman who is of the essence of 'Being',—and then subsequently when he comes to put forward arguments to prove that 'all this is unreal', there arises a suspicion as to there being in this a self-contradiction; and when, in order to explain this suspicion it is declared that 'the world is neither real, nor unreal, nor real-unreal, nor neither-real-nor-unreal, —being just like the water in the mirage; as any of these would be opposed to reason',—this comes to mean that the world, like Brahman, is an absolute non-entity; and it is in answer to this that we have the *Sūṭras* referred to. The sense of the reply is that Brahman is not a 'non-entity', *i. e.* not a mere void, because it is actually cognised as real entity, by valid means of knowledge; and the Nihilist also must regard at least something as a real entity, otherwise there would be no limit or starting point for the sublation (necessary for the unreal character of things).

This sense of the *Sūṭra* is not incompatible with the view that the world is unreal. This has been thus declared—'The absolute denial of things has been refuted by valid means of knowledge; and the *practical* validity of these means cannot be asserted without having for the basis of such assertion a certain thing that is essentially real.'

Nor is it impossible to explain the propriety of the Sūtra speaking of the 'difference from dreams'; as this Sūtra only points out a 'vitiating condition' in the following inferential reasoning—"The thing under discussion is an absolute non-entity, like the water in the mirage,—because of any other view being opposed to reason",—the 'vitiating conditions' pointed out being in the shape of—(1) 'the capability of being sublated', (2) 'non-amenability to any valid means of knowledge', (3) 'the character of orginating from certain discrepancies', and so forth.

Page 65.

Even if those *Sūtras* be regarded as aimed at the refutation of Idealism, there is no incongruity. As in that case the connection of the Sūtra might be thus explained:—The Vedanta texts having been shown to point to the fact of the world having for its material cause Brahman *who is devoid of colour &c.*, this view is faced by the contradiction of such inferential reasonings as point to Ideas being in the form of the 'blue' and the like; and in explanation of this we have the Idealist view put forward in the following manner;—"The object must be in the form of the Idea, (1) because the "cognition (of things) is similar to dream-cognition, (2) be-"cause the thing is always cognised along with the cognition, "and (3) because the thing cannot be differentiated from "its cognition. That is to say,—(1) The cognition in "question has no substratum apart from the cognition,—be-"cause it is a cognition,—like dream-cognition; (2) if this "conclusion be not admitted then we shall be faced by the "absurdity of the object being known even in the absence "of any cognition of it; and (3) in the case of two "things that are different,—as for instance, the Horse "and the Buffalo,—we do not find them to be invari-

"ably concomitant with each other; hence we cannot "admit of anything as real besides the Ideas that we have." And it is in answer to this view that we have the two Sutras; the sense of the answer being that the Idealist's position is open to the following objections—(1) There is sublation (of the notion of the identity between the Cognition and its object), (2) the inferential reasoning is subject to a vitiating condition in the shape of 'the character of being sublated'; (3) the concomitance (between the cognition and its object) is due to the object being the means of the Cognition; and (4) even if you deny the external object in its gross form, you will have to admit a certain difference between the Cognition and its object,—because of the 'similarity' (that you admit to exist between the Object and its Cognition).

In this case the meaning of the *Sūṭras* would be explained thus:—*There is no abhāva*—or *unreality*—of the object apart from the Cognition; but it has the *reality*; and that consists in the capability of effective action, not sublated in the practical world of thought and action; *because of Upalabdhi*; that is to say, because it is actually known by valid means of knowledge, as apart from the Cognition. The 'difference from dreams' is put forward only for the purpose of pointing out 'incapability of sublation' as a vitiating condition' in the Opponent's reasoning; the sense being that the reasoning is faulty inasmuch as it is tainted by 'vitiating conditions' and is sublated. Thus then, there can be no suspicion of any contradiction. Hence it has been declared that the object is not of the form of the Cognition, but it is something *eternal*; and though this object is endowed with the *reality* that consists of the capability of effective action, yet, on the strength of the texts declaring 'non-duality', it is regarded as *imposed* upon, or assumed in, Brahman, and not as *absotutely real.* And herein lies the difference of the Vedānta from the Bauddha view. This has been thus declared in the *Ātmatattvavivēka* :—' There is no existence for the Cognition if we disregard its difference from the Cognised object; and the victory or credit of refuting this view belongs to the powerful Vedānta; and as according to the Vedānta, the illusory world is real as we know it, there can be no room, in this doctrine, for the theory of the Bauddha'. The arguments against cognitions apprehending objects has already been refuted by us. So that all is well and sound.

END OF SECTION 22.

Section (23).

The Unreal can prove the Real: Inferential Reasonings though themselves unreal can prove real 'Non-duality'.

Says the Opponent:—"The Inferential reasonings that "prove the *reality* of the world are superior in validity to "those that prove its *unreality*. Because if the latter were *not* "to indicate the unreality of the 'Subject' and other factors "of the conclusion, as also the premises of the reasoning that "proves *unreality*, then there would be no proving of the "unreality of *all things*; while, on the other hand, if it "were to indicate the unreality of those factors, then "there would be (1) *mutual contradiction* (the reasoning "proving the unreality of its own constituent factors and "*vice versa*), and (2) the '*Asiddhi*' or *Non-existence, of the* "'*Substratum*' &c. (*i.e.*, of the '*Subject*' and the other "factors, which being unreal, would be Non-entities)."

It is not so; because there can be no 'contradiction' even if the Inference in question were to indicate the *unreality* of its own constituent factors; and the reason for this is that the conclusion and the premises do not express that *reality* of these factors which consists in their not being sublated at any point of time.

"The *absolute reality* of these factors is necessarily "implied; as otherwise the propositions concerned could "not prove what they are meant to prove; as it is only "something *absolutely* real that can prove anything; for "the simple reason that such reality is involved in the "*capability to prove*. What is necessary for this *capability* "*to prove* (as belonging to premises) is, not that they "should be cognised, or that they should be directly or "immediately cognised; because the former will include "absolute non-entities also, and (these being in fact devoid

" of the said capability the said definition would become
" 'too wide' ; while the latter will not include the ceternal
" super-sensous things, and (these being endowed with the
" said capability) the definition would be 'too limited.'
" Nor again can the fact of the thing being *cognised as real*
" be regarded as necessary for the said *capability*; because
" as a matter of fact we find that even though fire may not
" be *known as fire*, it is found to have the *capability* of
" burning all the same; and conversely, even though the
" heap of the *guñjā* fruit is cognised as fire, the capability
" to burn is not found in it. Nor can the *capability* be
" dependent upon the fact that with regard to the thing
" there should be such a cognition of reality as is not
" sublated up to three or four stages; because if this were
" accepted, then the Self would have to be regarded as
" transient, because of its being cognised as 'fair' (in the
" ordinary conception 'I am fair'), and the *Ākāsha* would have
" to be regarded as tangible because of its being cognised as
" 'blue'; because both these notions—'I am fair'
Page 66.
" and 'the sky is blue'—are found to be *not-*
" *sublated* upto three or four stages; as for these being
" *sublated by* reasoning, this sublation is found in the case
" in question also (where the notion of unreality is found to be
" sublated by reasoning)."

It is not so, we reply. Because what is necessary for the aforesaid *capability to prove* is the character of being the object of such cognitions as are different in nature from the cognitions of the *blueness of the sky* and such other things, and which go to prove for you the reality of such things as the *Jar*. It is for this reason that what has been asserted in the *Iṣhtasiḍḍhi*—that what is necessary for a certain thing being regarded as of a certain character is that it should be known as such to the people—is quite right; and right also is the view that the necessary condition for a thing or premiss to be regarded as having the *capability to prove* is that with regard to it the two disputants and the umpire should have the idea that it is real,—this idea being such as is found to be correct (and not sublated or rejected) up to three or four stages. As regards the notion of fire with regard to the heap of *Guñjā fruits*, or that of 'fairness' with regard to the Self, or that of 'blueness' in the sky,—you also will admit that the idea that people may have are not of this kind (as none of these is entertained by both the disputants and the umpire). Otherwise the said characters would have to be accepted (by you) as real.

You may argue thus:—"According to the Vedantin, the reality of Brahman is proved by the verbal cognition (afforded by scriptural texts) that is free from all known discrepancies; and in the same manner the reality of the world would be proved by the sensuous cognition that is free from all known discrepancies; specially as the capability to prove is equally present in both cases."

But this is not possible, we reply. The notion of the reality of the world we do not find to be such as is not *sublated*, as we find in the case of the notion of reality of Brahman; for the simple reason that the *reality* which consists in not being sublated in the past, present or future cannot be cognised by Sense-perception (which applies to the *present* only), as we have already pointed out.

Nor would it be right to argue here that if the mere fact of a certain thing being the object of cognition were to be the condition necessary for its *capability*, then the fire, which is not cognised as fire, would not have the capability to burn, and the poison which is cognised as nectar would have the capability to bring back the dead to life. This, we say, would not be the case; because in fire there does exist the character of being the object of the said cognition,—a character which is known to all persons, from God downwards; and as for poison becoming like nectar, the notion referred to in this case would be similar to that of the *blueness* of the sky.

As a matter of fact however, all that is necessary for a thing to be *capable of proving*, is that it should have *practical reality*, and it does not matter whether it be cognised or not cognised; and this *practical reality* is nothing more more or less than the *incapability of being sublated by anything else save the knowledge of Brahman.* Nor does this latter character necessarily involve *unreality*; as it can belong equally to that which is *not sublated* at all (*e.g.*, the real Brahman, which being not sublated at all can be said to be 'not sublated by anything save the knowledge of Brahman') and that which is sublated by the knowledge of Brahman only. It is for this reason that this character has not for its invariable concomitant (*i.e.*, it does not necessarily imply) *absolute reality*; and *absolute reality* not being a necessary condition in the *capability to prove*, there is no discrepancy in the *capability* of a thing to prove something, even though it be itself devoid of *absolute reality*.

This also sets aside the following argument:—"What do you mean by the *practical reality* of a thing? (1) Does it mean that it is *sublatable by the knowledge of Brahman*? (2) Or, that while it is an object of practical activity (ordinary speech and action), it is real? (3) Or, that it is used (and spoken of) as real? The *first* is not possible; because until its *unreality* is established, you cannot prove its sublatability; and thus there would be an undesirable interdependence. Nor is the second tenable by you; and such 'practical reality', which is contrary to 'unreality', we also accept. Nor lastly, can the third be maintained; because unless the thing has *reality* it cannot be *capable of proving* anything." This reasoning, we say, cannot serve any useful purpose; because the explanation (of 'practical reality') that we have given above is free from all serious objections.

The Opponent might put forward the following argument:—"If the 'Probans' and other factors of your reasoning have only *empirical reality*, then the 'Subject' sought to be proved by their means also could have only *empirical* reality; because it is a well-recognised fact that the existence of the 'Probans' appearing in the premises is exactly of the same character as that of the 'Subject' of the Inference."—But this also would be futile; as in the first place we also admit that the reality of '*dṛishyaṭva*' as well as that of '*miṭhyāṭva*', is equally empirical; and secondly it is not an established fact that the existence or reality of the two must be of the same character; we find that from the presence of *Dust-cloud*, mistaken for 'smoke', we infer the presence of *fire* (which in some cases turns out to be *real*, though the 'Probans', in the form of 'smoke' is unreal); and again, before the odour has appeared in the jar by baking, we infer (wrongly) the presence of odour in it (which is *unreal*),—at any rate, until we have the notion to the contrary, that 'odour is not there'—from the right notion that it is a form of 'Earth' which is always co-existent with 'odour' (this Probans being quite *real*). For these reasons we conclude that even though the 'unreality' may itself be unreal, yet it is cognisable by means of those scriptural texts that describe Reality. Specially as, just as there is nothing incongruous in the fact of that which is real being cognisable *as* (*practically*) *real* by the ordinary right means of knowledge, so too there is nothing incongruous in our cognising, by right means of knowledge, that which is unreal, *as unreal*; and further, even though the scriptural texts may not make known reality as regards one factor (*viz.* the *unreality*), yet, as regards another factor (the real Brahman) it would make known what is *absolutely real*.

The Opponent says:—"As a matter of fact, the mere practical character of the reality of the instrument of knowledge is not a necessary factor in its instrumentality; as we find that this practical reality is not present in the Witness or Cogniser (who is real, absolutely), who yet brings about (and is an instrument of) Ignorance &c., (which are not real)."—This is not so, we reply; because even with regard to that which is absolutely undeniable, we have explained that what is meant by its being 'real' is that it is not capable of being sublated by anything else except the knowledge of
Page 67.
Brahman; and further, in the threefold division of *reality* (into Absolute, Empirical and Apparent), if we define 'Empirical Reality' as that which is *not* '*absolute Reality*', there would be no incongruity in regarding that (practically real thing) as the originator—even though the character of the originator might belong in common to the *practically* as well as the *absolutely real.*

As a matter of fact however, he who brings about Ignorance and the rest is the Witness himself as influenced by Ignorance. And such a Witness would have only a *empirical* reality; because in his pure uninfluenced or absolutely real form he is not the *sādhaka* or accomplisher of anything. Hence it is established that in all cases of instrumentality, what is necessary is that the agency should have only empirical reality. We have already shown under the section on '*Drishyatvahētūpapatti*' how there is no incongruity of the 'vicious circle' involved in the view that it is the Self influenced by Ignorance that is the 'witness.' We shall show this again later on.

Anything that is found to be brought about by an agency that has only *empirical* reality, is itself regarded as having only empirical reality; while when the agency is only *apparent*, the result brought about is also of the same character,—

and not *practically* real. And thus we can have no confusion as to the carrying out of injunctions and prohibitions.

This also sets aside the argument advanced by Uḍayana that—"by turning upside down the ordinary conceptions of men, the discussion becomes an entirely haphazard affair." Because we do not transgress the bounds of ordinary conception, inasmuch as we recognise the *practical* reality of all such things. As for the assertion of the great Bhaṭṭa Āchārya (Kumārila) that appear to be inconsistent with our view, we shall explain in course of our explanation of the three kinds of Reality, that our view is not irreconcileable with it. Thus we find that there is no inconsistency in regarding the 'Subject' and all other factors of Inference as *unreal*.

END OF SECTION (23).

Section (24).

Arguments against the preceding section refuted.

"It certainly appears to be much simpler to admit the "*reality* of the inferential factors than to regard them as "*something different from an absolute non-entity*; and such "being the case how can the demonstrative or proving power "of these factors be held to be dependent upon such charac-"ter?"

This is not right; no simplicity can attach to the postulating of such *reality* as consists in not being sublated at any of the three points of time; and as for that *reality* which consists in the form of Genus (Individuality, &c.), such reality would not be incompatible with *unreality*; and further, *absolutely true Reality* is not a necessary element in the demonstrative capacity of things; as is shown by the fact that such capacity actually belongs to things not quite real; *e. g.* (1) in the case of reflection the image demonstrates the existence of the thing reflected; in which case, even though the thing is real, it is not so in its reflected form; so that *reality* cannot be regarded as necessary for demonstrative capacity;—(2) even though the thing dreamt of is unreal, yet it is indicative (and to that extent, demonstrative) of future good and evil; even though in this case what is indicative of the good and evil is the actual (dream) perception,—as we learn from such Vedic texts as 'when one sees a dark man with black teeth &c.',—yet, as to attribute any indicative power to mere *perception* by itself would be palpably absurd, the perception has to be taken along with the object perceived;—(3) similarly again, the redness of the crystal (which is not real) demonstrates its proximity to a (red) accompaniment. It will not be right to urge that the case of the reflection in the crystal should not be cited as a separate example, in view of the fact the redness in the crystal is not exactly unreal, it is only the reflection of a particular property of the red object [and as such falls under the case of the reflected image";—this contention will not be right; as in the first place no reflection is possible of a mere property, independently of the face and such other objects; and secondly in a case of mere reflection it is found that the reflected image does not extend over the whole of the reflecting medium; so that if the case of the red crystal were one of mere reflection, it would not be possible for us to perceive the redness as pervading over the entire piece of crystal. Thus then, the distinction we draw between the two is that when the character of subsisting in the crystal is imposed upon the redness [*i. e.* when the redness is cognised as subsisting in the crystal], it is a case of mere *reflection*; while when the redness is imposed on the crystal [*i. e.* when the crystal is cognised as being of red colour], it is a case of *unreality* of that redness. It is in accordance with this distinction that the author of the *Pañchapāḍikā*, though upholding the reality of reflections, has shown that (in the case of the red crystal) the redness is *unreal*, by citing (as an instance

of unreality) the case of the redness in the crystal due to the proximity of a red object. (4) Similarly in the case of the written word we find that the thing denoted is indicated by the letters assumed in (and identified with) the form of the written signs (that stand for the letters). It is not right to urge that the thing is indicated by the real letters themselves (and not those that are assumed in the written signs), this letter being brought to the observer's mind by the written signs. For it is a fact known to all men, from the youngest child upwards, that the actual letter is brought to mind simply by reason of the identity that has been assumed (between the real letter and the written sign) in regard to the written signs, with regard to which such notions are commonly current as 'this sign is the letter *ka*', 'this is the letter *ga*', and so on (where there is a clear identity between the two); in fact, even when one becomes cognisant of the difference between the two, the idea of identity has taken such strong hold on his mind that he cannot altogether get rid of it; it is for this reason that we have such universally used
P. 68. expressions as—'he is reading and writing the letter *ka*', [when what is actually written is the written sign]. (5) So also, even though the 'shortness' and 'length' are merely imposed or assumed in regard to letters, yet they are found to be expressive of real things; as we find in the case of such words as '*naga*' and '*nāga*' [where the *lengthening* of the vowel in *na* alters the denotation of the word from the 'mountain' denoted by '*naga*' to the 'serpent' denoted by '*nāga*.'' "But in the case of these letters, what makes them expressive is that length which belongs to *sound* and is not assumed (but real),—or that which pertains to the manifestation of that sound [and hence the expressive power belongs to what is real]; and similarly with *shortness* &c. also." This cannot be maintained; as even when the letter-sound is not actually uttered (and the letter is not actually pronounced), we have such notions as 'this letter is

long' and so on [so that the *length* in this case cannot belong to the *Sound*]. "But how can the *real* thing be indicated by the assumed or fictitious length of the vowel-sound? Certainly, no *real* fire is ever indicated by the assumed or fictitious smoke." This is not right. All that is necessary for anything to be a true indicator is that it should be endowed with the character (capacity) of the true indicator; and it does not matter whether such capacity is *assumed* or *not-assumed*. That the fictitious or assumed smoke does not indicate or prove the real fire is due, not to its unreality, but to the absence, in its case, of that invariable concomitance which is the characteristic of all true indicators of fire; and the realising of the fact that it is not fictitious is necessary only for the purpose of being sure of the said invariable concomitance; just as the perception of its rising upwards (is necessary for the purpose of being sure of its being that with which fire has been seen to be concomitant in the kitchen). This is what has been thus described by Vāchaspaṭi Mishra :—' Even though both are equally real, yet it is *colour*, and not taste, that is cognised by means of the Eye; similarly even though both the length of letter-sounds and the fictitious smoke are unreal, yet the real thing is indicated by the former and not by the latter.'—(6). Similarly instances of the real being produced by the unreal we have in the following cases—real fear is produced by the illusory or assumed elephant, as well as by the rope mistaken as serpent; the perception of a hole in the solar disc is indicative of death; suspected poison leads to actual death.

" But in this last case what actually happens is that the " suspicion arouses and thereby brings about the derangement " of the bodily humours; so that what brings about death is the " suspicion (which is real), and not the suspected poison (which " is unreal); similarly in the case of the illusory elephant and " the hole in the Sun, what is effective in bringing about the real " result is only the *cognition* of those things (which is real),

" and not those things themselves. So also in every case " that has been cited, the result is brought about by *cognition* ; " and in itself Cognition is real. In fact, negative as well as " positive reasonings go to prove that it is Cognition that is " the real cause in all these cases; for instance, even though " the serpent be near the man, yet unless he actually *cognises* " it as snake, he is not afraid. 'But if mere Cognition by " itself, independently of its object, were held to be the cause of " fear, such a principle would have very undesirable appli- " cations (for in that case "very cognition could be the case " of any effect) ; so that in order to avoid this contingency, " the causal efficiency should be attributed to the Cognition " as qualified by its object; and in this way causal effic- " iency would belong to the *Object* also.' This is not right ; " as even though causal efficiency might belong to the cog- " nition as qualified by the object, yet in the bringing about " of the effect, the qualifying object would remain indiffer- " ent (inoperative), and as such devoid of real causal effic- " iency ; as for example—(*a*) even though the absolute nega- " tion and the destruction of the jar, as qualified by " the jar, occupy points in space and time different from " those occupied by the Jar, yet the jar itself does not " occupy that different space and time ;—(*b*) the desire for " the jar arises from the cognition of the Jar, and the " knowledge of Brahman arises from the Vedānta texts ; " and yet the jar itself does not arise from its own cognition, " nor does Brahman arise from the Vedānta texts ;—(*c*) even " though the prior negation of the jar is productive of the " jar, the jar itself is not so ;—(*d*) though the non-percep- " tion of distinctive features is the cause of the mistaken " cognition of a thing, the perception of those features is " not so ,—(*e*) even though the non-performance of the en- " joined act is productive of sin, the performance of the " enjoined act is not so ;—(*f*) even though the desire for " heaven is productive of the sacrificial performance, the

" heaven itself is not so;—(*g*) though the remembrance " of the past gives rise to pain, the past does not do so;— " (*h*) though the indirect cognition of the non-existent thing " gives rise to activity with regard to it, the non-existent " thing does not do so;—(*i*) though the cognition of the " jar to be built is the cause of the jar, the jar itself is not " so;—(j) though the knowledge of Brahman is destructive " of the ignorance of Brahman, Brahman itself, being abso- " lutely impartial in its character, is not so;—(*j*) even though " the ignorance of Brahman is the modificatory cause of the " world, Brahman itself is not so; [in all these cases, even " though a thing qualified by another thing has a certain " causal efficiency, the qualifying thing is devoid of that " efficiency]. 'With all this however, inasmuch as the " unreal thing has the capacity of distinguishing cognitions, " it must be regarded as having some sort of causal efficiency.'

P. 69. " Not so; for what is meant by a thing distinguish- " ing (a cognition) is, not that it is the *cause* of the " distinctive cognition of that, but, that it is the object of the " cognition of (and is recognised as) the cause of the distinctive " cognition; for instance, even when the stick is present, there " is no cognition of the distinguishing of the cognition of " that stick. 'But if the distinguishing thing is unreal, that " which is distinguished by it must also be unreal.' Cer- " tainly not,—(*a*) inasmuch as we do not perceive the " character of the absolute non-entity in either the 'cogni- " tion of the absolute non-entity' or the difference from ab- " absolute non-entity, (*b*)—as we do not perceive the 'appar- " ent reality' of the 'difference from apparent reality' " —(*c*) as we do not perceive the fourth kind of " 'inexplicability' in the cessation of the 'inexplicable " ignorance' in regard to that fifth kind of reality which " constitutes the essence of Brahman,—as we do not " perceive 'falsity' in the 'negation of the false Duality' " in regard either to the real essence of the Self or to

" that which is different from it,—it follows that the " notions are entirely indifferent as to 'Unreality' and " the rest; so also in the case in question (even though " the qualifying factor may be unreal, the qualified thing " need not be so)."

To the above the following reply is made:—[A] Firstly—It has been asserted above that in every case the qualifying factor, in so far as it is a purely adventitious adjunct, is wholly indifferent and unaffected (by anything that may be predicated of the *qualified* thing). But this is not right; as so long as the qualifying factor can be taken as an essential attribute, there can be no justification for its being regarded as a mere adventitious adjunct; the law being that before a character can be regarded as an adventitious adjunct, some reason has to be found for its not being regarded as an essential attribute. If it were not so, then, in the case of such Vedic passages as 'the priest with the stick recites the the *Praiṣa* mantras', 'the red-turbaned priests move along' and the like, the *stick* and the *red-turban* might be regarded as mere adventitious adjuncts, and (in that case) the sacrificial performances could be carried on even in the absence of these (the performance not being adversely affected by the absence of what is merely an adventitious adjunct) [and this is absurd]; similarly in Pāṇini's Sūṭra '*sarvādīni sarvanāmāni*', '*sarva* and other like words are Pronouns',—the word '*sarva*' itself might cease to be regarded as a Pronoun [as it might be taken as a mere adventitious adjunct of what is denoted by the compound '*sarvādīni*.];—so also in the Vedānta-sūṭra *Janmādyasya yataḥ*', 'that from which is the birth &c., of this world',—the *birth* might cease to be regarded as proceeding from Brahman [as it would be taken as an adventitious adjunct of what is denoted by the compound '*janmādī*, and hence, *ex-hypothesi*, not affected by anything that is predicated of this compound];—[there is this other advantage in the factor under dispute being regarded as an essential attribute] if we take it as an essential element, the compound may be taken as a Bahuvrihi of that type which includes the stated qualification; on the other hand, if it be taken as an adventitious adjunct, it could not form an essential element in what is denoted by the compound, which therefore will have to be regarded as a *Bahuvrīhi* of that type in which the stated qualification is excluded; and this would be highly undesirable; similarly in the case of such ordinary assertions as 'bring in the men with swords in their hands' and the like. (B)—*Secondly*—when causal efficiency (productiveness) can belong to the cognitions of the reflected image and such other things, there can be no objection to the same efficiency belonging to the things also, these latter being regarded as the essential attributes of these cognitions; so that there can be no justification for the view that these are only adventitious adjuncts. In the examples that we have cited, on the other hand, there are objections against such procedure. Herein lies the difference between the two sets of cases. For instance, (*a*) in the first example cited by us, it is only after the place and time of the jar has been apprehended that we can apprehend the fact that the absolute negation of that jar occupies a different time and place; for if the jar itself also were connected with this latter time and place, this would be a direct contradiction of the acknowledged fact that the place and time occupied by a thing are different from those occupied by its negation;—(*b*) in the second example, so far as the case of the jar is concerned, the contingency in question would not be altogether impossible, as in certain cases the jar-cognition does become the cause of the *jar* also, just as it is of the *desire* for the jar; but in the case of Brahman, if Brahman itsef were something brought about by the Vedānta texts, then this would be incompatible with its eternality;—(*c*) in the third example, if the jar were its own cause, in the same way as its prior negation is its cause,—there would arise the absurd contingency of the *prior negation of the jar* and the counter-entity of this negation (*i. e.*, the jar itself) occupying the same point of time; and further, inasmuch as in the very nature of causes, the cause of the jar must belong to a point of time anterior *to* the Jar itself, if the Jar were regarded as its own cause, this would involve the absurdity of the thing (jar) being anterior to itself;—(*d*) and (*e*) if the counter-entity and its negation co-existed, there would be no possibility of the appearance of wrong cognition and sin [*i. e.*, if the *perception* of destructive features co-existed along with the non-perception of those features, no wrong cognition would be possible];—(*f*) if the object of desire were productive of the sacrifice, it would mean that it exists already *before* the sacrifice is performed; so that there would be no possibility of any further *desire* for that object; for there can be no desire for bringing about that which is already in existence;—(*g*) if the something that has passed away were held to be productive (of pain &c.), we would have the absurdity of each product having for its immediate antecedent (not its cause) one of its own several past operations;—(*h*) if a non-entity were productive, it could not be held to be without form;—(*i*) if, like the cognition of the jar, the jar itself were the cause,—this would involve the aforesaid absurdity (that the jar, *as the cause*, would exist at the time that the jar, *as the product*, is non-existent);—(*j*) it is not possible for the *indifferent* Brahman by Itself to be destructive of ignorance; because that which forms the object of the (cognitive) Vṛitti ° is the *conditioned* Brahman; so that the pure Brahman by itself, not being the *object*, cannot serve as the destroyer of that ignorance; and as for the *conditioned* Brahman, this is certainly destructive (of Ignorance);—(*k*) even though the Ignorance of Brahman is the modificatory (or evolvent) cause, yet Brahman Itself

° Both editions read घद्दादृष्टया; but the sense requires स्वदृष्टता।

cannot be regarded as the cause of the world, for the simple reason that in the world we find *jadatva*, 'unconscious character', (which is not compatible with Brahman, which is pure Consciousness).

Thus then, it is clear that we must accept the particular thing to be an adventitious adjunct, because of these reasonings against any contrary idea. In regard to the case in question [i. e. the case of the reflected thing and its image] however, there is no such reasoning available; specially as such characters as that of being present at the immediately preceding time and place, and the like, belong also to such things as have mere apparent reality; e. g., in regard to the rope mistaken as snake, we have such notions as 'this snake is *here at the present* moment.' And certainly simply because in some cases the principal alternative has been renounced in view of the reasonings to the contrary, it would not be right to renounce it in each and every case. And there is a further reason:—The excellence, &c, of the product is in accordance with the excellence, &c., of the cause as pointed out by us. For instance, during the waking and as well as during the dreaming state, the perception of excellent gold produces excellent pleasure; the perception of the superior snake produces a superior degree of fear; and if the object (gold or snake) were not the *cause* of the effects concerned, the excellence, etc., of the latter would not necessarily follow those of the former; as there is the law that "the product does not follow the excellence of what is not its cause."* It will not be right to attribute the said excellence to the excellence of the *cognition*; for even in the cognition there can be no other excellence save that pertaining to its object. It might be held that the peculiar *jāti*, or class-character, to

* The Kumb. Edition reads पै... ., which gives better sense than पंमकार्यं... the reading of the litho. Edition, though the latter also can be made to yield the same sense.

which the cognition belongs would constitute its *excellence*. But this would not be right; as the postulating of such a class-character would constitute a 'cross-division' with such class-characters as 'visual' and the like;* and further, when the excellence of the effect can be accounted for on the basis of the excellence of the object, it would be a needless multiplication of assumptions to posit several sub-classes under the general heads of 'visual' and the rest; specially as there is no proof for the existence of such sub-classes. Then again, cognition being the cause of such effects as fear and the like, it must be the *object* of the cognition that determines its particular causal efficiency; otherwise if the cognition by itself were to be productive of the said effects, this would give rise to absurd contingencies [such for instance, as every cognition of any thing whatsoever, being productive of fear]

[To return to our main theme], it is found that the Cognition is actually unreal or false, when it is characterised by (related to) an Unreal Object; so that, when, in the case of a wrong Cognition, the Cognition by itself is found to have the causal efficiency, the fact remains that the causal efficiency belongs to something that is unreal; and thus when the Cognition has been found to be unreal in that form in which it is endowed with the causal efficiency,—even if it be *real* in some other form, that *reality* would be no better than *unreality*; for the simple reason that it would be absolutely futile.† This is what has been thus described by the author

* Class-characters should, by their very nature, be mutually exclusive; otherwise they lead to 'Cross-division'. *E.g.*, In the case in question, there are several cognitions which are both 'Visual' and 'Excellent', while some are only 'visual' without being 'excellent,' and others again are 'Excellent' without being 'visual'. This constitutes a 'Cross-division', a *Saṅkara*, which is one of the impediments to the postulating of a *class*.

† The reality of the thing is fruitful only when it brings about effective action; and as this can be brought about only when the thing has causal efficiency, if the Cognition is unreal, in so far as its that efficiency is concerned, what use would there be of its reality in any other form?

of the *Khaṇḍanakhaṇḍakhādya*—'The reality at some other time would be like the waking up of the guardsman after the house had been entirely robbed by thieves.'

Then also, as regards Wrong Cognition, it is, by its very nature also, unreal, for if in its own form it were (real and hence) not sublatable,—then, it might be impossible for it to be sublated even in reference to its Object (which would be absurd). "But in the reasoning 'if the wrong cognition were not sublatable by itself then it would not be sublatable in regard to its object also', you have a vitiating adjunct in the shape of the character of 'being produced by excellences', which vitiates your general proposition [in the form 'all that is unsublatable by itself is also unsublatable in regard to its object]'; for we find that the character of *being produced by excellences* is one which is concomitant with the character of *being sublatable in regard to the object*, and yet it is not equally concomitant with the character of *being unsublatable by itself*." This is not right; as the character that you have put forward as the vitiating adjunct is one that *is* concomitant with the middle term of our reasoning (*viz.*, unsublatability in regard to the object),—inasmuch as this character also is one that is inevitable, and hence one to be borne in mind, resembling in this aspect, *accessories of fire* in the case of the inference of fire;—and further, what indicates the unreality of the *object* is the fact of the accessory causes being tainted with such defects as tend to make the object unreal; and these would be equally effective in making the corresponding Cognition also unreal.

In the case of the *cognition of the nonentity* or its opposite, the non-perception of the character of *being a non-entity* does not necessarily sublate that cognition; for the simple reason that it is not admitted (by us) that in all cases there should be perfect similarity between the *differentiator* and the *differentiated*. In the case in question, on the other hand, there is such a similarity between the differentiator and the differentiated, inasmuch as both are endowed with a form conducive to unreality. We have made the assertion on the supposition that '*Kāraṇatva*' is a single character subsisting in common in all (causes). In reality however there is no such single character as '*Kāraṇatva*' subsisting in all such causes as the *stick*, the *yarn* and the like. For instance, you hold the differentiator (for all causes) to be *reality*, while we hold it to be *the character of being other than an absolute non-entity*; in fact however what actually differentiates the Cause is the character of 'stick', 'yarn' and the like, just as the effect is differentiated by such characters as those of the 'jar', the 'cloth' and the like;—and as these characters must be diverse, the characters of the 'Cause' must also be diverse. Just as, for instance, the 'similarity' between the cow and the Gavaya is different from the 'similarity' between the Brother and the Sister; as in this case the differentiator is not one, but diverse, in the shape of 'gavaya' and 'sister'; so also in the case of the Cause, what serves as the differentiator is the 'stick', 'yarn', &c., irrespectively of 'Reality' or 'Unreality'. So that whether a thing is 'real' or 'unreal' cannot be determined by the fact of its being *productive* (cause) or *unproductive* (not-cause). This is what has been thus described by the author of the *Khaṇḍana-khaṇḍakhādya*.—'Inasmuch as both of us are agreed as to previous relation being the necessary element in a *Cause*, any discussion as to its being real or unreal is absolutely futile';—and again, 'If reality enters into the Cause as a necessary factor, the Cause is on that account, unreal; and if reality does not enter into it, then also, on that same account, the Cause is unreal'. "But exactly the same might be urged against your view also: 'If reality enters to the substratum as a necessary factor, the substratum is on

° A 'na' is necessary, as read in the litho. Edition.

that account, unreal; and if reality does not enter
P. 71. into it, then also, on that account, the substratum is unreal'." This could not be rightly urged against us; as for us the substratum is real in its own essential form (and *reality* does not enter into it as an adventitious adjunct), while you regard *reality* to be something entirely different from the *Cause*; and this constitutes a great difference in our standpoints.

The Opponent raises a fresh question—"The object can-"not be regarded as the determinant or differentiator of the "productive or causal character of the Cognition; there is "no proof for its being so. Nor will the fact of the object "not being the said determinant lead to any undesirable "contingencies; as the fact of the *cognition of the snake* "being different from the *cognition of the not-snake* "is known irrespectively of the fact of the cognition "being determined by these objects; that is to say, the "difference between the said two cognitions is dependent "upon what distinguishes them; and certainly neither the "Object nor the relationship of the Object is what distin-"guishes them; as apart from their own forms there is no "such relationship as subsists in both the Cognitions; and "that which is not a relationship cannot serve as a distinguish-"ing feature. It might be urged that there would be such a "relationship either in the form a certain character belonging "to all Cognitions, or in that of the form of the Cognition "itself,—either of which, even in the absence of any other "relationship, would be capable of accomplishing all that "is necessary (in connection with the cognitions). But "this would mean that all the specific details of usage in "connection with the Cognition is accomplished, either "through the Cognition itself, or through some character "belonging to it,—entirely independently of the *Object*! Fur-"ther, we have the following inferential reasoning in support "of our contention:—The *cognition of the snake* must be "regarded as different from the *cognition of the non-snake*, "irrespectively of the fact of the two being related to "different objects,—(a) because the former is produced by a "cause different from the cause of the latter,—just as the "sprout of the *Kalama* corn is different from the sprout of "the *Yava* corn;—or (b) because the former produces effects "different from the effects of the latter,—just as the seed "of the *Kalama* corn is different from the seed of the "*Yava* corn'. It might be argued that what is put forward "as the Probans in this inferential reasoning can be explained "on the basis of the fact of the Cognitions being related to "different objects; and as such they would be futile in "proving the conclusion that is sought to be deduced from "them. But if this were true, then, in the case of the "*Kalama* and *Yava* corn also, even though the sprout and "seed of the former have causes and effects entirely different "from those of the latter, yet the difference between the "two would be reasonably based upon their *adventitious* con-"nection with something—the person, Chaitra for instance,—"regardless of any such difference of *Kalama* seed and sprout "from the *Yava* seed and sprout as consists in its own "*esssential* form! And Direct or Immediate Perception also "could be regarded as different from Indirect or Mediate "Cognition, simply on the basis of its relationship to some-"thing else! Thus then—(1) just as the 'negation of the "jar' is different from other negations irrespectively of the "counter-entity (jar),—(2) as the 'removal of stone' is a "different act from the 'removal of *māṣa* grains', irrespec-"tively of the object removed,—(3) as the 'cognition of the "past' and the 'mediate indirect cognition and usage in "regard to a non-entity' are different from other cognitions "etc., as otherwise there would be an admixture of their "effects,—so the 'cognition of the snake' also is different "from the 'cognition of the not-snake', either by itself, or

" by reason of its being the 'cognition of snake' brought " about by the causes of 'snake-cognition',—even though, " when it appears in regard to the *Rope* there are more " causes operative towards it (than those operative towards " the *snake-cognition* when appearing in regard to the real " snake). Thus then, there can be no objection to the view " expressed by us. Nor will it be right to assert that " the *counter-entity* also is a determinant of the *negation*; " because—(1) at the time that the negation in the shape of " *Destruction* is present, its counter-entity is non-existent; " (2) at the time that the action (of production) is going " on, its object is non-existent; and (3) when we have a cognition of a past (or future object), the object is non-existent."

The above view is not right. As a matter of fact, what distinguishes all *snake-cognitions* from *non-snake-cognitions* is, not the particular forms of the cognitions themselves; for the simple reason that there can be no such *form* as is common to all cognitions (of the snake); what serves as the differentiator must be some such property as is common to all. This property cannot be in the form of a *jati*, a *class-character*, pervading over every *snake-cognition*; for such a class-character would form a 'cross-division' with such class-characters as 'Perception', 'Inference' and the like [as 'snake-cognitions' may be both *Perception and Inference*]. That differentiator must be in the shape of an *Upāḍhi*, an adventitious adjunct. And this adventitious adjunct can be none other than the object which is related (to the Cognition) either by *Svarūpasambandha* (a natural relationship) or by the relation of 'imposition' (surmise, *adhyāsa*);—there being no proof of any other *Upāḍhi*.

On these same grounds we should regard as rejected that inferential argument* whereby it has been sought to be

* That the 'snake-cognition differs from 'non-snake cognition' irrespectively of its connection with a different object—because it is brought about by a set of causes different from those bringing about the latter, etc. etc.' Kumbakonam Text, P. 71, ll. 9-10.

proved that one cognition is different from another cognition irrespectively of their being connected with two different objects. Specially as such an Inference would be *too wide*. For instance, the 'jar-contact' differs from the 'cloth-contact', *not* through a class-character—as one is not the substratum of a class-character not subsisting in the other (both being 'contact'),—but it differs from it through its adventitious adjunct in the shape of the *jar*; so that here we have a case which shows that all 'cloth-contact' differs from the 'jar-contact', and that *entirely through its connection with a different object*; so that this is a case contrary to that which you seek to prove [*i. e.* by your Inference you seek to prove *difference irrespectively of the connection of another object*, while this is a case of *difference depending entirely upon the connection of another object*]; and yet what you have put forward as your probans—viz., the fact of being brought about by a different set of causes—is found to be present in the case cited [the 'cloth-contact' being brought about by causes entirely different from those by which the 'jar-contact' is brought about]; and thus your reason becomes too wide [being found applicable to what you seek to prove as also to its contrary]; and on the same grounds the said reasoning is *futile* also [failing to prove what it is sought to prove]. It might be argued that in this manner, the *kalama-sprout* may be regarded as different from other sprouts through even such accidental circumstances as its being connected with a particular sower in the person of Chaitra [while the other seed may have been sown by another person]. But even such a contingency will not be undesirable for us; specially

P. 72. as it would serve to set aside propositions contrary to our conclusion. Further, even in a case where differentiation is done by a *class-character*, the *adventitious adjunct* does not necessarily cease to be the differentiator; for instance, even though the *action of stone-picking* is differentiated from the *action of grain-picking* by its class-character (the *kind of 'action'* involved in the former being different from that involved in the latter),—yet there would be nothing incongruous if we regarded them as differentiated through their adventitious adjunct in the shape of the *object* (stone and grain) also. Inasmuch as *stone-picking* is accomplished by means of an Action that is characterised by a certain class-character,—if the action of *grain-picking*, which is not characterised by the same character, is not accomplished by the former action, there can be nothing incongruous in this. Then again, as differentiation can be done by other means also, even in cases where a class-character is postulated, it is done with a view to provide an explanation of such relations as that of cause and effect (that subsists between a class-character and any particular cognition). And in the case of cognition and usage in regard to *past* and *non-existent* objects we find that the necessary differentiation is done by the past and the non-existent objects themselves; and [as for these being not present at the time of the differentiation] the act of *differentiating* does not consist in *being the cause of the notion of difference*; and it is only if this were so that the *past* and *non-existent* objects could not be accepted as 'differentiators', on the ground that having *no existence* at the time, they would not have that *prior existence* or *antecedence* (which constitutes a necessary factor in the 'cause');—in fact, we have already pointed out that what is meant by anything being a *differentiator* is that it forms the object of the conception that people have in regard to the cause of the *differentiation* [*i. e.* when a certain thing is *conceived of* as being the cause of the differentiation, it comes to be known as the 'differentiator'; so that it is not necessary that it should actually *be* an active cause *at the time* that it is conceived of as such];—and certainly this condition can be easily fulfilled by *past* objects. This same reasoning also serves to set aside the example of Negation, etc., that the Opponent has brought forward; as the said condition of differentiation may be available in the case of an absolute non-entity also; and if it happens, in some cases, to be available in the case of really existing things also, we shall accept it in accordance with the maxim of '*Kimuṭa*'. [That is, when the condition is accepted as fulfilled even by non-entities, it is all the more acceptable in the case of real entities; *lit.* 'what then should be said in regard to entities?'].

" Even if we accept the Object to be the differentiator, " as it cannot be the (inseparable) *attribute* in all cases, it has " to be regarded as a mere *accident* (an accidental mark), and " all that an *accident* can do is to point to a certain charac- " ter (or attribute) of the object qualified,—this character " being different from the relationship of the object to that " Accident itself; for instance, when a house is indicated by " means of an accidental mark in the shape of the presence " of *crows*,—the house being indicated as 'the house on " which a number of crows are sitting'—all that the " '*crows*' (which are the *Accidents* in this case) do is to " point to the particular *location* of the house. Such being " the case, it is this latter *attribute* (*e. g.*, location) which " should be regarded as the *differentiator* [and not the " adventitious connection of an Accident]; so that in the " case of Cognitions also, their differentiation should be " regarded as being accomplished by means of a certain " attribute in the cognitions themselves, irrespectively of " their relationship to a certain *object*."

This reasoning is not right; as we do not admit that the *object* of the Cognition is its (adventitious) *Accident*, just as we do not admit that it is its (inseparable) *Attribute*. For as a matter of fact, when in regard to a certain object, the idea of its being different from other things is brought about by a certain character through the reflection that it casts upon (*i.e*, through its connection with) the said object,—this character is called its 'attribute'; by which it is meant that that character casts its reflection upon the object at the time that it is differentiated from other things;—as examples of such 'attribute' we have the class-character of 'cow', '*goṭva*'. On the other hand, when the idea of the Object being different from other things is brought about by a character (not by itself directly, but) through the indicating of a distinguishing property of the Object,—and the connection of the character itself is put aside (as not being of much consequence)—such a character comes to be called the 'accident' of that object; an example of this we have in the shape of the *crows* (seated on a house and serving for the time being to mark the *location* of the house, which distinguishes it from other houses);—but that which neither casts its reflection on the object, nor indicates another property of it,—and yet serves to differentiate it,—such a character is called its 'adventitious adjunct', '*upāḍhi*'; *e. g.* when the word '*pañkaja*' ('clay-born') is used, the character of the 'lotus' (which is one of several *clay-born* things), is its 'adventitious adjunct'; or when the word '*udbhiḍ*' (lit. 'Digging thing') is used, the character of a particular sub-class (named '*Uḍbhiḍ*') of the larger class of 'Sacrifice', forms the 'adventitious adjunct'. In these two cases we find that the two—(1) the class-character of 'lotus' and particular sub-class of the Class 'Sacrifice'—do not point to any other character of 'what is clay-born' or 'what digs up the result', respectively; for the simple reason that we have no idea of any such other character;—nor do they bring about a conception on which they themselves cast their reflection; for the simple reason that we do not admit of any conventional denotative potency in the whole words ('pañkaja', 'clay-born' and 'Uḍbhiḍ', 'Digging thing'), apart from that belonging to their component particles ;—with all this however, the class-character of the 'lotus' does serve to distinguish the *Pañkaja* from the Lily and such other *clay-born* things, and the particular sub-class of the wider class 'Sacrifice' does serve to distinguish the 'Udbhiḍ' from the Jyotiṣtoma and other sacrifices leading to results ;—and as such these two come to be regarded as '*Upāḍhi*', 'adventitious adjunct.' Both these examples that we have cited are such as are accepted by the two schools of Mīmāmsakas—the *Prābhākaras* as well as *Bhāttas*. As an example of '*Upāḍhi*' from the stand-point of the Naiyāyika we have the character of *being the receptacle of Sound*, as applying to cases where the word '*Ākāsha*' is used. It is in view of this explanation of the term '*Upāḍhi*' that *Nescience* and the rest are regarded by the Vēḍanṭin to be an '*Upāḍhi*' of the 'Witnessing Consciousness.' From all this we conclude that in a case where the object cannot serve as the *Attribute*—on the ground that it is not present at the time (that the Cognition appears),—if we regard it is an '*Upāḍhi*', an *adventitious adjunct*, there can be no room for those objections that refer to the case of its being regarded as an *Attribute*. In a case where there is doubt, whether it should be regarded as an *Attribute* or an *Adventitious Adjunct* (both being found possible), the thing is, by preference, regarded as an *Attribute*. Thus then, our final conclusion is that in the case of all *Cognitions*, it is the *object* that serves as the *differentiator*.

Against this conclusion the following objection may be raised—" As between the *direct cognition* and *remembrance* of one and the same object, we find that differentiation is done by their respective class-characters (of '*anubhava*' and '*smriti*' respectively), irrespectively of the fact of the *object* of one being present and that of the other absent ; and in view of this, it would be just as well to regard the *class-*

character as the real differentiator in all cognitions, irrespectively of the object."

It will not be right to argue thus ; as such a differentiator would not be available as between two such cognitions as are of the same *kind* (*e. g.*, when both are 'perceptions') and yet have totally different objects.

" But in this case also there would be differentiating class-characters available, like the *sweetness of milk* [which distinguishes one kind of sweetness from all other kinds ; so that the 'perception of the jar' would be of a different class or kind from the 'perception of the cloth.']".

The assumption of such class-characters would give rise to a 'cross-division' with such classes as 'visual', and the like, as we have already pointed out.

The Opponent takes up a view line of argument—" According to your Vedanta view, every cognition represents the reflection of Consciousness in the organic functioning (*Vṛiṭṭi*), which latter undergoes modification into diverse shapes ; so that in this view, every cognition is manifested in such distinct reflections. Similarly according to our view every individual cognition is conceived of as having a particular character of its own, which renders it capable of bringing about the said conception. So that under both these theories every cognition stands self-distinguished [and there is no room for an external differentiator.]"

Page 73.

This is not right : as in reality what imparts the shape to the *Vṛiṭṭi* is the *object* itself (in our view),—and (in your view) what serves to mark out the distinctive character of a cognition is the *object* itself ; so that in either case it is not possible to say that the differentiation (of cognitions) is independent of the *object*. And [as to whether the object is an *attribute*, or an *accident*, or an *adventitious adjunct*] we have already explained that so long as it can be regarded as an *attribute* or an *adventitious adjunct*, it cannot be regarded as an *accident*.

"But the Vedic text—'how can entity proceed from the non-entity?'—the Vedanta sūtra '*nāsatodriṣatvāt*'—and the Bhāṣya passage 'because no entity is found to be produced from such absolute non-entities as the *hare's horn*'—would be contradicted by what you have asserted [as you have asserted that the non-existent (past) object can be the cause of Cognition, while the authorities cited deny that any such causal efficiency can belong to non-existent things]."

Not so, we reply. For what these authorities deny is the causal efficiency of the *absolute non-entity*; and we have never asserted that any such efficiency belongs to *absolute non-entities* [certainly what is non-existent now, and which existed in the past, is not an *absolute non-entity*].

Thus then it is shown that the character of being *different from the existent* is a proof (*of unreality*).

END OF SECTION (24).

Section (25).

[There is no real relationship between *Cognition* and *Cognised*. Their relation can be no other than that of *Adhyāsa*, Imposition].

A fresh objection is raised—"The inferential arguments brought forward in support of unreality are absolutely futile; for the *cognisability*, *ḍrishyaṭva*, of things is possible also on the basis of *reality*."

This is not possible, we reply; as no relation of 'cognition and cognised' would be possible in the case. As a matter of fact, a Cognition cannot illumine (*i.e.*, render cognisable) the cognised object, without being, in some way or other, related to it; as if it did so, then any Cognition might illumine any object;—nor on the other hand, can it illumine the object, by being related to it; for Cognition being either the very essence of the Self, or a quality of it, it is not possible for it to bear to its object the relation either of Conjunction or of Inherence; and there can be no other relation except that which may be *imposed* or *wrongly surmised* (*aḍhyasṭa*). Nor is the relation of 'subject and object' possible between Cognition and its Object; firstly because the character of the 'subject' belonging to only one (*i.e.*, Cognition), and that of the 'object' also belonging to only one (*i.e.* the Object),—there can be no such relation as that of 'subject and object'; as every relation, as such, should subsist in both the members related;—and *secondly*, the exact notion of this relation cannot be determined. For, what is it that constitutes the 'character of the Object'? (*a*) Is it the fact that it is the receptacle of the result brought about by the Cognition? or (*b*) that the ideas of acquiring or abandoning, produced by the Cognition, pertain to it? or (*c*) that it forms the objective of the Cognition? or (*d*) that it imparts a shape to the Cognition? or (*e*) that it is perceived (or cognised) as such? or (*f*) that it is amenable to the activities resulting from the Cognition? or (*g*) that its cognition is brought about by its contact with the instrument of Cognition? or (*h*) that it appears in that particular cognition, and that which appears (is manifested) in a Cognition is the object of that Cognition? or (*i*) that it serves to distinguish the Cognition, without any other relationship to it?

(*a*) As regards the *first* of these *nine* alternatives, [*i.e.* the view that the *object* of a Cognition is the receptacle of the result brought about by that cognition],—it is not possible for the said *result* to be in the form of 'being known,' because in the first place we do not admit of any such character of 'being known'; and secondly such a character could not subsist in past and future things [and yet such things also are 'objects' of Cognition];—nor can *abandoning*, &c. &c., be regarded as the *result* (of Cognition), as nothing like it is possible in the case of *Ākāsha* and such things [and yet these also are 'objects' of cognition]; and secondly, under this definition the dirt attaching to a piece of gold (which also is picked up or abandoned along with the gold-piece) would have to be regarded as the 'object' of the Cognition, the Gold;—nor again can 'recognition' and 'description' be regarded as the said *result* (of Cognition), as these do not belong to the *cognised thing*; it might be argued that these two (Recognition and Description) belong to the cognised thing in this sense that this thing is the object of those two; but it would not be right to put it thus, as what we are considering is what the exact character of the 'object' is [and yet you are introducing this very term in your explanation].

(*b*) For the same reasons the second alternative also cannot be accepted [*viz.* the 'object' of Cognition is that to which pertain the ideas of abandoning and acquiring, produced by the Cognition].

(*c*) The third alternative also cannot be accepted [*viz.*, that the 'object' of a Cognition is that which forms the objective of that Cognition]; as the cognition of God and the cognitions of thing past and future are such as are not the product of (acted upon by) any *operative agency or 'Kāraka'* (such as the *Objective* is, along with the Instrument, the Dative and the rest) [God's cognition cannot be the product of anything, as it has no beginning in time; and past and future things being absent at the time, could not act upon any present cognition]; so that both these sets of cognitions would have to be regarded as *without objects.*

(*d*) Nor again is the fourth alternative tenable [*viz.*, that the 'object' of cognition imparts a shape to the cognition]; for inasmuch as there is complete non-difference between the Cognition and its shape, everything that helps in the bringing about of the Cognition would have to be regarded as its 'object'; and further, under this alternative, there would be no 'object' possible for *inferential* and other (non-direct) cognitions [as in the case of these, the object is not present to impart its shape].

(*e*) Nor can the fifth alternative be maintained; [*viz.*, that the 'object' of the Cognition is cognised (or perceived) as such]; for the character of 'being cognised' includes or presupposes that of *being the 'object'*; and hence the explanation involves a 'vicious circle.'

(*f*) Nor can the sixth alternative be accepted [*viz.*, that the object is that which is amenable to activities resulting from the Cognition]; because it is not right to postulate the 'amenability' (or 'capability') and then to attribute to that a further 'amenability, [*i.e.*, 'being an object' is itself an 'amenability' to cognition, and it is not right to assign to it the further 'amenability,' that to activities proceeding from the cognition]. "But 'amenability' itself can be 'amenable' without further 'amenability' being assigned to it, just as 'visibility' or 'cognisability' is 'cognisable' without another 'cognisability' being attributed to it." But so long as the exact nature of the 'distinguishing characteristic (of the 'object') has not been ascertained, there can be no Apprehension of any 'amenability' (belonging to it); and it will not be right to regard the character of 'being the object of cognition' as that 'distinguishing characteristic'; as this would involve a 'vicious circle.'

(*g*) The seventh alternative also cannot be maintained [*viz.*, that the 'object' is that whose cognition is brought about by its contact with the instrument of cognition]; for under this view God's cognition, which is eternal, would become *objectless* [as it is not possible for any *object* to be eternal, like God's cognition].

(*h*) Nor again is the eighth alternative admissible [*viz.*, that the 'object' is that which appears in the Cognition]; as in the term 'in the cognition,' '*samvidi*,' the Locative ending cannot have the sense of the 'container,' the 'receptacle'; because the Cognition can never be the *receptacle* of the cognised thing; nor can the Locative have the sense of 'object,' as in the first place it is the exact nature of the 'object' itself that forms the subject-matter of the present enquiry; and secondly, this explanation would make the Cognition the 'object' and the cognised thing the 'subject,' and thus the wellknown relation of 'subject and object' between the two would be reversed! Nor thirdly can the Locative be construed as being absolutive ('*samvidi*' being taken as a Locative absolute); for even so, inasmuch as the 'appearing in the cognition' implies or presupposes the character of 'being the object,' this interpretation would involve a 'vicious circle.'

Page 74.

(*i*) Nor lastly can the ninth alternative be maintained [*viz.*, that the 'object' is that which serves to distinguish the Cognition without any other relationship to it]; because in a case where a person has the idea that 'colour-cognition subsists in me,' this *subsistence* or *inherence, of colour-cognition* serves to distinguish the colour-cognition without any other relationship; so that under the ninth definition of 'object,' that *subsistence* should be the 'object' also of the Cognition in the form 'this is colour'!

[The Opponent offers another explanation of the character of the 'Object']—"The relationship between the Cognition "and its Object is 'based upon the assertion, by the learned, "that 'this is the object of that cognition'; just as the only "definition provided (by Jaimini 1-4) of *Mantra* is that it "is that to which the learned give the name 'Mantra.' Nor "will this involve a 'vicious circle'; as every use of the "term 'object' would depend upon a preceding assertion of "the learned [and thus there would be no mutual interdepen-"dence, the assertion of the learned not depending upon that "particular use which follows, and is based upon, it"].

This explanation also is not satisfactory. As this may suffice to show that the thing is 'cognisable' in general; it would not show that it is the 'object' of any particular cognition. Further, when the declaration of the relationship (between the Cognition and its Object) has a beginning in time, it cannot be held that one declaration is based upon a preceding declaration; as such continuous attributing to a foregoing factor is possible only in the case of a beginning-less series [for in a case where there is a beginning, similar attributing would not be possible for the first of the series]. Again, inasmuch as the said declaration also will be related to its 'object,' the explanation suggested would also involve a 'vicious circle.'

Another explanation is suggested by the Opponent—"When a Cognition happens to be the cause or basis of that "usage which consists in a certain thing being spoken of, "that thing is the 'object' of that Cognition. It may some-"times so happen that the instruments and agencies con-"cerned being defective, the usage does not actually appear "but even so, the Cognition concerned will be regarded as

"the 'cause' of that usage—fulfilling, as it does, that condi-
"tion of causal efficiency in which the non-appearance of the
"due effect is accounted for as being due to the absence of
"the necessary auxiliaries (in the shape of *efficient instru-
"ments* and so forth). It might be argued that under this
"definition of the 'object,' every *non-determinate* cognition
"will have to be regarded as being *without an object.* But that
"will not concern us, as we do not admit of any such cogni-
"tion. Another objection that might be urged against our
"definition of the 'object' is that, inasmuch as as it intro-
"duces the specific terms 'that' and 'which' (which restrict
"it to the case of individual particular cognitions), it cannot
"serve as a comprehensive definition. This objection also
"would be pointless; inasmuch as the definition has been
"put forward in answer to a similarly worded and non-com-
"prehensive question, in the form 'what is the object of
"which *cognition*?' [and the only correct of this answer will
"be '*that* thing is the *object* of that *Cognition which*, &c. &c.,
"exactly as we have put it]. Lastly, a third objection that
"might be urged is as follows—'It sometimes happens that
"on account of some mistake the usage that follows on the
"cognition of the *Jar* is that pertaining to the *Cloth* [*i.e.*,
"though the object actually perceived is the Jar, yet, by
"some mistake, the perceiver says *this is a cloth*]; and in this
"case, inasmuch as the cognition of the Jar will have been
"the cause of the usage consisting in the *Cloth* being spoken
"of, this *Cloth* will (under the definition) have to be regarded
"as the *object* of that Cognition.' But as a matter of fact,
"a Cognition can be the cause of only such usage as bears
"upon the same thing as the Cognition itself; so that in the
"case in question, inasmuch as the Jar-cognition will bear
"upon a thing (the Jar) other than the *usage* (which bears
"upon the Cloth), it could not be regarded as the cause of
"this usage."

This definition also cannot be accepted. The *capability to bring about the usage consisting in the thing being spoken of* (being a generic character) cannot be ascertained in regard to each individual cognition; as a characteristic feature (in its generic form) can be ascertained only from its effects, and no such effect is found to appear in connection with each individual cognition; and so long as no such effect has been brought about, there can be no ground for admitting any individual *capability*. In fact the said capability can be ascertained only by finding that the cognition in question has always, in every case, the same thing for its 'object', and [as this explanation involves the conception of the 'object', if we make it the basis of the definition of the 'object'] this leads to a 'vicious circle'.

For the aforesaid reasons we also reject the following explanation—"The 'object' of a cognition is that which forms its objective; and as the 'objective' does not represent a particular form of 'active agency', it is not impossible for past and future things to have the character of the 'objective'; in fact the 'objective' is that which is endowed with the peculiarity of being capable of bearing the operation dependent upon the action concerned; otherwise (*i. e.*, if the objective were anything different), in the case of such expressions as '*ghatam karoti*', 'he makes the jar', the Accusative ending (in '*ghatam*') would have no meaning at all; for if the '*ghata*' is not an accomplished entity, it cannot be productive of anything,—while if it is an already accomplished entity, it cannot be the objective of the action of '*making*' (*karoti*)."

Then again, the 'capability of being an operation' cannot consist in being actually imposed upon, or characterised, by a result in the shape of that *operation*; for this will not hold good in regard to the case where the operation has been suspended. Nor can it consist in its mere inherent potentiality (for bearing that operation, and not in actually bearing it at the time); for this 'potentiality' of the thing cannot be anything apart from its 'being the object'; so that this definition also will be open to the same objection as before (of its involving the *vicious circle.*) Nor will it be right to describe the said 'capability' as that by virtue of which the absence of the result is possible only on account of the absence of auxiliary agencies, [*i. e.*, the thing is so *capable* means that the operation is not there simply because of the absence of auxiliaries]—and this is something different from the specific character of the thing (which consists of its *being the object*) [So that there shall be no *vicious circle*]. This will not be right; because it is impossible to conceive of any such character without perceiving a comprehensive specific character (that would meet all the cases concerned). Further [by the explanation now put forward, the character of 'object' would apply to only such things as are not yet fully accomplished entities, but are *capable* of becoming so, not being so at present by reason of the absence of auxiliaries; but] as a matter of fact, in such expressions as '*ghatam karoti*', 'he makes the jar', what forms the 'object' of the 'making' are the fully accomplished entities in the shape of the potsherds (that constitute the jar); specially as it is only the fully accomplished entity that has been held to be the effect or product of the operations, and as such

P. 75. the 'object' of the action of 'making'. It is in view of this fact that philosophers, holding the view that before being produced the product does not exist, have declared that in cases where a word in the objective case is used in conjunction with a verb meaning to *bring about* or *accomplish*, the accusative word has to be taken in its indirect figurative sense, of *something related to the thing directly denoted by the word* [and not this thing itself; which according to these pulosophers, does not exist before the operation of the cause, and which therefore could not have the causal operation bearing upon itself]. On the other hand, as regards the philosophers for whom the product is an already existing entity (even prior to the causal operation), even though the thing already exists from before, yet it remains for it to be manifested (to have its existence rendered perceptible); so that it is not impossible for it to be an active agent as well as the 'objective' of the action of 'making'.

The above arguments serve to set aside the following assertion—"The eighth alternative (*h*) mentioned above (P. 73) may be regarded as unobjectionable, in the following sense:—the term '*samvidi*' is Locative Absolute, and 'appearing' should mean 'being capable of bearing the operation' [the definition meaning that the 'object' is that which becomes capable of being operated upon, when the Cognition is there]; that is to say, the object is that which, (when the Cognition is there) must be subject to the operation, whenever such other necessary causes happen to be present."

The Opponent put forward a fresh definition of the "object':—"When a certain thing characterises a Cog-"nition, irrespective of any other relation, and which, "in its own turn, does not have its own nature or form "affected or characterised by that Cognition,—this "thing is the 'object' of that Cognition Even though the "Self bears the relation of inherence to the Cognition of "itself (and as such the characterisation would appear to be "*not* irrespective of other relations), yet it does not require "this Inherence for the purpose of characterising the "Cognition; specially as in the case of the Jar etc., we find "that these things characterise their cognitions, even without "any such inherence. In the case of such cognitions as 'the "colour-cognition inhering in myself, which has been des-"troyed, was desired of me', it is found that even though "the *inherence in Self*, the *destruction* and the *desire* do not "form the 'objects' of the said Colour-cognition,—yet "they are found to characterise that Cognition, irrespective "of other relations. But even so the suggested definition "of 'object' does not become applicable to these; for they "themselves have their nature characterised by the Colour-"cognition, which is what *inheres*, which is *desired* and which "is the *correlate* (of destruction); as every *relation* (*e.g.* "Inherence), and Desire etc. have their nature always charac-"terised by the related things, the desired things and so "forth [so that the case of Inherence etc. does not fulfil the "last condition of the definition; that 'Object' should not "have its own nature characterised by that cognition]. On the "other hand, what forms the 'object' of a Cognition does not "ever have its nature characterised by that Cognition; as a "matter of fact, it is the Cognition that has its nature char-"acterised by the Jar and other things; and not these, Jar "etc., that have their nature characterised by the Cognition. "Though it is true that such cognitions as the *Inference of a* "*Cognition* or the Secondary or Representative Cognition, "which form the 'object' of the Cognitions apprehending "them, do *have their nature characterised by a Cognition* "[and as such may be suspected to be excluded from the "definition);—yet, as a matter of fact, none of the Cogni-"tions mentioned has its nature characterised by that "cognition of which it is itself the 'object'; and as such the "definition does not fail to apply to these."

This is not right, we reply. As this would mean that the cognition in the form 'this colour-cognition subsists in me' does not have the 'subsistence in the Self', for its 'object'; for the simple reason that the 'subsistence in the Self' being a form of relation, is naturally characterised by its own cognition, which is a factor in that relation; *secondly*, just as in the case of the conception in the form 'this is the cognition of the Jar', the Cognition has its nature charac-terised by the Jar,—so also in the case of the conception in the form 'the Jar is cognised', the Jar also has its nature characterised by the Cognition; so that the proposed definition of the 'object' (being inapplicable to the Jar) becomes an *impossible* one.

Another definition is suggested—" When a Cognition has the character of a certain thing, this thing is its 'object'. In the case of the conception 'the Colour-cognition subsists in me', it is the *Subsistence* that has its nature characterised by the Colour-cognition,—not that the *Colour-cognition* has its nature characterised by the *subsistence*. It may be pointed out that the definition here put forward is meant to apply only to the case where Cognition forms the 'object' of cognition; and is not intended to apply to the case of Desire etc. also; so that it cannot be objected to on the ground of its not applying to these latter, and as such being 'too narrow'."

This also is not right, we reply. The expression 'having the character of a certain thing', '*yadīyasvabhāvam*', is formed with a nominal affix (*chha* in '*yadīya*'); and if this affix signifies the thing *being the object*, then the definition involves 'self-dependence'; and it is not possible to attribute any other signification to the affix. Further, 'the negation of the negation of Colour-cognition' being the same as 'Colour-cognition', 'Colour-cognition' (thus) has the character of the said 'negation', this 'negation' would (under the proposed definition) have to be regarded as the 'object' of the Colour-cognition.

Another definition is put forward—"The 'object' of " a Cognition is that which forms the receptacle of the con- " tact of that Instrument which brings about that Cognition. " It might be urged that by this definition the Self would " have to be regarded as the 'object' of every Cognition, " as the Self forms the receptacle of the contact of Mind " which brings about the Cognition. But what is meant

"by the term 'Instrument' in the definition is that partic-
"ular Instrument which is specifically instrumental in
"bringing about the particular individual Cognition [and
"the 'Contact of Mind' or 'Mind' is not so, its instru-
"mentality being common to all Cognitions]. Even so, it
"may be argued, the Mind being the receptacle of the Con-
"tact of the Eye, which is the specific Instrument of the
"particular (visual) Cognition of Colour, this Mind should
"have to be regarded as the 'object' of that Colour-Cog-
"nition. But the word 'Contact' also in the definition
"stands for the contact of that particular Instrument which
"specifically brings about the particular cognition only
"[and the *Eye-contact* only, and not *Mind-contact*, would be
"such a 'contact' in the case of Colour-cognition].

This definition also cannot be accepted, we reply. As, in the first place in the case of visual cognition, the contact of the Mind and Eye also is a *specific instrument*, the Mind also would (under the definition) have to be regarded as the 'object' of visual cognition;—and secondly, the definition would fail to apply to such 'objects' as are not before the Eyes (are imperceptible; and as such cannot be the receptable of the contact of any instrument). "But as regards imperceptible things, what forms the 'instrument' in the case of their cognition is the 'Cognition of the Probans,' and certainly the 'Probandum' (which forms the 'object' of Inferential Cognition) bears (is the receptacle of) this relation to the said Instrument that it is its invariable concomitant." This is not right; as by this reasoning the Probans itself may be regarded as the 'object' of the inferential cognition, by reason of its bearing a distinct relation to its own Cognition (*i. e.*, the 'Cognition of Probans', which is the specific instrument of inferential cognition). Nor will it be right to argue (with a view to escape from this difficulty) that in the case of

P. 76.

Inferential Cognitions the particular form of relation that goes to make a thing its 'object' is only that of 'invariable concomitance.' As, if that were so, then the character of the 'object' could never belong to such things as *the relationship to the thing of wider extension*, which relationship forms the distinguishing feature of that thing being regarded as of wider extension (in comparison to the other thing).

"The 'object' of a cognition may be defined as that which, while being coexistent with the contact of the instrument of the Cognition, is the direct differentiator of that Cognition; and this definition may be regarded as applying to eternal and imperceptible things as well."

This also we cannot accept; as in the first place, this would mean that the 'object' of a cognition may be regarded merely as 'thing' in general; and secondly the definition would also become 'too wide;' being applicable to 'subsistence' (in the conception 'the Colour-cognition subsists in me'), which is a 'differentiator of the Cognition,' even though it is not the 'object' of the Colour-cognition.'

"The 'Object' may be defined as that which bears a natural relation' to the Cognition [*lit.* the character of the 'object' may be defined as consisting in the "natural relation between the Cognition and the Cognised]."

This also cannot be accepted; as it is wholly inapplicable. For if by the term 'natural relation' you mean merely a simple relation, then the definition proposed becomes 'too wide', being applicable to *Conjunction* and *Inherence* also. Nor will it mend matters to qualify the definition by adding the term 'excepting the two relations of Conjunction and Inherence'; as even so there might be a 'natural relation' between the Himālaya and the Vindhya mountains. "*Natural relation* may be defined as that which, in the absence of any other form of relation, is found capable of giving rise to the idea of the two things being qualified by each other." This also cannot be accepted; as in the first place, with this definition of 'natural relation', the proposed definition of 'object' will fail to apply to the case of the conception 'I know my-Self.'; for here (between the Cognition and the Self) there is present the relation of *Inherence* [and yet the *Self* is the 'object' of the Cognition];—and secondly, it will not apply to cases where *Negation* or Imperceptible things are cognised; for there is nothing to prove that either of these latter is capable of giving rise to the idea of things being *qualified*; and if these did have such capability, then it would be possible for these to give rise to the cognition of qualified things (which they cannot do; as it is only things that *are found to be present*, are positive and perceptible as such, that can serve to qualify anything). Then again, what is that form of things which consists in the 'capability to give rise to the idea of things being qualified'? (*a*) Is it something in the nature of a *property*? or (*b*) is it something in the nature of forms of the two things concerned? (*a*) If it be the former, then the 'form' of things loses its character of 'relation'; and inasmuch as the notion of 'cognition' enters into its constitution, it would become something not perceptible by the eye and such other organs of perception. (*b*) Nor can it be a something in the very forms of the two things themselves; as in that case, no comprehensive notion of it would be possible; and further, under this explanation, no misconception in regard to negation would be possible; as in that case also, the cognition of 'qualified' being possible, the necessary 'natural relation' would be present. Nor will it be right to incorporate into the said definition the notion of 'right cognition'; for whenever a real relation is present, the character of 'right cognition' comes in as a matter of course. Otherwise, it would mean that the 'absence of relation' is due to the absence of the 'character of right cognition', and the absence of the character of right cognition is due to the absence of relation,—which would involve an objectionable interdependence.

"But", says the Opponent, "a *relation* is so called when, "in the absence of any other relation, it happens to be "characterised by the capability of bringing about the Cog- "nition of being qualified; just as we find in the case of the "relation expressed in the expression 'with the stick', "where the relation is that of *Conjunction*. As for the Cog- "nition of being qualified, this has for its object the thing "cognised, and not what serves to characterise it. So that "there is no incongruity in the *visibility* of that *cognition of* "*being qualified* which is amenable to (or capable of) the "*natural relation*. The following argument may be urged— "'If such be the case, then, there would be nothing to dis- "criminate between the right and wrong Cognitions of "Negation; for both of these equally have for their object "only the two forms." This however will not be right; as "the required discrimination could easily be made by ascer- "taining whether the *cognition of negation* of the Jar is really "the cognition of that negation, or it is the cognition of some- "thing else [in the former case the cognition being right, "and in the latter case wrong].—'But if the objects of the "two (right and wrong cognitions) were not different, "then also there would be the same impossibility of "discrimination;—for according to you the cognition being "of the nature of both, and both, being present, there is no "*wrong cognition*, which consists in the cognition apprehend- "ing something different from what actually exists; and hence "no discrimination between right and wrong cognition would "in this case, be possible.' Not so; for the *negation of the* "*negation of the Jar* being the same as the *Jar*,—if in "regard to this one has the cognition of the 'negation of the "Jar,' this cognition comes to apprehend something different "from what actually exists. Then again, in reality the object "of the 'wrong cognition' (of the Jar) is something that "resembles the Jar; and inasmuch as this is not so of the "*right cognition* (of the Jar); so that the objects of the two "are actually different. Nor will the definition proposed "fail to apply to the case of imperceptible negation, for in "several forms of Negation, what forms the characteristic "feature of the capability to bring about the cognition of a "thing as *qualified* are as follows—(1) in the case of Absolute "Negation, it consists in its occupying a point in space other "than that occupied by its counter-entity; (2) in the case "of Previous Negation, it consists in occupying the same "point in space as the counter-entity, but appearing at a "time other than that of the counter-entity; and (3) in the "case of Mutual Negation, it consists in its occupying a point "in space other than that occupied by that which forms the "characteristic feature of the counter-entity, and characterisa-"tion by this is easily possible even in the case of the imper-"ceptible negation, even though this may, at that time, not "actually bring about the cognition of a thing as qualified. "For certainly the stick (which helps in the making of the "Jar), even while it may be only in the forest (and not "actually in the hands of the potter), it does not fail to be "distinguished by the character of being *capable of bringing* "*about the Jar.*"

This is not right, we reply. For if this were true, then, it would mean that all such eternal and imperceptible things as *Ākāsha*, Absolute Negation and the like,—being as they are distinguished by the character of being capable of bringing about the cognition of things as qualified,—must always necessarily be productive of the cognition of things as qualified; [which would be wrong] inasmuch as it is a fixed principle that every eternal thing, which has the inherent capability of bringing about a certain effect, stands (for its operation) in need of the presence of certain accessories (by reason of whose occasional absence the unceasing operation of the eternal thing is avoided).

Further, in the case of the expression *vishistasya pratyayah*, 'cognition of a thing as qualified,' if the Genitive ending (in '*vishistasya*') signifies only the *natural relation*, it involves the absurdity of the thing (*natural relation*) being dependent upon itself. While if the Genitive denotes mere *Relation* in general, the definition becomes too wide, being applicable to such objects as the Jar and the like, which form the object of such collective cognition as that of their *being related to the self which is characterised by the character of the 'Self'*; as the qualified relation of the two factors involved in this term is capable of bringing about the cognition of things as qualified. Further, under this theory, there would be no difference between the two conceptions, 'the negation of the cognition' and 'the negation is cognised'! For in both the conceptions the 'negation' and the 'cognition' both being of the nature of 'natural relation,' there could be no distinction based upon the difference in their 'objects.'

These same reasonings serve to set aside the view that in the case of 'Cognition' and 'Cognised things,' the 'capability to bring about the cognition of things as 'qualified' constitutes a relation of an entirely different kind (from the well-known *natural relation*). For even so, it would be inapplicable to the case of imperceptible eternal negations; as in this case there is no 'capability of bringing about the cognition of things as *qualified*'; firstly because such a view would involve the imposition of the result upon the eternal thing; and secondly, because the cognition of visible things, &c., would fail to have any 'object' at all.

Thus then, the conclusion is that, inasmuch as in the event of the relation between Perception and Perceived being real, the exact nature of the relation cannot be determined, the said relation must be regarded as purely illusory or surmised.

End of Section (25)

Section (26).

REASONINGS IN SUPPORT OF THE UNREALITY OF THE WORLD.

The Opponent comes forward with the following arguments against the Vedantin—"Even though the entire perceptible world is (according to you) only imposed upon "*Cognition*, which is Brahman, yet for the purpose of explaining the well-known phenomenon, that at any one point of "time only one particular thing appears in Consciousness, "you have admitted that there is some sort of relation "between the Cognition and the Cognised thing, through "a certain mental projection (Vṛiṭṭi) which takes the form of "the thing and is brought about by the contact of that thing "with a particular sense-organ; so that even though the "thing be 'unreal', it will have the said relation, even "though it be only through the said *Vṛiṭṭi*; why then should "you persist in your improper hankering after regarding the "said relation as only 'imposed' or 'assumed'? You do not "hold, as the Bauḍḍha Idealist does, that every individual "Cognition bears the impress of an individual object; "for as regards the *Cognition*, it itself in its purity can have "no diversity, and though it is beset with diversity when "it is accompanied by a limiting condition, yet, in this "limited form, it is as 'unreal' as any ordinary object like "the Jar; and as such cannot form the substratum (of any "imposed relation or impression)."

Our answer to the above is as follows:—As a matter of fact, every source of light illumines directly the object that comes into contact with it; and Consciousness (which is of the nature of light) cannot illumine an object indirectly, through the intervention of a relation. In fact, the Lamp does not illumine an object that is related to it only indirectly. Hence the conclusion is that the Consciousness that forms the substratum of an object illumines this object, without being intercepted (by any such extraneous thing as a *relation*); and it is the removal of such an intercepting thing that is done by the organic *Vṛiṭṭi* (postulated by the Vedantin); it is for this reason that even though, prior to this Organic *Vṛiṭṭi* there may be an *imposed* relationship, yet there is no cognition of the thing (such cognition being prevented by the intercepting obstacle, which can be removed only by the *Vṛiṭṭi*). It is for this same reason again that the said 'imposed' relationship has got nothing to do with the actual illumining (being rendered cognisable) of the Jar by the Consciousness reflected in the *Vṛiṭṭi*.

This also serves to set aside the view that—"inasmuch as all that is necessary for the illumining of the Jar is the Consciousness reflected in the *Vriṭṭi*, there is no need for assuming the manifestation of the Consciousness as the substratum of that object; an assumption which is involved in the theory that the illumining of the Jar is brought about by the Consciousness manifested in that Jar". As it is necessary to assume the manifestation of the Consciousness which has the object for its substratum, in order to account for the explicitness (or directness) of the Cognised thing, as distinguished from its indirectness. "But until the ultimate Direct Apprehension (of Truth) is reached, there is no manifestation of the *pure* Consciousness; and as for the Consciousness circumscribed by the Jar and such

P. 78. objects, that cannot be the substratum of those; as if that were so, there would be an objectionable self-dependence." This is not right; because as a matter of fact, even before the ultimate Direct Apprehension, the *pure* Consciousness does become the substratum (of objects), under the influence of Nescience; so that even though there is no *manifestation of the pure Consciousness* in the sense of the cessation of the root-Nescience, yet there *is* manifestation of It in the sense that there is cessation of certain phases of that Nescience; and thus *manifested* the Consciousness can be regarded as illumining the objects (cognised).

"If the cognition manifesting the Jar is unreal, then it cannot be the substratum (of the perceived Jar); while if it is *real* (true), then, since it is not brought about by a defect, it should be valid; hence its object being *real*, it could not be its substratum;—so that you are placed on the two horns of a dilemma".

There is no force in this argument; the mere fact of a certain Cognition *not being brought about by a defect* does not necessarily make it *valid*; because *Consciousness* is never *brought about by a defect*; what does make a cognition *valid* is the fact of its being circumscribed by an *Emanation* not brought about by defect; and as this condition is not present in the case in question, the object does not become *real*; so that it is only natural that the *real* Cognition should serve as the substratum of the *unreal* object.

"As a matter of fact, there can be an assumption of a
" superimposed (unreal) relation only where *real* relation is
" possible; but whence is there an impossibility of the real
" relation? In fact, just as in the case of the Substance and its
" quality, it being found that the well-known relation of *Con-*
" *junction* is not possible, it is concluded that the relation
" subsisting between then is that of *Inherence*,—in the same
" manner in the case in question, it being found that both these
" relations (Conjunction and Inherence) being impossible,
" there subsists between (Cognition and Objects) a third kind
" of relation. Nor is there no proof for the existence of this
" third relation; for its existence, like that of Inherence, is
" vouched for by Inference and Perception. For instance—
" (*a*) When two things are not either in Conjunction or in In-
" herence with one another, the notion of the one qualifying
" the other must appertain to the relation of *qualifier and*
" *qualified*,—because it is the notion of a qualified thing,—
" like the notion of the qualified thing, the *man with the stick*.
" (*b*) The said produced Valid Cognition must be based upon
" the relation of *qualifier and qualified*,—because it is such

"produced Cognition of a qualified thing as is not sublated,—
"like the cognition in regard to which both parties are agreed.
"(c) The cognition in question must have for it subject the
"unsublated relation of the *qualifier and the qualified*—because
"it is the unsublated cognition of a Qualified thing,—like the
"cognition of the Qualified thing, *the man with the stick*. Such
"conceptions as *Chaitra is possessed of an ox* and the like are
"also included under the 'subject' of these inferences; hence
"these conceptions cannot serve as the ground of doubts aris-
"ing in regard to the truth of the premises. Thus it becomes
"established that apart from Conjunction and Inherence, there
"is a third relation."

This is not right; the first two inferences are open to the charge of being 'irrelevant'; as the 'imposed relation' can serve as the subject as well as the cause or basis of the said conceptions; and as regards the second argument, it is open to the further objection of having the premisses *not true*, as is shown by the case of *mediate or indirect cognitions*. As regards the third argument, it is superfluous; as till the attainment of Brahma-knowledge, every cognition can remain unsublated; if, on the other hand, the Probandum is intended to refer to the subject of cognitions that are *never sublated*, then the Probandum itself becomes defective (no such Probandum being possible). "But as a matter of fact, an imposed relation is possible only when all real relation has been rendered impossible; so that no imposed relation can be assumed until the real relation, of a kind different from Conjunction and Inherence, has been rendered impossible; under the circumstances, how can there be any 'irrelevancy', 'superfluity' and 'defective Probandum'?" This is not right; as the real relation is rendered impossible by the simple fact that we do not perceive that with which it is invariably concomitant; that is, that with which real relation is invariably concomitant is 'negation, difference of time and place'; and this negation is not possible in the case of such cognitions as pertain to past and future things; hence how can there be any real relation among them? It will not be right to argue that—"like the relation of Inherence, the real relation would be rendered possible by the fact that the negation of the absence of the relatives is not impossible";—for even Inherence can not lead to two such things being regarded as *related* as are removed from each other in place and time; *e. g.*, even in the absence of the relatives, Inherence does not qualify the Jar that has been destroyed with the Colour that is to come into existence to-morrow.

Further, even if the relation be merely *imposed*, the nature of the Probandum does not become such as is incompatible with the cognition apprehending the Subject (*Relation*); for inasmuch as the cognition is of a qualified thing, what becomes accomplished in the first instance, is the mere 'relationship' in general, which is common to *real* as well as *unreal* relations. Further, that which apprehends the relation turns out to be that imposed relation which is accompanied by sublation in the shape of that non-apprehension with which the real relation is invariably concomitant. Hence there cannot be the least chance of any incompatibility with that which apprehends the *subject*.

"Inasmuch as we find Conjunction happening only between such things as exist separately from each other,
P. 79. inseparable existence should render Conjunction impossible."

Not so; because since in some cases we find that there is no sort of connection between things existing separately from one another, the mere fact of separate existence could not be regarded as a ground for relationship, on whose presence the relation is sure to be established. So that there being concomitance between the two, the mere non-perception of *separate existence* cannot serve to set aside the possibility of relationship. Though the reverse premiss (of concomitance) might be assumed, in the form—' when there is relation there is always separate existence'—yet there would be no proof on which such assumption could rest; specially because there are no reasonings favouring such assumption. On the other hand, we find that there is relation present among things not separated in time and place,—while there is no relation among things that *are* separated in time and place; and from this it is clear that there is invariable concomitance between *presence of relation* and *absence of separation in time and place,* and that this latter is a necessary condition for the former; so that whenever we do not perceive *absence of separation in time and place,* we have to admit that there is something that renders the presence of relation impossible; for when the necessary *condition* is absent the *conditioned* can not be present.

"In accordance with what you say, there would be no
" relation (*a*) of *Destruction* with the *Past Thing* (*b*) of *absolute*
" *negation* with its counter-entity, (*c*) of the *potency* with its
" objective, (*d*) of *Ignorance* with its object, (*e*) of *Desire* with
" the object desired, (*f*) of *Usage* with the object of which it
" deals, (*g*) of a *verbal expression* with the object expressed, (*h*)
" *of Cognition in the form of 'Emanation'* with the object cog-
" nised,—each former member of each of which couples falls
" within the definition of 'Unreality';—and thus there being
" no relation between *Cognition* and the *absence of relation*
" spoken of in your verbal expression, there would be several
" incongruities; such as contradiction of your own arguments,
" incompatibility of your own acts, and contradiction of your
" own assertions. Specially because the *counter-entity* and
" other things just mentioned are not *imposed* upon *negation*
" and the rest, in the manner in which (according to you) the
" *object* is imposed upon the *Cognition*."

Not so, we reply. Though it is true that in view of the said parity of reasoning, there is no real relation between Destruction and the rest with their counter-entity, &c.,—and the imposition also does not come about in the manner of the *cognition and the cognised*, both being equally unreal;—yet we do not absolutely deny 'the character of counter-entity,' 'relativity' and so forth, which are duly recognised in experience; what we mean is that they are all 'unreal,' falling within the womb of 'Cognition,'—and as such different from the 'real' as well as the 'imposed'; and whether those, like Conjunction, &c., are something quite distinct (from the things related), or they constitute the very form of the things themselves, or they are included under the categories postulated by other philosophers, or they are something different from these,—we do not concern ourselves with any investigation of these points; such investigation being as useless as an investigation into the question of the teeth of the crow. There would be no force in the argument that—"since before unreality is recognised the said relation itself could not be known, there is a mutual interdependence." Because as a matter of fact, what is known first, on the basis of the impossibility of any relationship between Cognition and Cognised,—is that every cognisable object is a product of 'imposition'; and from this it follows that all such relations as those of 'negation and counter-entity' and the rest, which are included under the category of 'cognisable objects,' must be *unreal*; and it is *not* that the unreality of the said relations of 'negation and counter entity' is first recognised, and then follows the conception of the unreality of the relation of 'cognition and cognised.' And thus, inasmuch as we do not absolutely deny all *relations* in general,—which alone are required for practical usage—there is no contradiction on our part of any assertions made by ourselves. This is what has been thus declared by the author of the *Khaṇḍana*—'The sublation of things being firmly established, if, on the ground of its standing on the same footing as these things, that sublation itself should become sublated,—let it be so; for those who regard all things as *Inexplicable*, whence can there be any clinging to anything at all?'

Nor can the sublation be said to be *not* firmly established; as we have already explained the reason for it, in the shape of the corroborative argument consisting in the fact that we do not perceive that with which the sublated thing is invariably concomitant; and also because we have refuted all antagonistic arguments put forward upon the basis of the allegation that our view involved incompatibility with well-known facts relating to the actual functioning of the things concerned. For the same reason our case is not analogous to that of the Casuist. What the Casuist does is to urge—against the reason of 'being a product' put forward in proof of 'non-eternality,' this reason being operative under certain conditions—the possibility of colour, &c., belonging to Sound, on the mere ground of its being found that there is no dependence upon any restrictive conditions;—while we do not urge anything on the basis of mere concomitance, irrespective of all restrictive conditions.

"In this manner, the relation of the *cognition and cognised* should stand on the same footing as that of the *Counter-entity and Negation.*"

Not so; because the said relation has got to be assumed, on the ground of the impossibility of any such relation as that of *mutual imposition.* In the event of such a relation as the latter being possible, that would constitute the required relation.

"Brahman, as the object of *Nescience,* can not be imposed upon the subject, *Ignorance*; so that the general proposition, that the object is always imposed upon the subject, cannot be accepted as true."

There is no force in this; as we do not hold any such proposition at all; all that we mean is that 'imposition' is the relation that subsists between 'Cognition' or 'Nescience' with their respective objects; and this is quite possible; it being found that the *cognised*

Page 80.

object is imposed upon *Cognition*, and that *Nescience* is imposed upon the *uncognised* object. It is for this reason that the relation between Nescience and the cognised object cannot serve as an effective counter-instance in the denial of 'imposed relation.'

"Under the circumstances no relation is possible between the *Hearing*, &c., culminating in *Direct Perceiving* and *Brahman*, which is held to be the *object* of these; for the simple reason that Brahman is never *imposed* either upon Hearing and the rest, or upon *Direct Perceiving*."

This is not right. 'Direct Perceiving' can be in the form either of 'Mental Projection', or of 'Consciousness manifested in the Projection.' If it is the former, then, it could be imposed upon Brahman; and as such the relation between them would be similar to that between 'Nescience' and the 'uncognised object'; for the same reason, it is not impossible for Brahman to be related to such mental processes as those of *Hearing* and the rest. If, on the other hand, Direct Perceiving is of the nature of 'Consciousness manifested in the Projection,' then, since the relation of identity (which alone is possible) could serve no useful purpose, the 'absence of relation' cannot affect the position adversely. The same reasoning also gets rid of the argument that—"if Brahman should be regarded as the object of the Final Direct Perception on the ground of this latter being imposed upon it, then, since the Direct Perception of the Jar also is imposed upon Brahman, Brahman should be regarded as the object of that Perception also." Specially because as a matter of fact, the *Perception of the Jar*, being, as it is, only a form of 'Consciousness manifested in the Jar', is not imposed upon Brahman; though in the form of 'Projection' it is imposed upon Brahman, yet Brahman, which only forms the substratum of that imposition, does not become the *object* of the said perception; and the reason for this lies in the fact that in this case there is not present that particular kind of imposition which could make Brahman the object of the Perception; in fact the presence of such Imposition is justifiable only when a well known fact cannot be explained except on that basis. As a matter of fact however, the 'form of Brahman' is not actually found to be present in the perception in question, in the same manner as it is in the case of the '*ultimate* Mental Projection.'

Between *Desire* and the *Desired object* there is relationship through cognition itself: So that there is no need of any separate relationship. "But in Cognition we perceive a relation of the object dependent upon contact; in Remembrance also we perceive a relation of the object dependent upon previous apprehension; similarly in Desire also we perceive a relation of the object dependent upon Cognition; —hence the relation in this last case must be held to be something distinct from the cognition; just as in the former two cases it is held to be something distinct from Contact and Apprehension." Not so; the said perception of relation can be explained as being due to the Cognition itself; so that there is no ground for the assuming of any relation apart from the cognition; specially as we are never cognisant of any other distinct relation dependent upon Cognition. In the case of Cognition, on the other hand, the perception of relation cannot be explained on the basis of *Sense-contact* &c.; as Sense-contact &c. being imperceptible, they could be apprehended only by Inference, &c., but even without such Inference the relation involved in the conception of the 'Cognition of the Jar' becomes duly apprehended. And as regards Remembrance, there is not the slightest suspicion of any relation based upon Apprehension; for the simple reason that at the time of Remembrance the apprehension has ceased to exist. And further, since both (Desire and Cognition) have the character of 'Cognition,' there would be equal possibility of relationship.

"In a case where there is Desire in regard to a single object, brought about by a comprehensive cognition of two things, both these things would have to be regarded as the objects of that Desire; for the simple reason that the cognition giving rise to that Desire has both of them for its object."

Not so; as the same may be said in connection with the view that the relation is something different from the cognition. It might be argued that—"if the cognition brings about the Desire in regard to a single thing, there is no possibility of two things being its object".—But the same might be said on our behalf also: in our case also what constitutes the relation (between the Desire and the Desired Object) is the fact that the cognition leading to the Desire has that thing for its object whereby it tends to give rise to that Desire. Nor could it be argued against us that no such relation to its object would be possible in the case of God's desire, which is eternal; for the simple reason that we do not admit of any such eternal desire.

Even though the Logicians may, on the strength of arguments proving the existence of God's eternal desire, postulate a peculiar form of relation to suit that case,—yet so far as the ephemeral desire and ephemeral cognition (of ordinary persons) are concerned, the relation to their objects has to be admitted to be of the form described above. Nor will this give rise to the incongruity of the son being 'the object of the pleasure produced by the cognition of the son (having been born),' on the analogy of desire. Because the two cases are not quite analogous; as a matter of fact, though the Cognition is the same in both cases, it is only in the case of Desire,—and not in that of Pleasure—that the object is the same as that of the Cognition; such is the nature of things: and you yourself have to set forth the same facts. If it were not so, then, just as the red colour of the *Japā* flower is transferred to the crystal, so should it also be to a piece of stone. "Inasmuch a there can be no imposition of the import in the Property, there can be no relation with the import." This is not right. What is meant by 'import' applying to a certain thing is that the conception of that thing is intended; and the conception can be related to the Property exactly in the same manner as to any other object of cognition; so that in this case also the relation would be of the nature of mere 'imposition'; and since the relation between the Property and the Import would be based upon conception, there would be no in congruity at all.

"Even though Cognition may be similar to the Lamp, in being of the nature of *Illumination*, yet it must be regarded as different from it, on the ground of its appearing within the body. Hence, like Desire, Cognition shou. l be related to remote things also. Otherwise, just as in the case of the Lamp, so in that of Cognition also, no *imposed relation* would be possible. Specially as in the case of Indirect Cognition, we do find the cognition being related to remote things."

This is not right; as a matter of fact, the absence of difference of time and place is a condition necessary for all relationship in general; so that there can be no ground for the assumption that the said condition is applicable to only such relation as is not one that pertains to *inner* things. As regards *Desire*, the relation with the *desired* thing is not direct; it is indirect, appearing through the Cognition,—as we have already explained. In the case of Indirect Cognition, though the relation with the Consciousness underlying the Substrate is *direct*, yet since the relation to the 'Projection in the form of the Object' is not direct, the relation of the *Object* with the 'Consciousness limited by the Object' must be *indirect*.

"Under your theory also, it cannot be necessary that every *Cognised object* must be imposed upon the *Cognition*; (*a*) because there can be no imposition on their own cognition of such things as (1) the absolute Nonentity, (2) the 'cessation of Nescience' of 'non-perception' which may be regarded either as a fifth kind of things, or as, uniformly non-different from positive entities, even though it is of the form of 'non-perception';—(*b*) because such ordinary things as the post and the like—, or the eternal supersensuous thing,—which are all imposed upon Brahman, which is of the essence of pure *Direct Apprehension*—could not be imposed upon their own cognition, which is of the nature of *indirect apprehension*;—(*c*) because the remembered thing cannot be imposed upon its own Cognition, which is of the nature of Remembrance;—and (*d*) the thing that has merely apparent reality cannot be imposed upon its own Cognition, which also has merely apparent reality; specially as under your theory, Cognition in the form of Misconception also has only an assumed (illusory) existence."

This is not right; for the *absolute nonentity* can never be cognised; so that it is only natural that there should be no imposition of it; it is only a *Cognisable* thing that can be imposed upon *Cognition*. We shall explain later on how the absolute non-entity can never be cognised. As regards the 'Cessation of Nescience,' regarded as a fifth kind of thing, its relation must be that of *Imposition*, for the simple reason that the destruction of a thing must subsist in the same substratum in which that thing itself subsisted. As a matter of fact however, the theory of 'the Cessation of Nescience being a fifth kind of thing,' as also that of all things being uniformly positive,—are to be rejected simply on the ground of their not being accepted by us. In what way 'Cessation of Nescience' is of the nature of 'Brahman,' and how there is 'non-duality of all things,' we shall explain later on. Then again, as regards the past and future things that are imposed upon Brahman, which is of the essence of Direct Apprehension,—even though these are not imposed upon the inferential and other kinds of cognition, yet that same Consciousness upon which they are imposed becomes circumscribed by the 'Projection' in the form of Inference and the rest; it is thus that Imposition becomes possible. Though, for the avoiding of undesirable contingencies, Consciousness, for being related to its object, has been regarded as standing in need of being affected by 'Projection,'—yet, in being a substratum, it does not stand in need of any such affectation. Lastly, in the case of eternal and super-sensuous things,—in the case of Remembrance,—and also in the case of things having merely apparent existence,—even though they may not be imposed upon a mere *apparent* 'Projection,' yet they are imposed upon that Consciousness which is manifested in the Projection bearing upon the substratum. Thus then there is no such incongruity as those urged by the Opponent.

"[When the shell is mistaken for Silver], the shell (according to the Vedāntin) is imposed upon the Consciousness circumscribed by the notion of 'this,' and yet it is illumined by the Consciousness reflected in the Projection of Nescience;—how then can there be any imposition of the object on the Subject, the Cognition?"

Inasmuch as the limitation by means of one is cast upon what is also limited by another, there is no distinguishing force; just as there is none in the case of an *accidens* which is not dependent upon anything else. It is for this reason that learned men have declared that Cognition is one by reason of the singleness of the result.

"If the Silver is imposed upon its own cognition, then, in the first place, it would be possible to have a misconception when the 'Cognition of the Silver' is not cognised; and secondly this misconception would be set

Page 82.

aside by the cognition of that 'cognition of silver'; and further inasmuch as, in the appearance of the Imposition,' the 'projections' are brought about by the cognition and non-cognition of its substratum, it would be possible to have the conception 'the cognition is silver.'"

Not so, we reply; because as a matter of fact, we do not admit that the 'Consciousness circumscribed by the Projection in the form of silver' is the substratum of the 'misconception of silver; in fact, what forms the substratum of the misconception of silver is Consciousness circumscribed by the notion of 'this'; and it is by mere chance that 'the Consciousness circumscribed by the Mental Projection in the shape of silver' also becomes a substratum of it. But this does not make this latter a necessary condition for the misconception. And what serves as the cause of the misconception is the non-cognition of the thing in the form of 'shell'—which would render the misconception impossible; and the cognition of the thing as 'shell, would set aside the misconception. For these reasons it is not possible for the misconception to appear in the form 'the cognition is silver.' Specially because the cognition is cognition only when circumscribed by the Mental Projection, and such cognition is not the substratum of the misconception. And inasmuch as the illusory (misconceived) thing is always cognised as identified with the substratum, the misconception can only appear in the form 'this is silver'.

"Inasmuch as such objects as the Jar and the like must exist before they are cognised by means of the sense-organ in contact with them, it is not right that there should be any imposition in this case. Nor will it be right to argue that the Jar is not illumined by that Mental Projection which is produced by the contact of the Jar and the sense-organ; whereas it *is* illumined by Consciousness subsisting in the Jar, which is not produced by contact;—because there is nothing to prove that there exists 'Cognition' apart from the 'mental projection'; and the cessation of Ignorance also follows from the same."

This is not right; as in order to explain the existence of things before the appearance of the *Mental Projection*, it is necessary to accept the existence of 'Cognition' as something distinct from the 'Mental Projection.' Otherwise, there being nothing to establish the existence of the things, they would be mere non-entities like the 'hare's horns,' there would be no justification for assuming their previous existence, as the basis (cause) of contact and of the cognition born of that contact. For these reasons it is necessary to admit the presence of proof for the existence of the Jar in that form in which it becomes the cause of 'cognition' by serving as the substratum of the contact of sense-organs. If this be not admitted, then no concomitance, positive or negative, being perceived (as between the Jar and its cognition), there could be no conception of the relation of cause and effect between them, and this would put an end to all notions of 'cognition' and 'objects of cognition.'

This Cognition is not in the form of 'Mental Projection'; as at that time the causes of the Projection are not operative. The Cognition must be regarded as something of a character totally different from 'Mental Projection,' as eternal, as one as self-illumined; (*a*) because such a conception of it is much simpler than any other, (*b*) because it is not touched by such properties of 'Mental Projection' as *production*, *destruction*, and *non-intelligence* The said Cognition comes to form the subject of various practical usages, through its connection with various accidental qualities; just in the same way as *Ākāsha* becomes diverse by reason of such accidental relatives as the Jar, the Gem, and the Flower; and since it is what brings about ignorance, it can not, by itself, serve to set aside ignorance; it does so, when affected by 'Mental Projection'; and herein lies the use of the 'Projection.' Such being the case, what incongruity can there be in the view that there is imposition of the Jar, &c., upon the witnessing Consciousness, which imposition brings about all Ignorance? This is what has been thus declared by the revered Surēshvarāchārya:—

'How can the conception of that be denied, on the basis whereof depends the fulfilment of the desired conception of all philosophers?'

'The notion of Right *Cognition* that all philosophers accept is that it apprehends the thing not already apprehended; and this is found incompatible with your theory:'

'The Body and such other things that exist, are they by themselves *cognised* or not *non-cognised*? In either case the character of *Right cognition* becomes impossible.'

'If the Body, &c., are cognised, even without the *Right Cognitions*, then tell us, what is the use of these *Cognitions*? What is already cognised cannot be made apprehended?'

'If, on the other hand, the Objects of Cognition are not cognised, by themselves, then what is non-existent cannot be manifested by Right Cognition. For instance, the shining Sun never illumines the Hare's Horn!'

"When the Vedantin says that 'in view of the illumination of the Mental Projection in the form *this is Jar*, the Conception the Jar, as 'cognised' should arise only from the relation of *Brahman*',—this is not consistent with the assertion that 'the apprehension of the Jar is of the nature of that Consciousness *which is reflected in the Mental Projection*, and *which is not the substratum of the Jar*."

This is not right; as there is no difference between 'Consciousness reflected in the Mental Projection' and 'Consciousness which is the substratum of the Jar';—'Consciousness, being *one*. How the *one* Consciousness illumines *all* things has been explained in detail by the Author of the *Bhāṣya* under the Sūṭra *Nābhāva upalabdhēḥ*, 'there is no non-existence of things, as they are actually apprehended' [Brahm-Sūṭra II—ii.]

"When you seek to establish *unreality* on the ground that on any other supposition, *cognisability* would not be possible,—(a) do you *intend* this argument to be one based upon Presumption? or (b) a mere corroborrative reasoning in the form that 'if things were *real* they could not be *Cognisable*? (a) The former view cannot be maintained; as the necessary details of Presumption are wanting. The details of Presumption consist of the following conditions:—(1) That which is *presumed* should be one that explains the well-known fact, and it should be one which is itself not incompatible with well-known facts of Cognition, and (2) that upon which the presumption is based should be one that cannot be explained except on the basis of what is persumed, and it should be a fact well-ascertained. In the case in question however the *unreality of the relatives*, which is what is sought to be presumed, is not one that explains the *relation*, upon which the presumption is based; in fact it is quite the contrary. It would not be right to argue that—'the relation *being imposed* is not unfavourable to the said presumption';—for inasmuch, as such a relation has itself still got to be proved, it cannot serve as the basis of any presumption. Further, what is sought to be presumed is quite contrary to facts of perception &c. Nor can it be right to renounce several well-known facts for the sake of the single fact of *cognisability*. Again, *being imposed upon Cognition* cannot serve as the basis of presumption; as in reality that is what is sought to be presumed. Nor could the basis of presumption consist of that relation of Cognition which is in the shape of forming the object of cognition; for the simple reason that any such relation is not admitted by you. Nor could the basis consist of the character of depending for existence upon the Cognition; for such a character in no way differs from that of being the object of cognition. (*b*) The second alternative also cannot be maintained [*viz.*, that what is put forward is a mere corroborative reasoning, in the form that 'if things were real they could not be Cognisable]—for even if things are *real*, their *Cognisability* can be explained, in the manner shown above, on the basis of some other relation; so that, there is no *inconsistency* at all (which could form the basis of the corroborative reasoning).'

There is no force in all this, we reply. Inasmuch as we have already started with the declaration that what we we were putting forward was a *Corroborative Reasoning*,—there is no room for the question as to whether it is such reasoning or Presumption, Further, there is no incongruity whether our reasoning be regarded as one or the other. If things are *real*, there can be no possibility of any such relation as that between *Cognition* and the *Cognised* object;—while what makes such relation possible is the *unreality* of things. Nor is *unreality* unfavourable to relationship; as we find that even though the shell-silver is unreal, yet it is related to 'this' by the relation of *being imposed*; so that *unreality* cannot be regarded as incompatible with all *relationship*. As regards the basis of Presumption, this also consists of the *relation of cognition*, in the form of being the object of cognition. We also admit of such character of *being the object of Cognition* as consists in *being imposed*; what we do not admit is only a *real* relationship is that form. Nor can it be argued that *imposition* itself has still got to be proved. For as a matter of fact, what forms the basis of presumption is the general relationship to cognition; and even though we may deny a particular form of such possible relationship, what it ultimately turns out to be is the relation of *being imposed*; and in this way it cannot be said to be something still to be proved or unknown. What forms the basis of presumption is not *being related by imposition*, but only *leing related*: and the said character of *being related* cannot be denied, even though there may be a possibility of the *imposed relation.* "As a matter of fact, *being imposed* cannot be a peculiarity of the general relation comprehended in the notion of 'the Cognition of Jar'; for there is no such conception as the *shell of the silver.*" There is no force in this reasoning; as even though there is no such conception as 'the shell of silver', yet the *shell* is recognised as the substratum of the *silver*; and in this way the relation becomes one consisting of *being imposed.* Just as, even though there is no such conception as 'Maiṭra of Chaiṭra', yet we have such a notion as 'Maiṭra is the father of Chaiṭra'; and as there is nothing incompatible with reason in this case, so is there nothing unreasonable in the case in question. As for the incompatibility of facts of Sense-perception &c., we have already answered this.

For that which serves as the basis of presumption, it is not necessary that it should itself be duly cognised; for in the case of the reflection it is found that even though reflection is not duly cognised, yet it serves as the basis for the presuming of the reflected thing. Nor can our reasoning be regarded as futile, even when it is regarded as corroborative reasoning; as we have already explained, by refuting your arguments, that if things are real, there can be no relationship among them.

Then again, the *reality* that would make things cognisable may be regarded as consisting either in the absence of indescribability or in non-sublatability at all three points of time. In either case there would be nothing incongruous. It might be argued that—"in the case of the absolute *non-entity,* which is cognisable, being comprehended by indirect apprehension,—*absence of indescribability* is not concomitant with *reality.*" This however is not right; for even though by the force of causes operating in the case there does appear a mental projection of the form of the nonentity, yet, *the character of cognisability*, which is incompatible with that of *absolute nonentity*, and which consists of being related to cognition, is not present at all. Though the form of the absolute nonentity enters into the Mental Projection, yet the relation of the Projection cannot be present in the said Nonentity.

Page 84.

It will not be right to argue that—"It is the *real* Jar that is related to its cognition, just as it is the *real* Brahman that is related to all activity relating to It";—because in the case of Brahman which is cited as an instance, it is *Imposition* alone that constitutes the relation to activity. So that if both correlates were real, there would be no relation of subject and object; and this impossibility could not be set aside by any argument based upon futility or some such thing.

This same reasoning also sets aside the following argument—"Is the *imposed relation* only the relation that is imposed? or is it merely the character of being imposed? If the former, then, even though the relation be unreal, the relative cannot be so; just like the cognition of the cognised thing. If the latter, then, inasmuch as cognition also is only *imposed*, there could be no further imposition upon it; for if one were to postulate impositions upon a series of cognitions, it would lead to an infinite regress."—For *cognition* is only Consciousness circumscribed by the Mental Projection; hence even though the circumscribing Projection, which is non-intelligent, is imposed,—yet the circumscribed Consciousness, which is luminous in its character, is not imposed; hence the cognised thing being imposed, and as such unreal, there is no possibility of an infinite regress.

This also disposes of the following—"Brahman, which is an object of verbal operation, is not assumed (or imposed) upon the operation; and as the object of Nescience, Brahman, is not imposed upon Nescience, so the cognised object also is not imposed upon the cognition. It is thus that the relation between the cognition and the cognised thing is real. And all undesirable contingencies having been set aside by this general relationship, any further enquiry into particular details or any further explanations would be without use."—For even though Brahman is not imposed upon either the Verbal Operation or upon Nescience, yet the required relation comes about by these—Operation and Nescience—themselves being imposed upon Brahman. So that there being no real relation in the case of Brahman, how can the relation between the cognition and the cognised thing be regarded as *real*—on the basis of that between Brahman and Nescience? Thus a particular fact having become duly explained, it is the generic conception that becomes open to the contingency of being sublated; so that further enquiry into particular details and particular explanations cannot be futile.

What we have just said also disposes of the following allegation—"If the relation is true, there will be found some sort of a definition of it. For instance, if the relation is included under 'Conjunction' or 'Inherence,' the definition of these would serve as its definition. If it is not included under these, then it would be defined as a relation distinct from the relations of Conjunction and Inherence."—For we have already shown that the reasons propounded above have demolished the possibility of the real relation, as also its inclusion under Conjunction and Inherence. As for the relation being distinct from Conjunction and Inherence,—this we also do not deny; all that we deny is the reality of the relation.

Further, the relation between the Cognition and the Cognised object is not real. For if the relation were something distinct from the related things, then there would be an infinite regress. "But just as the cognised object is self-contained, not needing a further cognisability,—in the same manner the relation also would be self-sufficient (and no infinite regress would be involved)." This is not right; for 'cognisability' also is only *relation to cognition*; and the self-sufficiency of this could be possible only if it were of a purely illusory character; so that what the 'loved of the Gods' has said is not unacceptable to us. If, on the other hand, the relation be the same as the related things, then it ceases to be a *relation*.

This objection does not lie against the hypothesis that the relation is *imposed*; for the relation, in this case, is purely illusory, and Illusion is capable of accomplishing even impossible things; so that all incongruities tend to add to the beauty of this hypothesis.

Page 85.

"The subject in hand was the explanation of the relation between cognition and cognised object, for the purpose of removing the undesirable contingencies; and the explanation of the character of the object is not what has been undertaken. So that the refutation of the character of *object* turns out to be an attack upon what has never been alleged."

Not so, we reply. From the refuting of the character of the *object* follows also the refutation of the *relation* that has been postulated by the Opponent. "But as a matter of fact, even though the character of the Subject has not been explained, yet reality would belong to the Subject; exactly in the same manner even though the character of *Object* is not explained', the object would be real." Not so; even though the character of the Subject (cognition) is not explained, yet it is only right that it should be regarded as *real*, because the appearance of the cognition can be explained on the basis of the imposition of the *object*, but until the nature of the object has been explained, it can not be regarded as real. For the simple reason that the Subject cannot be imposed, and hence the appearance of the Object cannot be explained on any basis except that of its being imposed. In cases where there is imposition of the Subject, the object is certainly real. *E. g.* Brahman is the object of cognition, and yet there is no imposition of either; the postulating of imposition in this case would mean *Nihilism*. Between two things, whether there is imposition of one or the other is determined by ascertaining which is inclusive and which exclusive, which is luminous and which non-luminous, and so forth. From all this it follows that, since there can be no imposition of Subject, which is of the nature of eternal cognition, the imposition must be of the Object only. "With all this it behoves you also to explain the nature of the Object; since you propound such arguments as 'the Instruments of Cognition in the hiding of these objects &c., &c.'; and since you put forward as probans the character of *cognisability*, which consists in being the *object* of Cognition". There is no force in this; for even though the object cannot be described in its essence, it can be described as something *imposed*, being exactly on the same footing as the Jar and such things.

"How can the object of *valid* Cognition be regarded as *imposed*?"

There is no force in this; you may accept the explanation that in the case of cognition relating to the phenomenal world, there can be no true *validity*,—which consists in making known the real essence of this. It is for this reason that no value attaches to the following reasoning of the Opponent—"The *objectivity* of the cognised object in relation to the Cognition is exactly similar to objectivity, according to the Vedantin, of the Conscious Self, in relation to the Mental Projection." Specially because even though there is no imposition of the Conscious Self, the Mental Projection is imposed upon it; but this non-imposition cannot be urged in the case in question, merely on the analogy of what happens in the case of the Self.

The following might be urged by the Opponent—

"When you have described *Unreality*, it behoves you to describe *Cognisability* also, which is your reason for unreality. Until there is cognition unmixed with the form of the *Jar* and such things, there cannot be any specific activity in regard to them. If such activity were possible merely on the basis of the Cognition, undescribed and unmixed in character,—then the same might be possible for me also. The only difference is as follows:—For you the *form* is different from the *real*; while for us, the form as that reality which is proved by the proof that shows that it differs from what in your philosophy is known as 'seemingly real.' The mention and non-mention of the definition does not either demolish or establish difference from real and unreal or indescribability. For on the strength of the reasons showing that Brahman cannot be a cause, it can be shown that Brahman cannot have the character of being the cause of the Universe,—even though its being so is declared in the Shruti. If it be asked—'what sort of Supreme Self would you posit?'—our answer is that the Supreme Self is that to which we cannot apply the notion of either 'like this' or 'like that.' Further, since Brahman also has been described as difficult of determination, the phenomenal world also would be amenable to a definition, similar to the 'indescribability' posited by you; and Earth &c. also would found capable of being defined, in such forms as—'the Earth is that which is solid,' and so forth. From all this it follows that *indescribability* is not incompatible with *Reality*, specially as the Real also could be *indescribable*, by reason of its not being produced. Nor does *describability* necessarily make a thing *real*; for in the shell-silver, the *silver-character*, which serves to distinguish it from other things can be easily *described* as belonging to an imaginary genus. Further, inasmuch as by refuting the fact of Brahman possessing the characters of 'bliss', 'consciousness', 'truth', 'self-luminousness', and so forth, it may be shown that Brahman would come to be regarded as *not* of the nature of Bliss &c. From all this it follows that the character of the 'object,' even though undescribable is real.—just like the sweetness of sugarcane, milk and such other things."

Our answer to the above is as follows:—Is *Cognisability* 'indescribable' as regards its *reality* or its *form*? It cannot be the former; for even though it were indescribable as regards its reality, it could be cited as a reason, simply in the form that it is not affected by the character of mere resemblance of this or that thing; so that no *description* of it would be necessary. Nor can the second alternative be right; for it is quite possible for the character of 'object of cognition' to be described as consisting of 'being related to cognition,' which can apply to the real as well as the unreal thing. You have asserted that—"the mention and non-mention of the definition cannot either demolish or establish either difference from the real and unreal, or indescribability." This however is not right; for what makes a thing *indescribable* is the *non-mention of its definition*, as accompanied by the aforesaid non-perception of its concomitants. You have further argued that—"Inasmuch as Brahman is difficult to describe either as consisting of Bliss, &c., or 'like this or that,' It also should be regarded as indescribable."—This also is not right. Even though it is difficult to describe Brahman as being of the nature of Bliss, &c.; yet It can be described as existing in such form as is characterised by opposition to Pain. This method of describing *reality* is not possible in regard to the phenomenal world; as in this case, there are sublating causes present. This same reasoning also disposes of the following argument—"With regard to earth and such things we do have such descriptions as 'being solid' or 'tangible,' and so forth, and their 'reality' also may

P. 86.

be described as consisting of *being produced*." For we do not assert 'indescribability' merely on the ground of *absence of description*; we base it upon *absence of description as real*; and this is certainly present in the phenomenal world, in whose case sublating causes are present.

"If the Object is imposed upon the Cognition, it is not possible for that to form the object with reference to the imposition produced by the ignorance of that object, and set aside by the cognition of it; nor would it be possible that there should be absence of cognition related to that object."

This is not right; as we have already explained that the phenomenal world consisting of the Jar and such things are the product of the ignorance of Consciousness only, and it is set aside also by the knowledge of that same Consciousness; and the said things are also actually found to be cognised as related to the Substantive Consciousness which is duly apprehended.

From all this it is firmly established that if things are real, the relation of Cognition and Cognised is not possible at all.

End of Section (26).
